FIRST CHOICE

FOR PROFICIENCY

Peter M

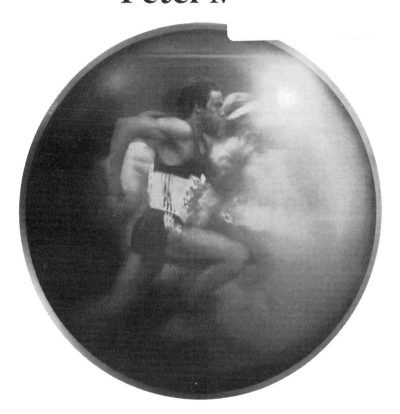

HEINEMANN

Heinemann International
A division of Heinemann Publishers (Oxford) Ltd
Halley Court, Jordan Hill, Oxford OX2 8EJ

OXFORD LONDON EDINBURGH
MADRID PARIS ATHENS BOLOGNA
MELBOURNE SYDNEY AUCKLAND
SINGAPORE TOKYO IBADAN NAIROBI
GABORONE HARARE PORTSMOUTH (NH)

ISBN 0 435 28800 8
© Peter May 1991

First published 1991

The author wishes to thank the following: the students,
teachers and library resources staff of the British Council evening
school in Madrid; Bill Anderson, Jill Florent, Karen Jacobs,
Jenny Duke and David Brancaleone of *Heinemann International*;
Herme.

**The author and publishers would like to thank the
following for the help:** Jackie Newbrook, Helen Naylor, John
Webber, Jon Naunton.

**We would like to thank the following for their permission
to reproduce copyright material:** *Aitken and Stone* 'The Folly
of Children's rights' Germaine Greer (p. 146); *Association of
British Insurers*, Holiday Insurance leaflet, (p. 55); *Kent Barker*
'From our own correspondent' (p. 62); *BBC Ariel Books* 'Use your
head' (pp. 103, 174); *BBC World Service* 'The story of English'
David Crystal and Tom McArthur (p. 22), 'The Man in the Moon'
Captain E. Cernan and Patrick Moore (p. 72); *Colourama* (p. 132);
Controller of Her Majesty's Stationery Office 'What a consul can do'
(p. 48); *Cambridge Univesity Press* 'Study skills in English' (p. 37),
'Keep talking' (p. 144); *Curry's* (p. 132); *The Daily Telegraph*
'Towards Olympic War Games' Christie Davies (pp. 76, 77); *Data
Protection Registrar* 'Are you in on the Data Protection Act?'
(p. 153); *Friends Provident* – Stewardship unit trust advertisement
(p. 156); *Michael Grade* 'Langham Diary' (p. 36); *Grafton Books*
'Hotel du Lac' Anita Brookner (p. 110); *Greenpeace* Information
leaflet; *The Guardian* 'Mind games grip the West Coast' Alex
Brummer (p. 84); 'Domestic dreamland' Malcolm Dean and
Martin Kettle (p. 112); *Guardian Weekly* 'Bulldozer revenge on
bank' David Rose (p. 63), 'Sea turning into desert' Martin
Walker (p. 100); Art Auction (p. 121); *Tim Haines* 'Breathe deep
as fishes do' (p. 190); *Hamlyn* 'ST guide to movies on T.V.' Angela
and Elkan Allan (p. 122); *Heinemann Educational Books* 'Teaching
Reading Skills' C. Nuttall (p. 9); *The Independent* 'Labours with a
Hercules' (p. 87) Hugh Herbert, 'Why tourists deserve to be
treated with disdain' Stephen Glover (p. 46), 'Teacher fails in
appeal over marriage rules' (p. 113), 'Hey rock and scroll' Giles
Smith (pp. 116, 117); *Kogan Page* 'Case studies in personnel
management' Michael Armstrong (p. 110); *Terry Jones* 'Input –
the end of the human race' (p. 98); *The Listener* 'Graham Greene
and Omar Torrijos' Paul Johnson (p. 56), Letter to the editor by
Graham Greene (p. 60), Letters – Paul Johnson (p. 60), Ronald
White (p. 60), Richard O'Slater (p. 60), J. Plested (p. 60),
'Marathon Mentality' (p. 80), 'Going for a song' David Bernstein
(p. 126); *Longman Group UK Ltd.* 'Teaching Writing Skills' Don
Byrne (p. 11); *Martin, Secker and Warburg* 'The return of heroic
failures' Stephen Pile (p. 175); *Richard Mayne* 'Dirty linen in the
cinema' (p. 122); *New Statesman and Society* 'This England' (p. 164),
'Ministry of Agriculture' (p. 164), 'A street mugging' (p. 164),
'The latest fashion…' (p. 164), 'Martyrs to labour' Jeremey

Seabrook (p. 174); *Newsweek* 'Drugs open up a generation gap' B.
Beck, P. Abramson, S. Hutchinson and K. A. Brown (p. 113); *The
Observer* 'Foil or fail' (p. 113); *The Observer EFL* 'Pedlar of White
House dreams' (p. 26), 'Life of the monarchy' (Ice princess…)
(p. 38), 'Amnesty, the first 25 years' Peter Benenson (p. 150),
'Sales talk' Sarah Mower (p. 192); *The Observer Magazine* 'Sad but
true?' Christine Doyle (p. 136); *The Ontario Institute for Studies in
Education* 'Helping language learners' Anita Wendon (p. 15);
Pluto projects/Pan Books/Heinemann 'New State of the World
Atlas' 1987 Michael Kidron and Ronald Segal (p. 90); *Postman &
Weingartner* (p. 73), 'Teaching as a subversive activity'; *Penguin
Books* 'The Quiet American' Graham Greene (p. 160); *Pergamon*
'Grammar in action' Frank/Rinvolucri (p. 69); *Phillips* (p. 132);
Prentice-Hall Inc. 'A history of the English language' Baugh/Cable
(p. 19); *Private Eye* 'Money – Government' (p. 164); *Radio Times*
'Film synopsis 2001' (p. 124); *Walter Schwartz* 'Tracking the
single truths' (p. 187); *Philip Short* 'Letter from the Pyranees'
(p. 52); *Sofa Sleepers* (p. 132); *Solo Syndications* 'Sunset for the sun
set' Vicki Woods (p. 140), 'Lives and loves of Jackie and Joan'
Joe Collins (p. 40); *The Sunday People* (p. 132); *Sunday Telegraph*
'What is happening to our weather?' Richard Asquith (p. 102);
Sunday Times 'Ice highway to warm up trade traffic' John Newell
(p. 170); *Times Newspapers Ltd.* 'Dictionary finds wellness
potential…' Charles Bremner (pp. 17, 18), 'The proposed shift
in the Earth's axis' (p. 105), 'Bruised American males…' Charles
Bremner (pp. 106, 107); *Telecom Security* (p. 132); *Megan Tressider*
'Exercise is bad for you' (p. 84); *World Press Network* 'Why the
computers days are numbered' Richard Parlour (p. 66),
'Pollution – it's only natural' Derek Ager (p. 96), 'Perspiration
beats inspiration' Michael Hove (pp. 106, 107), 'What Americans
find stressful' (p. 143).

*While every effort has been made to trade the owners of copyright
material in this book, there have been cases where the publishers have
been unable to locate the sources. We would be grateful to hear from
anyone who recognises their copyright material and who is
unacknowledged.*

Artwork acknowledgements: *Greenpeace* (p. 104); *Pluto
Projects/Visionslide* (p. 86, 102, 104, 128, 168); *David Austen*
(p. 103); *Variety* (p. 123); *Guardian Weekly* (p. 18); *Spectator*
(p. 162).

Photographic acknowledgements: *All Sport* Javelin Thrower
(p. 76); *J. Allan Cash* 1943 scene (p. 44), Monaco (p. 134), Home
(p. 134); *Bell Educational Trust* computing (p. 12), video making
(p. 12), language lab. (p. 12), social scene (p. 14); *Columbia
Pictures Inc.* The Last Emperor (p. 122); *Format* crowd (p. 33),
nurse (p. 65), pilot (p. 65), fireman (p. 65), policeman (p. 65),
market (p. 94); *Hulton Deutsch* Bletchley (p. 44), Suffragettes
(p. 106), Einstein (p. 166), Mozart (p. 166); *Image bank* aerobics
(82), executives (p. 164); *Martin Chillmaid* record covers (p. 116);
Network canal/river pollution (p. 96), rowdy tourists (p. 54); *Rex
Features* De Niro (p. 32), Live Aid (p. 34), Princess Diana (p. 39),
Jackie and Joan (p. 40), Geldof (p. 88); *Science Photo Library* space
(p. 72), surgery (p. 74), volcano (p. 96); *Tate Gallery* The Tate
Gallery by Tube (p. 127); *Zefa* couple (p. 24), computer (p. 72),
jogging (p. 82), tennis (p. 82), swimming (p. 82).

Tapescript acknowledgements: John Haycraft of
International House (Intro. Unit), James Richardson, Liz Hunter
and Peter Thompson (Unit 7) and Ken Wilson (Unit 16).

Designed by Mike Brain
Cover design by Mike Brain
Recorded by James Richardson at studio AVP
Illustrated by Maxine Rogers, *Hardlines*, Judith Lawton

Typeset by Tradespools Ltd, Frome, Somerset
Printed in Scotland by Thomson Litho Ltd.
92 93 94 95 96 10 9 8 7 6 5 4 3 2

CONTENTS

INTRODUCTORY UNIT   **LEARNING   PAGE 8**

Overview of the Examination. How the course will take students to CPE standard.

Reading: Predicting text content. Exploiting existing knowledge. Faster reading. Skimming. Scanning. Words from context. Responding to the text.

Grammar: General tense revision.

Writing: Summary 1: recognising main points.

Listening: Predicting. Exploiting existing knowledge. True/false. Advising.

Functions: Advising.

Oral: Pronunciation of individual sounds. Photograph: topics.

Study skills: Efficient learners.

Exam skills: Reading information.

UNIT 1   **LANGUAGE   PAGE 16**

Reading: Words from context: clues to meaning, connotations, synonyms, hyponyms. Style: formal, figurative, euphemistic.

Grammar: Narrative tenses and time links. Adverbial positioning.

Writing: Narrative essay.

Listening: Choosing a title. Labelling. Events in chronological order. UK and US spellings. Language varieties.

Functions: Telling a story: speaker's and listener's role.

Oral: Pronunciation: vowels. Photograph: previous events. Communicative activity: problem solving.

Study skills: Using the dictionary: vocabulary.

Exam skills: Essay planning.

UNIT 2   **PUBLIC LIFE   PAGE 26**

Reading: Words from context: clues to meaning. Structures. The writer. Vocabulary: descriptive adjectives, abbreviations.

Grammar: Passive 1: intransitive and stative verbs, *got* + past participle, + infinitive/perfect infinitive. 2nd conditional. Emphatic conditionals.

Writing: Punctuation: quotation marks. Topic sentence. Time links. Conditional links. Descriptive essay: systems and scenes.

Listening: Putting names to description. Descriptive adjectives in table.

Functions: Describing people: appearance and character.

Oral: Pronunciation: consonants. Photograph: identifying and describing people. Reading passage: identifying the source.

Study skills: Note-taking from speech: recognising important information, writing shorter notes.

Exam skills: Answering multiple choice questions.

UNIT 3   **PRIVATE LIVES MADE PUBLIC   PAGE 36**

Reading: Words from context: near-synonyms, connotations, The writer.

Grammar: 3rd conditional. Reference words. Prepositions of place. *Used to/would*.

Writing: Summary 2: identifying relevant parts of the text. Narrative/descriptive essay.

Listening: True/False/Not Stated. Taking sides. Comparing with opinions in reading text. Writing: topic sentences, description, reference words.

Functions: Talking about the past: descriptive story-telling.

Oral: Pronunciation: diphthongs. Photograph: descriptive and time contrasts. Discussion: roleplay.

Study skills: Using the library.

Exam skills: Essay writing: which approach?

UNIT 4   **GOING PLACES   PAGE 46**

Reading: Words from context: connotations. Reference words. Understanding complex sentences. Contrasts. Discussion.

Grammar: Modals 1: *may/might/can/could/must/have to/need to/should/ought to*. Cause and result links.

Writing: Contrast links. Enumerating and paragraph building. Discursive essay organisation.

Listening: Discourse markers. Gist: listening for reasons. Imagining a scene.

Functions: Asking for, expressing and responding to opinions.

Oral: Pronunciation: weak syllables. Photograph: Opinions.

Study skills: Extensive listening.

Exam skills: Sentence transformation type 1.

UNIT 5   **UNIFORMS   PAGE 56**

Reading: Words from context: contrasts, context, hyponyms, connotations. Ignoring difficult words. Roleplay.

Grammar: Reported speech: backshift. *wish/if only*.

Writing: Formal letter: writing to the editor, job applications.

Listening: For/Against/Not Stated. Vocabulary: gap-filling. Roleplaying characters.

Functions: Coercing.

Oral: Word stress 1: simple words, parts of speech. Discussion: information gap. Reading passage: identifying the purpose.

Study skills: Extensive reading.

Exam skills: Predicting from the listening tape introduction.

UNIT 6   **WHAT NEXT?   PAGE 66**

Reading: Words from context. Ignoring difficult words. Style: metaphor, simile, personification. Text organisation: stages.

Grammar: Prepositions of place. Phrasal verbs 1: with *off, on, away*. Future perfect.

Writing: Writing about the future: what readers want to know, future or conditional? Seeing into the future, tense sequences, text organisation.

Listening: Predicting from introduction. The speakers. Points actually made. Evaluating predictions. Using historical parallels. Continuing the discussion.

Functions: Making and reacting to predictions.

Oral: Word stress 2: words with suffixes, compound words.

Study skills: Personal aims.

Exam skills: Interview photograph: predicting the questions.

UNIT 7   **TAKING PART   PAGE 76**

Reading: Reference words. Text organisation: paragraphing. The writer.

Grammar: Relative pronouns 1: omission. Modals 2: past.

Writing: Balanced discursive essay: organisation, introductory expressions, balance.

Listening: Listening for agreement. Advantages/disadvantages. Evaluating arguments.

Functions: Likes and dislikes.

Oral: Stressed words. Reading passage: the content. Preparing a talk.

Study skills: Looking for mistakes.

Exam skills: Sentence transformation type 2.

UNIT 8   **SHARING IT OUT   PAGE 86**

Reading: Connecting ideas. Expressions from context. Style: informal, neutral, nonstandard.

Grammar: Contrast links 2. Phrasal verbs 2: with *round, out, up*. Mixed conditionals.

Writing: Summary 3: relevant points, economy with words.

Listening: Writing answers. Completing a table. Speculating. Roleplay: relating to students' own country.

Functions: Communication strategies.

Oral: Weak forms of words. Photograph: contrasting.

Study skills: Self assessment.

Exam skills: Essay timing.

UNIT 9

CLEANING UP PAGE 96

Reading:	Register. Idioms. Style: personification. Inferring.
Grammar:	Dependent prepositions: *on, with, about, at, from.* Verbs followed by the gerund. Conditionals: *were to/should/happen to.*
Writing:	Directed writing task.
Listening:	Reasons actually given. Labelling a map. Inferring. Comparing.
Functions:	Asking about and expressing preferences. Expressing indifference.
Oral:	Intonation: falls, rises, fall-rises. Reading passage: link to theme. Discussion: evaluating advertisements.
Study skills:	Reviewing to remember.
Exam skills:	Key words in essay titles.

UNIT 10

INTERACTING PAGE 106

Reading:	Vocabulary: synonyms, affixes, compound words. Reference words. Transformation type 1.
Grammar:	Phrasal verbs 3: with *back, down, over.* Hypothetical forms: *I'd rather, it's time, as if he were, it isn't as though.* Inversion: subject and verb following place adverbial, subject and auxiliary after negative adverbials.
Writing:	Dialogue: reporting verbs, informal speech connectors.
Listening:	Points actually mentioned. Focusing on one speaker only, forming a mental picture, comparing and identifying in a photograph.
Functions:	Handling conversation: involving others, changing the topic, hesitating.
Oral:	Intonation: friendly (fall-rise) and unfriendly (fall). Discussion: roleplay.
Study skills:	Practising with people.
Exam skills:	Sentence completion.

UNIT 11

TIME OUT PAGE 116

Reading:	Connecting ideas. Contrasts. Style: metaphor.
Grammar:	The infinitive. Reported speech 2: indirect ⇒ direct, reporting verbs. Relative pronouns 2: formal/informal positioning, with determiners.
Writing:	Informal letter: functional language.
Listening:	Speaker's aim. Labelling. Reasons actually given. Relating to students' own country.
Functions:	Praising and criticising.
Oral:	Intonation: new information (fall) contrasted with shared information (fall-rise). Reading passage: special features. Discussion: completing a story, informal, anecdote using the narrative present.
Study skills:	Grading vocabulary.
Exam skills:	Gap-filling.

UNIT 12

THE HARD SELL PAGE 126

Reading:	Sentence completion. Reference words. Style and register.
Grammar:	Introductory *it.* Phrasal verbs 4: with *through, at, into.* Conditionals without *if.*
Writing:	Describing objects: descriptive and compound adjectives, colours.
Listening:	Tones of voice. Table completion. Identifying advertising techniques and target groups. Potential customer's response.
Functions:	Persuading and being persuaded.
Oral:	Intonation: assertive rises. Discussion: describing and persuading.
Study skills:	Getting help.
Exam skills:	Group interview.

UNIT 13

FIRST PERSON SINGULAR PAGE 136

Reading:	Transformation type 2. Relative pronouns. Gap-filling.
Grammar:	Phrasal verbs 5: separable/non-separable. Verbs followed by infinitive or gerund.
Writing:	Summary 4: identifying weaknesses.
Listening:	Rapid note-taking. Tone of voice. Personalisation.
Functions:	Worrying, fearing and reassuring.
Oral:	Intonation: low key. Discussion: talking about yourself.

| Study skills: | Using the dictionary: verb patterns. |
| Exam skills: | Predicting from listening comprehension questions. |

UNIT 14   **RIGHTS AND WRONGS**   **PAGE 146**

Reading:	Reference words. Style: formal and neutral. Sentence completion.
Grammar:	Infinitives as relatives. Introductory *there*. Adjective order.
Writing:	Use of English section B (excluding summary).
Listening:	Note-taking. Speakers that agree. Interruption/counter interruption.
Functions:	Interrupting, countering interruption.
Oral:	Intonation: high key. Discussion: quotations.
Study skills:	Defining terms.
Exam skills:	Answering open-ended questions.

UNIT 15   **TALKING MONEY**   **PAGE 156**

Reading:	Open-ended questions. Register. Transformation type 2. Text organisation: patterns.
Grammar:	Phrasal verbs 6: compound words. Forms + gerund or infinitive.
Writing:	Describing character.
Listening:	Speakers' attitudes. Adjectives of emotion.
Functions:	Expressing surprise, irritation and anger.
Oral:	Elision and linking. Photograph: describing likely character. Reading passage: identifying the message.
Study skills:	Dictionary examples.
Exam skills:	Set Book essay.

UNIT 16   **SUCCESS**   **PAGE 166**

Reading:	Open-ended questions. Sentence completion. Transformation type 1.
Grammar:	Phrasal verbs 7: passive use. Conditionals: inverted forms.
Writing:	Beginnings and endings (narrative/descriptive essays).
Listening:	Comparing reality with predictions about speakers. Multiple choice questions. Evaluating the speakers' linguistic performance.
Functions:	Expressing optimism, pessimism and satisfaction.
Oral:	Assimilation. 3 part interview: students make up the questions.
Study skills:	Revising: general, language areas, individual items, skills.
Exam skills:	1 The written papers. 2 The interview.

INDEX OF FUNCTIONS AND STRUCTURES **PAGE 176**

PROGRESS TESTS   **PAGE 178**

KEY TO PHONETIC SYMBOLS

Vowels and diphthongs

1	iː	as in **see**/siː/	8	ʊ	as in **put**/pʊt/	15	aɪ	as in **five**/faɪv/
2	ɪ	as in **sit**/sɪt/	9	uː	as in **too**/tuː/	16	aʊ	as in **now**/naʊ/
3	e	as in **ten**/ten/	10	ʌ	as in **cup**/kʌp/	17	ɔɪ	as in **join**/dʒɔɪn/
4	æ	as in **hat**/hæt/	11	ɜː	as in **fur**/fɜː(r)/	18	ɪə	as in **near**/nɪə(r)/
5	ɑː	as in **arm**/ɑːm/	12	ə	as in **ago**/əˈgəʊ/	19	eə	as in **hair**/heə(r)/
6	ɒ	as in **got**/gɒt/	13	eɪ	as in **page**/peɪdʒ/	20	ʊə	as in **pure**/pjʊə(r)/
7	ɔː	as in **saw**/sɔː/	14	əʊ	as in **home**/həʊm/			

Consonants

1	p	as in **pen**/pen/	9	f	as in **fall**/fɔːl/	17	h	as in **how**/haʊ/
2	b	as in **bad**/bæd/	10	v	as in **voice**/vɔɪs/	18	m	as in **man**/mæn/
3	t	as in **tea**/tiː/	11	θ	as in **thin**/θɪn/	19	n	as in **no**/nəʊ/
4	d	as in **did**/dɪd/	12	ð	as in **then**/ðen/	20	ŋ	as in **sing**/sɪŋ/
5	k	as in **cat**/kæt/	13	s	as in **so**/səʊ/	21	l	as in **leg**/leg/
6	g	as in **got**/gɒt/	14	z	as in **zoo**/zuː/	22	r	as in **red**/red/
7	tʃ	as in **chin**/tʃɪn/	15	ʃ	as in **she**/ʃiː/	23	j	as in **yes**/jes/
8	dʒ	as in **June**/dʒuːn/	16	ʒ	as in **vision**/ˈvɪʒn/	24	w	as in **wet**/wet/

MARKING SCALES—SPEAKING

1 Fluency

5	Virtually native-speaker speed and rhythm, and coherent presentation of thoughts.
4	Foreign, but with minimal hesitation in all contexts.
3	Minimal hesitation in everyday contexts, but some hesitation when discussing more abstract topics, though not such as to demand unreasonable patience of the listener.
2	Hesitation not unreasonable in most contexts, but impedes understanding on abstract topics.
1	Speaks haltingly even in everyday contexts.
0	Not capable of connected speech.

2 Grammatical accuracy

5	Virtually native-speaker over a wide range of structures and contexts. Few errors.
4	Few errors even in complex structures when discussing abstract topics. No basic errors.
3	Structures adequately controlled and varied in most contexts. Few if any basic errors.
2	Structures adequate in everyday contexts but limited in range. Basic errors not infrequent.
1	Frequent basic errors.
0	No awareness of basic grammatical functions

3 Pronunciation: Sentences

5	Virtually native-speaker stress-timing, rhythm and placing of stress; intonation patterns and range of pitch within sentence; natural linking of phrases.
4	Stress-timing, rhythm, placing of stress, intonations, etc. sufficiently native-like as to make comprehension easy and listening pleasurable.
3	Stress-timing, rhythm, placing of stress, intonation, etc. sufficiently controlled.
2	Foreign speech patterns make the candidate occasionally difficult to understand.
1	Foreign speech patterns severely impede comprehension.
0	Not intelligible, through faulty stress and intonation

4 Pronunciation: Individual sounds

5	All individual sounds virtually as a native speaker.
4	Most individual sounds virtually at native-speaker level.
3	All sounds sufficiently correct to be understood without difficulty.
2	Some individual sounds poorly articulated so that comprehension is sometimes difficult.
1	Individual sounds so poor that comprehension is often impossible.
0	Unintelligible judged on individual sounds.

5 Interative communication

5	Wholly effective at communicating both actively and receptively in all contexts.
4	Communicates effectively and with ease in most contexts, experiencing few difficulties.
3	Communicates with ease in everyday contexts and adequately in more abstract contexts.
2	Communication effective in everyday contexts but needing patience in abstract contexts.
1	Communicates poorly even in everyday contexts.
0	Communicates nothing.

6 Vocabulary resource

5	Wide-ranging, varied, precise and appropriate in all contexts.
4	Shows few vocabulary gaps other than in specialised areas. Rarely needs to paraphrase.
3	Adequate on general tasks, though sometimes needs to resort to paraphrase.
2	Vocabulary though adequate for everyday tasks seldom rises above the mundane.
1	Lack of vocabulary makes performance even in everyday contexts inadequate.
0	Vocabulary too slight for communication at this level.

THE EXAMINATION

Paper 1 of the Examination, **Reading Comprehension**, consists of forty multiple choice questions. Each question has four possible answers.

Section A (25 items) – sentence blank filling. Only one of the given alternatives is both grammatically and contextually correct. There are no technical or specialised terms included, but lexical features such as collocations, synonyms, antonyms, modal and phrasal verbs are tested, as are grammatical rules.

Section B (15 items) – text comprehension. Three or more reading passages are used to test the Candidate's understanding of:
1 the text as a whole.
2 specific details.
3 shades of meaning (in some texts); variation in language according to the context or circumstances; the writer's technique in communicating his/her message.

All passages are of the kind of material that could be read and understood by proficient English speakers anywhere.

You are not required to understand every word in every text.

THE COURSE

When we read (or listen) we are constantly making connections between our previous knowledge of the subject and what the writer (or speaker) is saying. We are also predicting the answers to questions we have subconsciously asked ourselves about the content of the text.

First you will be asked questions to focus on what you already know about the subject in general:

1 The topic

a In groups, look at the cuttings on the right. Where is each taken from?

b What differences are there in the way you read each of them?

c What differences are there between the way you read in your first language and the way you read in English? Why?

Then you are asked about your expectations of the text content.

CABIN BAGGAGE
For security and safety reasons only one piece of hand baggage, which must not be larger than 115 cm. (length x width x depth), will normally be allowed in the cabin.
The following additional items are also allowed:
One small size handbag/purse.
One coat or one cape or one blanket.
One umbrella or one walking stick.
One pair of crutches.
One small camera/binoculars.
An infant's carrying basket or invalid's fully collapsible wheelchair, which are carried free of charge, will normally be carried in the cargo compartment.
A reasonable amount of reading matter for the flight.
Infants' food for consumption on flight.

GUNMEN in a speeding car shot and killed two Syrian soldiers in Muslim West Beirut. Police said the gunmen sprayed the soldiers with rifle fire as they walked through the Zokak Blatt residential neighbourhood.

In a number of branches you can use your SERVICECARD to obtain specified amounts of cash – up to the SERVICECARD limit previously agreed with your branch – from the Rapid Cash Till. The whole operation need take no more than 15 seconds.

DOWN
1. After hash it's time for soup (6).
2. Country alternative to poet (6).
3. A regulation in a motorway in Africa (6).

IF EVER there was a record to conjure up the beer-swilling, head-swimming ambience of a suburban house party in full flow then this is it. 'Wow' manages, through the intuitive tastefulness peculiar to K-Tel, to feature almost every song you've *hated* in the past two years, which is no mean feat.

But is there really, in the present state of weapons technology, no other option — no means of stunning rather than killing, so that the gunman's fate can be decided by due judicial process rather than instant execution?

A VOYAGE TO LILLIPUT
cable, and marked with black figures which we humbly conceive to be writings, every letter almost half as large as the palm of our hands. In the left there was a sort of

---

2 Before reading

How can you improve your reading speed in English? Discuss in groups.

The next step is to read (or listen to) the text in order to get a general impression of its meaning.

3 While reading

Read the text below quickly and decide which of the following titles best fits the text:

**HOW TO READ LESS IMPORTANT MATERIAL.
THE DIFFERENCES BETWEEN FIRST AND SECOND LANGUAGE READING.
HOW TO READ FASTER – AND WHEN NOT TO.
FASTER READING IS ALWAYS BETTER READING.**

You may then be asked to go quickly through the text again, this time to find specific details.

4 Reading for detail

Look at the text again and briefly note down all the ways *you* can improve your reading.

Throughout the course, you will be encouraged to look for clues to meaning from within the text. The objective is to increase your independence so that your reading is not interrupted by over-use of the dictionary. The following activity is an example of how we can find out enough about new vocabulary for general understanding of the text.

An essential element in learning a foreign language is extensive reading of as wide a variety of text-types as possible. As you read more, so your confidence and enjoyment grow; in 5 the process you will also *acquire* a lot of useful language without, in many cases, noticing you are doing so, your reading speed will steadily increase, and this can be further improved by 10 adopting the following technique:

1 Look at the title and sub-headings.
2 Read the introduction and the conclusion.
3 Look at any pictures (and their 15 captions), graphs, tables, etc.
4 Read the text from beginning to end.

There are texts, of course, that *do* require slower reading: a contract 20 needs careful examination;

instructions in a repair manual should be followed very carefully; literature is often best enjoyed at a leisurely, relaxed pace. But often we are more 25 concerned with the *gist* – the main points or the general sense – rather than the details, as when reading a newspaper, a magazine or an advertisement, for instance. 30
Some would say that the best way of learning to read in another language is simply to read enjoyable, interesting material and so transfer the techniques used in reading your 35 first language to your second. Many students, however, still study foreign-language texts on a word-by-word basis instead of concentrating on the overall meaning. By the time 40 they have reached the end of the text, paragraph or even sentence, they will probably have forgotten

what came before. Research has also shown that an efficient reader makes 45 fewer eye movements than a slow one, by focusing on groups of related words:

If you look at
each group of words 50
arranged like this
you will notice
they can be absorbed
by focusing
on each line. 55

Obviously, texts are rarely laid out in columns, so a good reader divides the word groups as follows:
Think about reading/in your first language./Do you look/at every 60 single word/or do you concentrate/on a group/at a time?/ Why not/do the same/in your second language?/

---

5 Words from context

Which part of speech (noun, verb, etc.) is each of the following words? Work out the approximate meaning of each word, using the clues which follow.

1 *sub-headings* (line 12) ....
What does the prefix *sub* tell you? What word is *headings* derived from? How does the meaning differ from *titles*?

2 *captions* (line 16) ....
Imagine a photograph in a magazine. What usually accompanies it?

3 *leisurely* (line 24) ....
Is the meaning likely to be similar to or different from *relaxed*?

4 *overall* (line 40) ....
Find a word in the previous paragraph which means the same.

When we have read (or listened to) a text we often demonstrate our understanding of it in some way: if it is a recipe, by cooking the meal; if it is a letter, by replying to it etc. Consequently, texts in the course also invite reactions.

6 Responding to the text

a Look at the three stages on lines 12–16. In pairs, think of a book you both know and decide what you can find out about the subject in general, the content of the text and the writer.

b Write a paragraph for your partner, giving him/her some advice on books, magazines or newspapers. Divide it up into groups of words (as shown on lines 49–55) and get him/her to read it quickly.

PRACTICE

THE EXAMINATION

Paper 3 of the Examination, **Use of English**, tests both the linguistic and communicative functions of language items.

Section A consists of four exercises that require the Candidate to fill in blanks or rewrite sentences.

Section B consists of an authentic text with questions. This provides a further test of reading comprehension, but, unlike Paper 1, alternative answers are not supplied. It also tests the Candidate's capacity to interpret and summarise, preferably in his or her own words.
Once again, you do not need to understand every word in the text to successfully complete the tasks.

THE COURSE

A systematic and comprehensive advanced-level syllabus presents and practises the uses of grammar in preparation for *Section A*. The emphasis is on what native speakers actually say in the 1990s, not on what they 'should' say (or used to say). This also applies to vocabulary, pronunciation and language functions. Preparation for *Section B* is covered in READING and WRITING.

Here, as elsewhere in each unit, you will notice how recently introduced vocabulary appears in different contexts in order to reinforce the meaning. Words that may be new to you, and those which you will read or hear later in the unit are also used. They should then be more familiar and make gist comprehension easier.

Activities follow the presentation of new language and grammar analysis; you are not being tested on your existing knowledge by out-of-context transformation exercises, gap fills, etc. (although you will be shown how to do these in EXAM SKILLS).

1 General tense revision – time lines

Time lines illustrate the relationships that exist in English between tense and time.

x	= single event or action
x x x x	= repeated actions or events
- - - - - - -	= state
vvvvvvv	= continuous action
|	= definite point in time

Examples:

I'm a student.   = $\underline{\qquad \text{- - - -}\,|\,\text{- - - -} \qquad}$
                          past   now   future

He lays out his work very clearly.   = $\underline{\qquad \text{x x x}\,|\,\text{x x x} \qquad}$
                          past   now   future

At last! I've been standing here for hours!   = $\underline{\quad \text{vvvvvvv}\,| \qquad}$
                          past   now   future

a In groups, match the sentences below with the time lines.

Example:
1–d

1 I'll arrange everything tomorrow.

a) $\underline{\qquad \text{vvvvv}\,|\,\text{vvvvv} \qquad}$
   past   now   future

2 He was finishing his essay.

b) $\underline{\text{x x}\,|\,\text{x x} \qquad\qquad}$
   past   now   future

3 We're starting later on Thursday.

c) $\underline{\quad \text{x}\,| \qquad\qquad}$
   past   now   future

4 She wasn't very studious as a girl.

d) $\underline{\qquad\qquad\qquad \text{x}}$
   past   now   future

5 He's planning his homework timetable.

e) $\underline{\qquad\qquad \text{vvv}\,|\,\text{vvv}}$
   past   now   future

6 I'd been to New York before.

f) $\underline{\qquad\qquad\qquad \text{x}}$
   past   now   future

7 I used to read word by word.

g) $\underline{\text{- - -}\,|\,\text{- - -} \qquad\qquad}$
   past   now   future

8 They'll be taking the exam at 9 a.m.

h) $\underline{\text{vvv}\,|\,\text{vvv} \qquad\qquad}$
   past   now   future

b Draw time lines for the following sentences:

1 They'd been doing a lot of revision for First Certificate.
2 I've only been to Paris once.
3 I'll have passed Proficiency by then!
4 The term begins next Monday.

WRITING

THE EXAMINATION

Paper 2, **Composition**, consists of choosing two of the following types of essay:

1 descriptive
2 narrative
3 discursive: expressing an opinion OR a balanced discussion (dialogue form may be an option)
4 a shorter, more structured and specific writing task
5 an essay based on one of the optional set books

Overall, the Examiners are looking for the Candidate's ability to *communicate* and the ideal composition should demonstrate the following (in alphabetical order):

☐ accurate punctuation
☐ accurate spelling
☐ appropriate and varied sentence structure
☐ appropriate and varied vocabulary
☐ examples and indirect references
☐ expression of experience or knowledge
☐ liveliness and imagination
☐ natural and appropriate style
☐ paragraph organisation
☐ relevance to the instructions
☐ sufficient length
☐ text organisation

Which of the points above do you think you will have to work on most? Make a note of them and check them in each essay you write.

In Paper 3, **Use of English**, summary writing is assessed for the following:

☐ The number of points that are relevant to the instructions.
☐ Concise, fluent expression in, where possible, your own words.
☐ Good linking within sentences and the paragraph as a whole.
☐ Not adding to the facts or opinions in the text.

THE COURSE

Each type of essay is covered in WRITING, leading to a guided writing activity; freer practice is given in REVIEW, when language from FUNCTIONS can also be incorporated.
Summary writing (as for essay type 5 and, often, type 4) also requires efficient reading of a text. Recognition of the main points is the first step in successful summarising.

1 Summary writing – 1

a Read the text and then, in pairs, suggest a title.

> When we speak, it is not necessary to be quite so explicit as we have to be in writing: many references are clear within the situation. If, for example, we refer to 'that thing over there', we assume that this is sufficiently clear to our listener. 5
>
> Secondly, the person (or persons) we are addressing is normally present – even on the phone we are in direct contact – so that there is continuous interaction and feedback, both verbal and non-verbal. The person we are addressing acknowledges what 10 we say (and we *expect* him to do so) in a variety of ways: perhaps only by a murmur or a grunt, but more commonly by asking questions or by making comments. We know immediately, therefore, how he is reacting to what we say, while non-verbal feedback 15 in the form of facial expressions, for example, makes it clear if we are getting our message across.
>
> In speech we use a great variety of prosodic features, such as pitch, loudness, speed, rhythm and pauses, as well as facial expressions and gestures 20 when we feel that these will help us to convey our meaning.
>
> When writing, by contrast, the person we are addressing is not present, so there can be no interaction between writer and reader. Prosodic 25 features are not available, and although we can employ graphological devices such as punctuation, capitalisation or underlining, in general we have to get our meaning across through the linguistic elements alone. 30
>
> While it is true that in writing we have to organise our sentences carefully because we do not have the help of feedback from our reader, on the other hand we do not normally have to write quickly: we can rewrite and revise our sentences until we are satisfied 35 that we have expressed our meaning. Equally, the reader is in a more privileged position than the listener in some respects: he can read at his own pace and re-read as often as he likes. Word and sentence boundaries are also clearly marked in the written form 40 of the language. To some extent, then, the disadvantages of communicating through the written medium are offset.

b Read lines 1–22 again. Which lines do each of these points correspond to?
Example:
The other person can often see what we are referring to. *Lines 3–5*
1 Any sound the listener makes tells us something.
2 We get information from body language.
3 We vary the characteristics of our speaking voice.
4 We adjust what we say according to the response.

c Read lines 23–43 again, and note the main points.

LISTENING

THE EXAMINATION

Paper 4 of the Examination, **Listening Comprehension**, consists of three or four realistic texts preceded by verbal instructions. Each is usually played twice, and the Candidate may be required to answer Multiple Choice or TRUE/FALSE Questions, re-order or match information, label diagrams or fill in blanks. The recordings are taken from: radio programmes, dialogues in situations, public announcements, phone calls or discussions. The speakers may or may not have 'standard English' accents.

The Candidate must get the information from the recording and interpret what the speakers are communicating, taking account of English stress and intonation.

As in the case of reading texts, you are not required to understand every word.

THE COURSE

The recordings are similar to those used in the Examination and are not graded for difficulty. The activities, however, do become progressively more demanding throughout the Course and include all the types of task that make up the Examination format.

As the skills of reading and listening have so much in common, several relevant points have already been made in READING. There are, though, a number of key differences – look back at the last paragraph of the text in WRITING for some of them.

1 Pre-listening

a In groups, discuss what qualities an efficient language learner has.
Think of people you know who are 'good students', e.g, they know why they are learning and are keen to do so.

b Discuss in what ways you learn outside the classroom.

c Look at the photographs. Which of these methods do you like best? Which do you think have been most useful? Which would you like to try?

2 While listening

a Listen to the recording and decide whether the following statements are TRUE or FALSE:

Efficient language learners:
1 are highly motivated.
2 know they must only speak 'good English'.
3 never use dictionaries or keep notes.
4 often feel depressed about their progress.
5 are interested in the countries where people speak the language.

Outside the classroom learners should:
6 listen only to British English.
7 practise English only with language teachers.
8 read any material in English they can find.

Preparing for the Proficiency exam should include:
 9 reading only high quality literature.
10 compiling lists of new vocabulary while you read.

b Listen again, and note down any other points which could be useful to you as a language learner.

3 Post-listening

In groups check your answers and list ways you can follow John Haycraft's advice.

FUNCTIONS

THE EXAMINATION

Language function – the purpose of a particular spoken or written form – must be recognised in all Papers of the Examination. Production of the forms used to express the appropriate functions is required in Papers 2, 3 and 5.

THE COURSE

A good command of grammar and vocabulary is not, by itself, sufficient for effective communication, as our choice of language is also determined by the situation and the people we are speaking (or writing) to. A given structure may perform a number of different functions, and there are always different grammatical forms that can be used to express any one function.

Examples:

I'd like a nice cold beer, please.	=	*requesting*
I'd like a nice cold beer, in this heat.	=	*wishing*
Why not spend some time in the USA?	=	*giving advice*
Have you ever thought of spending some time in the USA?	=	*giving advice*

a Look at the sentences below and match them with the functions on the right.

Example:
1 – d

1 It might be a good idea if you did a summer course.	a *inviting*
2 I really don't like learning lists of vocabulary.	b *making suggestions*
3 Shall we enrol for the Tuesday/Thursday class?	c *expressing dislikes*
4 What do you think of this dictionary?	d *giving advice*
5 Would you like to come for a meal after the lesson?	e *asking for permission*
6 Would you mind if I left early this evening?	f *asking for opinions*

b Look at the following sentences and decide which category of function they all belong to:

I suggest you have a good look through your notes.
I'd buy myself a more up-to-date grammar book.
You could always record yourself, and compare your pronunciation to a native speaker's.
Personally, I think you should subscribe to English-language magazines.

c Using the forms in italics in **b** (and others on this page that express the same function) talk to your partner, imagining he or she:

1 is always late for the lesson.
2 enjoys reading English and American literature.
3 has just bought a new home computer.
4 has got illegible handwriting.
5 would like to meet English-speaking people of the opposite sex.
6 is the laziest person you've ever met.

STUDY SKILLS

In every unit, there is a section headed STUDY SKILLS. Each one deals with a different aspect of the techniques and strategies you need if you are to make the most efficient use of your time spent studying.

Efficient learners

Look back at the corrected answers to the questions in LISTENING, and look at more characteristics of good learners in the list below. Compare yourself with 'efficient learners', making notes about each point.

☐ They know that learning a language is not easy, but do not become discouraged.
☐ When they are learning new vocabulary, they form mental images of the objects.
☐ They contrast words in their first and second languages.
☐ They have their preferred ways of studying, but know that there is always something new to be learnt in any situation.
☐ They frequently make comparisons between what they say in the foreign language and what other people say.
☐ They make notes of what they have learned and check their progress.
☐ They can think in their second language.

Now exchange notes with your partner and give him or her advice.

ORAL

THE INTERVIEW

The Examination

Paper 5 of the Examination offers a choice of an individual or a small group interview. In either case, there are normally three stages based on one general topic:

1 responding to the Examiner's questions about a photograph and related issues.
2 reading a short text (not aloud): saying where it is probably taken from, why it was written and how it is connected to the overall topic.
3 discussion of an authentic text: this could be an article, an announcement, an advertisement, etc.
   AND/OR
   a communicative activity: expressing an opinion on a topic (Candidates are given time to consider and prepare this), roleplay, discussion or finding out/exchanging information.
   OR
   discussion of *one* of the optional Set Books.

The Candidate may be asked to discuss topics of virtually any kind, including those of an abstract nature. He or she will be expected to speak at considerably greater length than at First Certificate level. For the marking criteria, see page 7.

The Course

A comprehensive phonology syllabus, with recorded material on cassette, is complemented by pair and group work that reflects the Examination format. Students assume the roles of Candidate and Examiner, giving each other marks on simplified Cambridge scales. A sensible balance between fluency and accuracy is the aim throughout.

a Look at the phonetic chart on page 6.
   Which of these sounds are not used in your first language? Make a list of them and write two English words which contain each.

b Now listen to the words in the phonetic chart and repeat.

c Listen again and write down another word that contains the same sound.
   Example:
   cut – run

d Look at the picture. In groups, make a list of all the topics which the people could be discussing.
   Examples:
   politics   fashion   computers

e In pairs ask your partner to tell you what he or she knows about one of the topics.

   Give him or her marks as explained on page 7; paying particular attention to *fluency*, *grammatical accuracy* (in this case, especially verb tenses) and *the pronunciation of individual sounds*.

f Now advise your partner on any difficulties you may have noticed.
   Examples:
   I think you should be careful with the difference in usage between the present simple and the present continuous. Well, I'd advise you to practise the sound /ʃ/, as in 'shout'.

THE COURSE

The REVIEW, brings together the language and skills that have been introduced and/or practised in a freer activity, or as revision and a check on progress.

1 Individual Sounds

a Say the following words aloud.
1 /kæpʃəns/ 2 /leʒə/ 3 /pɑːtnə/ 4 /əreɪndʒ/
5 /leŋθ/ 6 /wɪðɪn/ 7 /rɪfɜː/ 8 /rɪkwaɪə/ 9 /ɪʃuː/
10 /peəz/ 11 /hɪə/ 12 /dʒenrəl/

b Write down the spelling of the words above.

2 Tense Revision

Use the time lines below to write six sentences about your study habits.

Example:
1 – *I used to translate everything I read.*
1 x x x│x x x

	past	now	future
2		x x x│x x x	
	past	now	future
3			x x x│x x x
	past	now	future

3 Reading/Summarising/Advising

a The text that follows is about learning in general. How do you think it will describe a 'good learner'?

b Read the text quickly. Which of the following best expresses the text content?
1 Good and bad learners compared.
2 What good learners believe and what they do.
3 Learning made easy.
4 Learning techniques – past and present.

c Read the text again and note down the main points. Where do they tend to occur in each paragraph?

d In your own words, give your partner advice on how to become a better learner.

Good learners:
● have confidence in their ability to learn. If they fail at one problem, they are not discouraged.
● tend to enjoy solving problems. The process interests them, and they tend to resent people who want to 'help' by giving them the answers.
● are apt to resent being told that something is 'good for them to know', unless, of course, they feel that it *is* good for them to know – in which case, they resent being told anyway.
● prefer to rely on their own judgement.
● are usually not fearful of being wrong. They can change their minds.
● are emphatically not fast answerers. They tend to delay their judgements until they have access to as much information as will be available.
● are flexible. They frequently begin their answers with the words 'It depends'.
● are skilful in making distinctions between statements of fact and other kinds of statements.
● know how to ask meaningful questions; they are persistent in examining their own assumptions and are apt to be cautious in making generalisations.
● do not need to have an absolute, final, irrevocable resolution to every problem. The sentence, 'I don't know', does not depress them.

EXAM SKILLS

In every unit, there is a section headed EXAM SKILLS. The aim is to make the most efficient use of your knowledge and abilities in preparation for, and when actually taking, the Exam.

Look back at all the information in this unit under the heading The Examination, decide whether the following statements are *true* or *false* and say *why* in each case:
1 Paper 1 *Section B* involves more than just understanding the individual words.
2 In Paper 2, you have to write an essay about one of the Set Books.
3 Your own personality should not be too apparent in compositions.
4 In Paper 3 *Section B*, you should copy your answers from the text.
5 The content of the Summary must come only from the text.
6 You should read the questions on Paper 4 carefully before the recording begins.
7 The speakers' accents are always those of South-east England.

UNIT 1 LANGUAGE

READING

1 The topic

a In groups make a list of English words that are used in your first language.

b Now make a list of words from your first language that are used in English.

2 Before reading

a Why do we 'import' foreign words? Do some people in your country complain about this?

b What other criticisms are made of the way your first language is spoken or written nowadays?

3 While reading

a Look at the first sentence of the text. Now read the rest of the text. How is the question answered?

b Suggest a title for the text.

4 Responding to the text

a Do you agree with the editors' conclusion in paragraph 7? Why/Why not?

b Have there been similar changes in your first language? Why/Why not?

5 Words from context

a Which part of speech is each of the following words? Work out the meaning of each word using the clues.

Clues to meaning:

1 *bloated* (1)	What effect does *inflation* have?
2 *wrought* (30)	Which other verbs could be used with *by*?
3 *VCRs* (34)	Look back at the first sentence.
4 *coinage* (48)	What are the *computer-related terms* doing now?
5 *outcome* (80)	Look at the expression *terminal episode*.

b *Connotation:*

You may only need to know if a word suggests a positive (+) or a negative (−) idea in the context. Write + or − next to each of the following words:

1 *appalling* (8) 2 *mentality* (18) 3 *slick* (19)
4 *thriving* (27) 5 *humble* (73) 6 *notorious* (85)

c *Synonyms:*

Find four expressions in the text which mean *books* and five which mean *words*.

Is the English language dying, bloated by the inflation of advertisers, politicians and other word-abusers of the video age? The old question is being put with some urgency in America these days. Two current best-sellers castigate the failures of the school system, commentators are lamenting the state of American culture and reports seem to be testifying almost daily to appalling ignorance among the country's youth.

'You don't have to make sense any more as long as what you are saying sounds good,' Russell Baker, a columnist of *The New York Times*, pronounced recently in a typical attack on linguistic abuses. The reduction of American television news to ever-shorter 'sound-bites' – often lasting only five seconds – suggests that people are giving up listening at all and just watch, according to some critics. Many blame not only the mentality of the pop media and advertising, but also the slick hyperbole of the President and his speech-writers.

But this week a powerful defence of present-day English appeared in the form of the first new unabridged American dictionary to be published for more than two decades. The editors of *The Random House Dictionary of the English Language* have tracked the explosion of new words and idioms of the past 20 years and found the language to be thriving. A read through some of the 210,000 new words or entries revised from the 1966 edition gives a fascinating glimpse of the vast changes wrought in American and, inevitably, global English by the electronic age.

'In 1966 no one had walked on the Moon, bought a sun blocker or running shoes, VCRs were unknown . . . Heavy metal, punk rock music, post-modernism, yuppies and soft contact lenses didn't exist,' the editors say.

They have included a vast range of vocabulary and colloquial terms that might not make it to the pages of the 19-volume *Oxford English Dictionary*, but which help record the preoccupations of the late 20th century. Among these are: *wimp, networking, chocoholic, monoclonal ability, catch-22* and *wysiwyg*. The last of these ('what you see is what

d *Hyponyms:*

What is a general term for *crêpes, hummus, chapati, tofu, linguine* and *sushi* (55)? Do we need to understand precisely what each word means? Find other groups of hyponyms in the text. Think of a general term for each group.

you get') is one of hundreds of computer-related terms that are increasingly invading daily life in the way that psychoanalytical jargon became current coinage in earlier decades.

Dozens of new business *buzz-words* are listed, reflecting the birth of global markets and the take-over boom. These include: *golden parachute, greenmail and money market zero-coupon.* Food is another big growth area as cuisine has become international, and hitherto exotic items such as *crêpes, hummus, chapati, tofu, linguine* and *sushi* can be found at the local supermarket.

Though they define their work as descriptive rather than proscriptive, the editors have combed their earlier volume to remove all sexist references and avoid 'man' and 'he' when they can keep to a genderless definition. One entry gives this as an example of the use of the word 'master': 'She is a master at interpreting financial reports'. They conclude that the language is not deteriorating or on the verge of death, and blame individual users for the ugliness and obfuscation that is so remarkable in modern American.

Though America has no monopoly on linguistic corruption, its citizens seem to be inventing euphemisms and unnecessary variations faster than ever. Anyone who listens to an airline or train announcement will notice that the word 'now' has been discarded as too humble. Instead, passengers are told 'at this time' to fasten seatbelts. Doctors no longer talk about health, preferring to return their patients to 'wellness'. A hospital recently announced the relapse of an important patient by saying he 'did not fully achieve his wellness potential'. He later experienced a 'terminal episode', or 'negative patient-care outcome', previously known as death.

Professor William Lutz, a Rutgers University professor and guardian of linguistic clarity, recently issued a list of horrendous public doublespeak. Much of it, of course, came from the Pentagon, lately notorious for describing tents as 'frame-supported tension structures'. According to Professor Lutz, official doublespeak 'avoids or shifts responsibility and conceals or prevents thought, and it is getting worse'.

6 Style

a Formal language

Find formal expressions in the text which mean the same as the neutral terms below.

Example:
attack (paragraph 1) – *castigate* (line 5)

1 showing (para. 1)   3 cooking (para. 6)
2 said (para. 2)   4 until now (para. 6)

b Figurative language

Find figurative words in the text which mean the same as the literal expressions below.

Example:
coming into in large numbers (paragraph 5) – *invading* (line 46)

1 sudden increase (paragraph 3)
2 appearance (paragraph 6)
3 looked very carefully through (paragraph 7)

c Euphemistic language

Give a more direct expression for the euphemistic expressions from the text.

Example:
terminal episode (79) – death

1 *at this time* (74)
2 *wellness* (76)
3 *did not fully achieve his wellness potential* (77–78)
4 *negative patient-care outcome* (79–80)

STUDY SKILLS   USING THE DICTIONARY

The vocabulary of English is constantly growing, so buy the most comprehensive and up-to-date dictionary possible.

1 The introduction will tell you how to find an item; its meaning(s), style, pronunciation and grammatical characteristics.
2 Practise looking up some words and phrases you already know.
3 When you are reading English, only look up a new word if you are sure that:
   a) its meaning is essential for understanding.
   b) the context does not give sufficient information for you to guess the meaning.
4 Use one notebook just for vocabulary items. For each new item check its spelling and which part of speech it is. Make a note of its meaning(s), pronunciation (note GB/US differences) and style. Write an example of its usage for each different meaning.
5 For every new item, decide which of the following categories it belongs to:
   a) language for active use, such as structural words and useful expressions.
   b) language that only needs to be understood when it is heard or read.
   c) language which you don't think would be particularly useful to know.
6 Practise the **category a** expressions (see above) the next time you are speaking or writing. Make a note of the contexts in which you read or hear **category b** expressions.

In pairs, look at all the new vocabulary in **Words from context** opposite. Decide which category each word belongs to.

Б Сейреулхова

PRACTICE

1 Narrative tenses and time links

a Look back at the sentence on lines 33–37 of the text. Which verb tenses are used?

b In pairs, decide which tenses are used in the following sentence:
The indigenous people had been using writing implements for centuries; when the Europeans started to arrive in the 1650s they found, and later destroyed, a culture which was creating its own literature.
Now draw time lines for each of the finite verbs.

c The past perfect and past perfect progressive tenses are often used with time links.

Examples:
He read the text again. He began to write a summary.
As soon as *he* **had read** *the text again he began to write a summary.*

He was living in Rome for three years. His Italian was fluent.
His Italian was fluent ***after*** *he* **had been living** *in Rome for three years.*

Join the following sentences in the same way, using these time links:
when   after   as soon as   until   by the time

1 She watched a few films in English. She decided to buy a VCR.
2 He looked carefully through his notes. He wrote the essay.
3 He listened to the tape three times. He finally understood.
4 They were studying German at university. They went to Berlin.
5 She spoke English in public several times. She felt more relaxed.
6 They compiled a new dictionary. They realised it was already out of date.
7 The last native speakers died. People took an interest in the language.
8 He was making very slow progress. He started to participate more in the lessons.

d Make a list of the stages of your progress in English. Use time links, the past perfect and the past perfect progressive.
Examples:
Until *I was twelve I* **hadn't studied** *any foreign languages.*
By the time I'd finished *the first course book I could understand some English.*
When I'd been studying *for two years I went to America.*

e Now use the past progressive to add descriptive information to each of your sentences above.
Examples:
I **was only learning** *my own language.*
We **were having** *lessons in the evening.*
I **was feeling** *more confident.*

f Use the simple past for shorter occurrences or interruptions. Write down similar events from your learning experiences.
Examples:
I was spending the summer in Boston when I first **read** *a novel in English.*
I was practising with the word processor when a friend **rang** *and* **said***, 'You've passed First Certificate!'*

Role play

Work in pairs.

Student A You are the Personnel Officer for a company. You are interviewing a candidate for a job which requires English. Ask the candidate about his/her progress in English.

Student B You are applying for a job which requires English. You are at the interview. Tell the Personnel Officer about your progress in English.

Change roles when you have finished.

English is our lingua franca, which is the Italian for French.

2 Adverbial positioning

a Different kinds of adverbs and adverb phrases are usually placed in different parts of the sentence. In pairs, look at the adverbials a) – 1) from the READING text. Decide which type each is (1–6) and write the letter in the column corresponding to its position (some types can be in more than one position).

The first one has already been done as an example: g) is an adverbial of place and it is the final expression in the sentence.

b When adverbials occur together at the end of a sentence, they tend to be in a certain order. Look at the sentence on line 4 of the READING text. What do you think the rule usually is?

All the adverbials a)–l) are in the most common position for each type. When you have completed the table correctly, use it for reference.

Adverbial

a) *with some urgency* (4)
b) *almost daily* (8)
c) *In 1966* (33)
d) *the late 20th century* (41–42)
e) *increasingly* (46)
f) *in earlier decades* (48)
g) *at the local supermarket* (56)
h) *faster than ever* (70)
i) *fully* (78)
j) *previously* (80)
k) *recently* (82)
l) *lately* (84)

Type + *example*	Position in sentence		
	BEGINNING	MIDDLE	END
1 Place (*in the north*)			g
2 Definite time (*in the 1980s*)			
3 Indefinite time (*already*)			
4 Frequency (*often*)			
5 Manner (*fluently*)			
6 Degree (*totally*)			

c Look at the map on the right and add the following adverbials to the text below, punctuating and using capital or lower case letters where necessary. The adverbs are all in the correct order.

The first one has already been done as an example.

about the year 449
profoundly
in that year
commonly
for more than a hundred years
in the south and east of the island
eventually
in the west and north

About the year 449 an event occurred which affected the course of history. As stated, certain Germanic tribes, the founders of the English nation, began the invasion of Britain. Bands of conquerors and settlers migrated from their continental homes in the region of Denmark and the Low Countries and established themselves. Then they extended the area which they occupied until it included all but the highlands.

d In groups talk about the roots of your own language. Either illustrate on the map where any significant influences came from, or draw a rough map of the world and mark them in.

WRITING

THE NARRATIVE ESSAY

1 A Narrative Text

a Look at the picture. What do you think the story will be about?

b Read the text, then suggest a title.

It was his last chance. The capital had been taken, cities were falling by the hour and border towns like this one would soon be subjected to military 'protection'.

He had known that a through ticket would have meant suspicion followed by questions; his accent would have immediately identified him as a foreigner. But as soon as he stepped down off the train, ten minutes before the customs post closed for the night, he realised he would have to ask for directions. Two words: *¿La frontera?*. He had practised under his breath, just in case, for the last 200 kilometres. He had worked on the vowels – no diphthongs, keep them clear; the consonants – roll both 'r's; the intonation – start low, rise a little.

Then he saw the stationmaster. His uniform and bearing reeked of authority. But there were no porters, there were no other passengers; it had to be him. A shiver as the sweat on his back turned suddenly cold, a few determined paces forward, eye-contact established and the question was asked. Not the question he had intended, though. At the last moment the name of the town across the frontier flashed into his mind and he pronounced it faultlessly.

The answer was brisk and dismissive; there would be no repetition for a native speaker. Had he said *derecho* – straight on, or *derecha* – to the right? The railway line – no lights, no bends in sight – seemed both the safer and the quicker option, but after covering a few hundred metres he found himself in a winding cutting where the trees blocked out such moonlight as there was. Still no sign of the border, and although he could not see his watch in the gloom he knew it was very close to midnight. His senses were scalpel sharp; he had already picked up the characteristic smell of eucalyptus wafting on the lazy warm air when he heard low voices ahead. He was getting near. He turned off to the right, following a path for some minutes, and miraculously found himself right outside the border post just as the sound of helicopter blades clattered through the night.

The building was in darkness except for one office; he strode in and greeted the seated policemen with a well-rehearsed *buenas noches*, simultaneously registering the unfamiliar uniforms. He was wondering whether they were part of a newly-arrived specialist force, and what the implications of that would be, when one of them answered him in Portuguese and took his passport. It dawned on him; he had unwittingly walked right across the frontier. He had made it.

But just then the peace was shattered once again. From nearby came the sound of heavy vehicles pulling up and orders being shouted in Spanish. The phone next to the younger policeman shrilled and he picked it up. He listened, his mouth hardening into a grim line, hung up and then quickly explained to the sergeant. It appeared that an elite unit from a third country had slipped in, neutralised the track patrol, picked up a number of foreign nationals and disappeared into thin air. They had been helped by a railway employee from the station on the other side – a former officer who had been cashiered by a cowardly government for revealing an earlier conspiracy. The sergeant flicked through the passport, glanced through the window at a faded sign ten metres away that said *frontera* and then looked up coldly.

'Without an exit stamp you'll have to go back', he said.

2 Tense Sequence

In groups, put these events from the story in chronological order:

a) He smelt something familiar.
b) Foreign refugees left the border area.
c) The frontier closed.
d) An officer was dismissed from the army.
e) He noticed the way the policemen were dressed.
f) He heard military activity on the other side of the border.
g) The train arrived in the station.
h) He left the railway line.
i) He heard people speaking.
j) An officer disclosed plans for a coup.
k) He crossed the border.
l) He was given directions.
m) He came to a section of the line which was in darkness.
n) He rehearsed a question.

3 Narrative essay organisation

a A scheme for a narrative composition may look like this:

PARAGRAPH 1 INTRODUCTION
Arouse the reader's interest. Scene setting and background.

↓

PARAGRAPH 2 BUILD UP
Involve the reader in the action. First difficulties arise.

↓

PARAGRAPH 3 BUILD UP
Keep the reader in suspense. Difficulties or dangers increase.

↓

PARAGRAPH 4 CLIMAX
Intensify the suspense. Crisis point is reached. Tension drops.

↓

PARAGRAPH 5 ENDING
Briefly tell the reader how or why events happened. Explain any subsequent events.

Which of the above are not used in the story on page 20?

b Which of the narrative writing techniques below are used in the story on page 20, and where?

- Varying sentence length to change the pace.
- Dialogue.
- Surprises (including the ending).
- Hints that there might be surprises.
- Mystery.
- Clues to the mystery.
- Moving backwards or forwards in time.
- Changing to another scene.
- Changing to other characters.
- Predicting events that happen later in the story.

In pairs, think of ways to incorporate the techniques not used in the story.

Imagine how the story continued and write your own final paragraphs.

EXAM SKILLS   ESSAY PLANNING

Before starting to write an essay, you should spend up to ten minutes writing a plan. Doing so has the following advantages:

- ☐ The essay will be better organised into, and within, paragraphs.
- ☐ Timing will be more systematic: allocate eight minutes per paragraph, for instance.
- ☐ If for any reason you do not have time to finish an essay, at least the Examiners will know what your intentions were.

Try to follow these stages:

1. Note down ideas as they occur to you – probably in no particular order.
2. Read the essay title again and group the ideas with headings, discarding any irrelevant points.
3. If you have more ideas while you are writing the essay, add them to the plan after checking their relevance to the title.
4. When you finish the essay, draw a single diagonal line through the plan.

The notes below are stage 1 of a plan for the following essay:
Write a story that ends with the words: '. . . and at last I understood'.

a In pairs, do stage 2, adding or leaving out points as you wish.

headlights appear / shadowy figures close in / go to police – not interested / leave on foot at night / outcome and explanation / bus driver looks and refuses to stop / someone whispers phrase in the street / travelling – strange looks from people / first man attacks – hit him and get away / hear footsteps – look back – apparently no-one / nearly exhausted – crowd getting closer / but there's a bus in half an hour / research the language – it's very difficult / friendly face / knock on the door – written message – boy runs away / start running – people chase – shouting phrase / try to leave town – no train for 2 days / see figures moving in the fields by the road / arrive in town – people watch through windows / plan visit to remote country / back in street – first threats – gestures with knives / hotel – phone rings – phrase shouted / arrive in the country / ask meaning of phrase – angry response /

b Write the essay, incorporating stages 3 and 4.

LISTENING

1 Pre-listening

a In groups, think of a country where each of the following languages is widely spoken, apart from its country of origin:

Example:

English – *USA*

Arabic	French	Greek	Portuguese
Chinese	German	Italian	Spanish

b Choose any country where your language is spoken. List the differences between the way your language is spoken there and in your own country. Consider vocabulary, grammar, spelling, intonation, word stress, sounds, etc.

In pairs, make a list of the differences you have noticed between British and American English.

2 Listening for gist

You are going to hear an extract from the BBC World Service programme *The Story of English*. The first time you listen, decide which of the following titles is the most appropriate:

1 American English – the language of the future.
2 Noah Webster – the man who revolutionised the language.
3 American and British English – two different languages.
4 American English – evolving, influencing and merging.

3 Listening for detail

Now listen again and write 'Br' for British, 'Am' for American or 'both' next to each of these people, present-day spellings and language varieties:

Example:

Noah Webster – *Am*

1 Samuel Johnson	6	Robert Burchfield
2 colour	7	Gullah
3 center	8	Cockney
4 magic	9	Aberdeenshire
5 Technicolor	10	World Standard English

4 Post-listening

a Put the following events in the order in which they actually happened:

a) Burchfield's prediction
b) The American Revolution
c) Webster's first dictionary
d) The article in *Royal American*

b Look at the words below. Are they British or American? Write down the British or American form of each word.

vigor	sabre	honour	kilometer
specter	armour	favorite	sombre
labourer	clamor	honorable	fiber
odourless	vapor		

c In pairs, decide which is the American form of the following words:

1 fetus/foetus   2 anaesthetic/anesthetic
3 defence/defense

Now discuss the advantages and disadvantages of American spelling.

d Look at the words below. Are they British or American? Write down the alternative form of each word.

traveler	prologue	dialing	dialogue
councillor	libeled	levelled	catalog
totalling	epilogue		

What do you think the spelling rules usually are?

e In pairs, discuss all the national, ethnic, regional, social or generational variations in the way your language is spoken and/or written.
Is the tendency towards:

1 diversity – wider differences as society becomes more complex?

OR 2 unity – a 'smaller' world in which language is standardised?

TELLING A STORY

1 The speaker

Like a written narrative, spoken story telling also tends to follow a pattern:

a) introducing the story.
b) setting the scene and describing the background.
c) beginning the action.
d) holding the listener's attention.
e) creating suspense by delaying the climax(es).
f) ending the story.

In groups, match the following informal expressions with the functions above:

1 To cut a long story short . . .
2 You can imagine how I felt when . . .
3 Well believe it or not . . .
4 So we arrived at this . . .
5 That reminds me of the time . . .
6 Well in the end . . .
7 Have I ever told you about . . .
8 Well, you'll never guess what . . .
9 Well who should I see but . . .
10 Then the most incredible thing happened . . .
11 Anyway . . .
12 So there I was . . .

2 The listener

The listener's role is not passive. He or she responds by gestures, facial expressions, laughter, etc., as well as by verbally:

a) showing interest.
b) showing that he or she is paying attention and understanding.
c) expressing emotions such as surprise, anger or sympathy.
d) prompting the speaker.
e) encouraging the speaker to quicken the pace.

In groups, match the following informal expressions with the functions above:

1 What happened next?
2 You/that must have been . . .
3 Hm.
4 What a . . .
5 So what happened in the end?
6 Yeah.
7 How did you feel?
8 So what did you do/say?
9 Go on!
10 No, you haven't.
11 How long did you have to . . .?
12 Really?

3 Practice

a In pairs, put the pictures in the correct order. Is any other order possible?

b Imagine you are one of the characters and tell your partner the story of how you learned English.

c Imagine that you arrive late for a lesson one day. Invent a story as an excuse and tell your partner.

1 Phonology – vowels

a Look at the vowels and example words in the phonetic chart on page 6. Which sounds are difficult for you to distinguish or pronounce? Why?

b Listen to the recorded words and repeat.

c Listen again and write each word.
Put /iː/, /ɪ/, /ʊ/, /uː/, /e/, /ɜː/, /ɔː/, /æ/, /ʌ/, /aː/ or /ɒ/ above each vowel sound.

d Now say the following words aloud:
coughed, trauma   coup, pushed   merged, ate
greet, women   apt, par, buzz

2 Interview

Photograph

In pairs, look at the picture and describe the couple.

They are not from the same country and they speak different first languages.

1 Imagine the events that led up to the scene.
2 Make notes (two minutes) to prepare a story.
3 Tell the story, and give your partner marks for how well he or she responds as a listener.
4 Listen to your partner's story and give marks for; *pronunciation* – individual sounds, particularly vowels; *grammatical accuracy*, especially the use of past tenses.

3 Discussion

Work in pairs.
Tell your partner about the origin of each word or phrase in **bold** type below.

Your partner should tell you whether what you say is true or false, and try to give the true explanation when a false one is given.
Cover your partner's section before you begin.

Student A

boycott – Captain Charles Boycott was silently ignored (*boycotted*) by impoverished Irish tenant farmers when he was hired by the Earl of Earne to collect very high rents. (true)

jumbo – one hundred years ago a particularly big African elephant was so famous that its name became an international word which has now come to mean anything very large. The elephant was called *jumbo*, which means chief in Swahili. (true)

yuppy – to contrast with the generation of the late sixties and early seventies who were approaching middle age by the mid-eighties, *yuppies* – or 'young hippies' – began to appear. (false)

Now choose six of the following and give a true explanation if you know the origin; a false one if you do not.

walkman   diagnosis   kilometre   badminton
suspense   morse code   penalty   doublethink
whisky   hamburger   braille   wellington boots

Student B

sandwich – the Earl of *Sandwich* was so keen a gambler that instead of leaving the card table for a meal during a game he would eat a slice of meat or cheese between two pieces of bread. (true)

Molotov cocktail – bottles filled with petrol, with a piece of cloth as a fuse, were used as bombs in the Russian city of *Molotov* – where the Bolsheviks first seized power in the 1917 Revolution. (false)

Coca Cola – John Pemberton, an American chemist, wanted to develop a safe, non-alcoholic drink and so in 1886 the world's biggest selling soft drink was first produced: a mixture of cocaine and an African nut known as the Kola. The cocaine was later replaced by caffeine. (true)

Now choose six of the following and give a true explanation if you know the origin; a false one if you do not.

rock music   rugby   guillotine   software
chauvinism   voodoo   chocolate   malaria
influenza   sadism   Nobel prize   bar

1 Which sound?

a Listen, and put the words in the correct group.
Example:
seize – 1

a) **1** /iː/   **2** /ɪ/
b) **1** /ɔː/   **2** /ɒ/
c) **1** /uː/   **2** /ʊ/
d) **1** /ɜː/   **2** /e/
e) **1** /aː/   **2** /æ/   **3** /ʌ/

b Listen again and write down each word. Put the appropriate symbol above each vowel.

c Look back at the words in 1 Phonology – vowels, on the previous page, and at those you have written above. Make a note of the spellings which correspond to each vowel sound.

Example:
/iː/ is often written -ee-, -ie- or -ea-.

2 American or British?

a Find the American spellings in the following text and write down the British equivalent for each one.

We were in a hurry to get to the theater but we hadn't gone more than a few hundred meters when a policeman stopped us. He gave us an icy look, demanded my driving license and wanted to know what I did for a living – 'between jobs', I replied. After a monolog about dangerous drivers, he informed me he would be reporting the offense. Satisfied, he jumped back into his car, cut sharply into the stream of traffic without signaling and was promptly hit from behind by a speeding vehicle. With a humorless smile, the local Inspector climbed out of the wreckage.

b Read the text again and find:
1 a figurative word which means 'very cold'.
2 a formal expression which means 'said to me'.
3 a euphemism for 'unemployed'.

3 Adverbials

In groups, correct the word order of each sentence. What variations are possible?
1 She watches every night at home a video by herself in Greek.
2 US English already was by the early 19th century being described as uniform relatively.
3 Always we studied at school Latin by word for word translating Virgil.
4 Some sounds in English at the time of Shakespeare were differently quite pronounced.
5 Machine translation recently dramatically has improved, but still post-editing in the forseeable future will be needed.

4 Vocabulary

a Put the following expressions from this unit into **category a**, **b** or **c**. (see STUDY SKILLS on page 17).

idioms   range   jargon   buzz-word
on the verge of   brisk   euphemism
connotation   figurative   synonym
hyponym   discard   doublespeak
conceal   fluently   eventually   pace
under my breath   rehearse   just in case
unwittingly   it dawned on me   verbatim
whisper   gesture   household word
standard   homogenous   lead up to
sympathy

b Practise saying the **category a** words which contain vowel sounds you find hard to pronounce.

5 Story telling

Tell your partner about an occasion when English, or any other foreign language, was useful to you. Make brief notes first and use some of the expressions above.

6 Narrative writing

Write a composition of about 250 words which ends: '. . . *and I never saw him/her again.*'
1 Make a list of **category a** items you can use.
2 Plan the essay in class.
3 Write it for homework.

7 Now do the Progress Test for Unit 1 on page 178.

READING

1 The topic

a Does your country have a written constitution? If it has, how long has it been in force?

b In groups, discuss the positive and negative aspects of your constitution and make notes.

2 Before reading

a Look at the title of the text. What do you know about the American political system?

b Write down ten words you think will appear in the text.

3 While reading

Read the text quickly and decide whether the following statements are true or false:

1 The President can set the dates for elections.
2 You could become President of the United States.
3 All Democrats are to the left of the Republicans.
4 The US system has always been democratic.

THE AMERICAN POLITICAL SYSTEM

The United States has the world's oldest written constitution and elections have been held under it with clockwork regularity since it came into force in 1789 – every four years for the President and every two years for the House of Representatives. The dates are fixed by law and there is no margin for discretion. This contrasts with the British system which gives the Prime Minister wide power to choose a convenient date. The US President can serve two four-year terms and is then barred by law from further service. He must be a native-born American, which was a significant point in the days when the United States was a country of mass immigration. This would still affect a well-known public figure if he were ever considered for the highest office. It has always been a fable that a poor foreigner could emigrate to America and hope to end up as a President.

The two big American political parties, the Republicans and the Democrats, can appear baffling to outsiders. Since the Republicans all believe in democracy and the Democrats all believe in a republic, what can be the difference between them?

In fact the names derive from historical roots and are simply convenient labels. Historically the Republicans were the party of estab-lished American society and the Democrats represented the less affluent, particularly the immigrant populations of the teeming cities. The two parties were (and to some extent still are) interest groups dedicated to looking after their own people rather than campaigners for any distinct political creed. Within each party, 'liberals' and 'conservatives' battle for power and left-wing Republicans are to the left of right-wing Democrats. Both parties support – indeed revere – the free enterprise, capitalist system. But in today's conditions the Democrats have become identified with publicly-financed welfare measures and Republicans with the principles of minimal government interference in the free market. Provided the terms are not pressed too far, the Republicans can be identified as the American 'conservatives' and the Democrats as the 'liberals'. Most politicians, however, pursue their principles within their own parties and to switch from one to the other is exceptional.

For the election of the President, the constitution has never worked quite as originally intended. The founding fathers thought that the ordinary voters would be too ill-informed to be fit to choose the head of state. So the constitution provides an 'electoral college' which was meant to be a group of wise men, chosen by the ordinary voters, and this would make the final selection. In fact mass parties, with electioneering organisations, came into existence from the beginning. The ordinary voters were swamped with information about the candidates offered to them. Each member of the 'electoral college' is mandated in advance by the voters and its meeting is only a formality. For all practical purposes, the candidate who becomes President is the one with the greatest popular vote.

4 Reading for detail

How many of the words you thought would appear in the text were actually used by the writer?

5 Responding to the text

In pairs, compare the system in your country to that in the USA.

6 Words from context

Which part of speech is each of the following words? Work out the approximate meaning of each word using the clues which follow.

1 *discretion* (7)
   Read the end of the sentence.

2 *barred* (11)
   Look at the expression *by law* and the contrast with *can* in the same sentence.

3 *office* (17)
   Which word does the use of *highest office* avoid repeating?

4 *baffling* (22)
   Look at the next sentence; the fact it is a question should help you.

5 *outsiders* (22)
   Find the expression in the previous paragraph which, in this case, means the opposite.

6 *teeming* (31)
   Look back at the expression *mass immigration* (14–15). Is the meaning essential for comprehension of the text?

7 *revere* (39)
   Does the use of *indeed* tell you that the meaning is stronger or weaker than that of *support*? Do you need to know exactly what it means?

8 *ill-informed* (54)
   Does the prefix *ill-* sound positive or negative?

9 *meant* (56)
   Find another word in the same paragraph which means the same.

10 *swamped* (62)
   Contrast *swamped with information* with *ill-informed* (54). *Swamped* is used figuratively; do you need to know the literal meaning?

7 Structures

a Is the *public figure* (16) being considered for *the highest office* at present? Has he ever been considered? Why is the form *were* used?

b What verb form could come after:
   1 *Republicans* (43)?   2 *Democrats* (47)?
   Why did the writer omit them?

c *Provided* as used on line 45 means:
   1 unless.   2 on condition that.   3 although.

8 The writer

What nationality do you think the writer is? Why? Who do you think the text is written for?

EXAM SKILLS   MULTIPLE CHOICE QUESTIONS

In the Examination, *Section B* of the **Reading Comprehension** consists of a number of questions or unfinished statements followed by four alternatives: A, B, C and D.

After you have read the text quickly for gist, look at the first part only, not A, B, C and D – three of these are designed to cause confusion by giving information which is *not correct*. It is a good idea to cover the four possible answers at this stage.

If the first part is a question, find the answer in the text, then see which of A, B, C or D matches it. If it is an incomplete statement, transform it into a question and then follow the same procedure.

Now find the information that is relevant to these questions and statements about the text on the opposite page. Do not look at the alternatives below them until you have found answers to them all.

1 Who can be President for 10 years?
   A A public figure.
   B Anyone born in Texas.
   C Nobody.
   D A poor immigrant.

2 The role of the 'electoral college' is:
   (Transform to: What is the role of the 'electoral college'?)

   A to ratify the voters' decision.
   B as the founding fathers intended.
   C to give information to the voters.
   D to represent the voters.

3 The Republicans can be identified as the American 'Conservatives' because:
   (Transform to: Why can the Republicans be identified as the American 'Conservatives'?)

   A the Republicans believe in capitalism.
   B the Democrats believe in a republic.
   C the Republicans do not campaign for any distinct political creed.
   D the Republicans are seen as favouring less government spending.

For this type of multiple choice question in the Listening Comprehension, the same technique can be used: the first time you listen, look only at the first part, not the alternatives.

PRACTICE

1 The passive

Look back at the second line of the text on page 26. The form *have been held* is an example of the passive used for processes; the action is of more interest than the person or thing that does it. The use of an active form here would require an unnecessary subject such as 'The country' or 'The USA'.

Passive forms do not usually have an agent: in the example above, 'by the country' or 'by the USA' is not needed. But on line 6 of the text the verb *are fixed* is followed by an agent – *by law*. Why do you think the agent is used here?

Some verbs cannot be used in the passive. These include:

- ☐ Intransitive verbs (i.e. *emigrate* on line 18).
- ☐ Verbs used to refer to a state (i.e. *want, own, believe*, etc. – verbs which do not usually have continuous forms).

Passive sentences are often impersonal in style, but a common informal variation from the *be* + past participle form uses *get* + past participle.

Example:
*The vase **got broken** during the party.*

a Transform the following phrases from the text on page 26 to the active.
Example: *The dates are fixed by law and there is no margin for discretion.* (lines 6–7)
*The law **fixes the dates** and there is no margin for discretion.*

1 *The US President can serve two four-year terms and is then barred by law from further service.* (lines 10–12)
The US President can serve two four-year terms and then . . .

2 *This would still affect a well-known public figure if he were ever considered for the highest office.* (lines 15–17)
This would still affect a well-known public figure if people . . .

3 *Provided the terms are not pressed too far, the Republicans can be identified as the American 'conservatives' and the Democrats as 'liberals'.* (lines 45–48)
Provided we . . .

4 *The ordinary voters were swamped with information about the candidates offered to them.* (lines 61–63)
They . . .

5 *Each member of the 'electoral college' is mandated in advance by the voters and its meeting is only a formality.* (lines 63–66)
The voters . . .

b In groups, write down as many questions as possible about past, present and future political life, using the passive form of the verbs below.

Examples:
Who was appointed Minister for Education after the last election?
When will the next general election be held?

appoint   hold   fix   bar   consider   represent
support   assassinate   identify   intend   mean
choose   inform   elect   manipulate   sack
accuse

Then, ask another group your questions.

c Media reports of public affairs often use the passive with the infinitive or the perfect infinitive. Write the answers to your questions in exercise **b**, as they might appear in a TV, press or radio news item. Use the following verbs:
expect   believe   say   report   rumour
understand   think   feel   fear

Examples:
*He is expected **to be appointed** leader of the party.*
*They are believed **to have been accused** of planning an armed revolt.*

2 The second conditional

The form *if* + simple past/*would* + infinitive can mean:

A hypothetical, impossible present

Examples:
If we had elections every two years, people would get tired of political campaigns.
(But in reality we have them every four years.)
If I were President I would spend more on welfare.
(But I am not the President.)
If we didn't have a written constitution, the politicians would behave ever worse.
(But we have a written constitution.)

An improbable future

Examples:
If he became Prime Minister, he would reduce taxes.
(There is a possibility he will become Prime Minister, but we don't expect it to happen.)

If she were asked to resign she would refuse.
(She might be asked to resign, but we do not think so.)

If they weren't supported by the Liberals, they would lose the vote of confidence on Monday.
(They probably will be supported.)

In less formal styles, the following are often contracted:

I would	→	I'd /aɪd/
Ann would	→	Ann'd /æn əd/
would not	→	wouldn't /wʊdnt/

The first and third person singular *was* is often used instead of *were* when speaking.

Example:
If I was the interviewer, I'd ask about that new yacht of his.

Imagine a constitution which included the following points. Ask your partner about the effect the rules would have on the system in your country.

1 Any politician who does not give clear answers to questions will be barred from public life.
2 All politicians will be tested by a lie detector when speaking in public.
3 Those who break promises will be prosecuted.
4 Ministers' salaries will rise (or fall) by the same percentage as the increase (or decrease) in gross national product.
5 Members of the government will only use state-run services: schools, hospitals, transport, etc.

3 Emphatic conditional forms

a *As/So long as, provided (that), providing* and *on condition (that)* all imply only if. Write four sentences about voting in your country on the following issues, using *as/so long as, provided (that), providing, on condition (that)*.

Example:
The Conservatives would vote against arms sales to dictatorships provided that they were left-wing regimes.
☐ Arms sales to dictatorships
☐ Stricter drug controls
☐ Immigration restrictions
☐ Action to reduce acid rain
☐ Increased welfare expenditure

b *Unless* can usually replace a negative conditional. Transform your sentences from **a**, using *unless*.
Example:
The Liberals would support immigration restrictions as long as they were not racist.
The Liberals would support immigration restrictions unless they were racist.

c Compare the following sentences:
The Conservatives would support action against acid rain on condition that company profits were not affected.
The Socialists would support it whether profits were affected or not.
= They would support it with or without the condition.

The Greens would support it whatever (no matter what) the consequences.
= They would support it unconditionally.

Write four sentences about voting on other issues in your country, using . . . *whether . . . or not . . . .*

Now write six more sentences using: *whatever, whoever, wherever, whenever, whichever* or use the more formal variations: *no matter what/who/where/when/which.*

Examples:
The Liberals would be against the idea whoever proposed it.
The Communists would be in favour no matter where it were put into practice.

WRITING

1 Punctuation

Quotation marks (inverted commas) are used:

a) For exact quotations from spoken or written language; including book titles, the names of newspapers, songs, etc.
Examples:
'the highest office', 'Hamlet', 'The New York Times', 'Yesterday'

b) To focus on the expression itself.
Examples:
What does 'that' refer to?
The noun 'ballot' means the process of voting.

c) For special uses of expressions.
Example:
The 'marriage' of the two parties has not yet been 'consummated'.

d) For expressions the writer would not normally use.
Example:
The Bill to make 'video nasties' illegal is being debated in Parliament.

e) For expressions used ironically.
Example:
The Minister promised more 'government action' to combat crime.

a In pairs, decide which category each of the following belong to. Could any of them fit into more than one?

1 He claimed there was a 'mole' within the Cabinet itself.
2 The MP denied he had been 'legless' at the party.
3 The 'Employment' Minister regretted the factory closures.
4 'Deprived' is used here to mean living in poor conditions.
5 Attempts to censor 'Spycatcher' made its author rich.
6 He was present at every major debate in 'The House'.
7 A dirty, sticky mark is called a 'smear'.
8 'Z' was one of the best political films ever made.
9 The Democrats 'will form the next Government'.
10 A senior diplomat said there had been 'a frank and open exchange of views'.

What could the use of quotation marks tell you about the writer's attitude in sentences 3, 9 and 10?

b Why are these expressions from the READING text on page 26 in inverted commas?
1 *'liberals' and 'conservatives'* (36)
2 *'electoral college'* (56)

c Write six sentences about yourself, punctuating them with quotation marks. Then, show them to your partner and see if he or she agrees.
Examples:
I always mix up 'do' and 'make'.
I'm reading 'Catch 22' at the moment.

2 The topic sentence

This indicates the main idea of the paragraph, and in the first one it may also specify the subject of the text in general.

a Look at the text on page 26. The sentence on lines 1–6 mentions:
☐ The country
☐ The constitution
☐ Regular elections
☐ The period of time covered
☐ The President
☐ The parliament

Which of these six points tell you about the content of:
1 the first paragraph?
2 the rest of the text?

b Now find the other topic sentences in the text. Are they at the beginning, middle or end of each paragraph? What does each one tell you about the content?

3 Time links

As the political system is a process, time links (see page 18) may be used to show the sequence of events. The simple present, often in the passive, is the most common tense.

Examples:
*The voters **are bombarded** with opinion poll predictions **until** the day before the election.*
***After** a very close result, a coalition **is** sometimes **formed**.*

Write an 80 word paragraph about the process in your country. Use time links and the following topic sentence:
As soon as Parliament is dissolved, the election campaign begins.

4 Conditional links

Notice how these short sentences can be connected:

Our elections usually take place every four years. The President sometimes changes the date.
Unless the President changes the date, the elections take place every four years.

The Lower House has the real power.
It doesn't matter what the Upper House decides.
Whatever/No matter what the Upper House decides, the Lower House has the real power.

a Join the sentences below, using the emphatic conditional forms from page 29.

1 Anyone can become President.
Foreigners are the only exceptions.
2 The party which obtains the most votes forms a government.
Of course, it must have a majority over all the other parties.
3 The Prime Minister can call a general election at any time.
However, there must not be regional elections within 90 days of the date chosen.
4 Most people are Republican.
They are not interested in what the Monarchists say.
5 The Prime Minister decides national policy.
The King's opinion is irrelevant.
6 Our system is difficult for outsiders to understand.
It is easier to do so if you have lived here.
7 Our constitution has traditionally maintained democratic rights.
However, this was not the case when extremist parties were in power.
8 The original aim was to legalise political parties.
Nevertheless, some more radical groups would be excluded.

b Using four of the sentences you have written (or similar ones) as topic sentences, write an essay of about 250 words describing the political system in your country for an English-speaking visitor. Use quotation marks where appropriate.

Use the text on page 26 as a model for your essay format:

PARAGRAPH 1
INTRODUCTION – the main points of the system: constitution, President/PM, Parliament, elections.

↓

PARAGRAPH 2
The difficulties foreigners have in understanding it.

↓

PARAGRAPH 3
Compare your system with that in the US and explain the differences. Describe the parties.

↓

PARAGRAPH 4
Explain any differences between how the system was originally meant to work and how it works in practice.

Notice how the model text ends with a reference back to the introduction. Try to do the same in your essay.

STUDY SKILLS NOTE TAKING

1 Recognising important information

a Speakers often signal the important points by emphasising them, repeating them, including them in a summary.
In pairs, match the following expressions with the techniques mentioned above:
As I said . . .   I'd like to stress . . .   To sum up
. . . In other words . . .   The essential point is that . . .   What you must remember is . . .
To run over the main points again . . .

Organising notes may be helped by the speaker listing the points.

b Speakers also tend to focus on the main ideas by talking more slowly and clearly, and in a louder voice.

2 Writing shorter notes

a Note-taking can be made more efficient by using symbols. Match the following symbols and meanings.

>	Is more than	<	Is less than
∴	Female	≠	Male
±	Because	♂	Approximately
♀	Therefore	∵	Is not the same as

b Study the abbreviations listed in your dictionary. In pairs, decide what these mean:
1 ie   2 NB   3 It   4 esp
5 pass   6 E   7 usu   8 Fr
9 sbdy   10 sthg   11 Mon
12 euph   13 fml   14 Apr

Which symbols would be useful in your own studies?

1 Pre-listening

a What is 'charisma'? Are people born with it?

b Look at the photograph. Why is this person so popular?

c In pairs, make a list of famous people who have had films made about them.

d Make a list of adjectives to describe the appearance and personality of the people in **c**.

2 While listening

a Look at the table below. You will hear descriptions of six famous people. Listen and guess who they are talking about. Check your answers in pairs.

b Copy and enlarge the table. Now listen again and complete it. Some answers have already been filled in.

1869 1953 1888   1926

	1	2	3	4	5	6
Nationality	Indian	Pak.	Russian	New York	Br.	American
Personality		forceful	shy	cunning	warm	electric
Features	bold		small head	blue eyes	abr. sun	broad face
Hair		longish	dark	blonde	grey	looks fair
Height	short	medium			tall	
Build	slight	slim	strong	slim	well b.	powerful

3 Post-listening

Add any more details you know about the people in **b**. Think of their complexions, eye colours, voices, habits, facial expressions and clothes.

FUNCTIONS

DESCRIBING PEOPLE

1 Vocabulary

a Copy the diagram below and in pairs, write in the following adjectives:

blue   curly   fair   red   dark   straight   black
long   wavy   blond   grey   brown

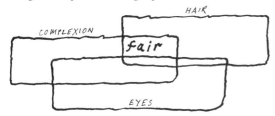

Now check the collocations in your dictionary. Notice the adjectival forms: *brown-eyed, fair-haired* but *a dark complexion*.

b On another similar diagram write in these adjectives:

regular   strong   short   round   weak   slim
long   tall   average   fat   heavy   thin

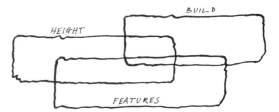

Check the words in the dictionary. Which have negative connotations? Notice: *They're tall; She's slim;* but *He's got thin features, a big chin,* etc.

2 Expressing appearance and character

a Look at the expressions below and decide which answer the questions:
  1 What does he/she look like? (Appearance)
  2 What's he/she like? (Appearance and character)
  a) He's rather thin.
  b) She seems very confident.
  c) She looks like a film star.
  d) He looks rather serious.
  e) He sounds fairly sensitive
  f) She's in her early twenties.
  g) She's quite intelligent.
  h) He's a tall man with glasses.

b In groups, look at the picture. Choose one of the people and describe his or her appearance to the rest of your group.

See who can identify the person you have chosen.

c Your partner is going abroad to stay with an English-speaking family, but they won't recognise him or her when he or she arrives at the airport. Write a description of your partner for the family.

ORAL

1 Phonology – consonants

a Look at the consonants and example words in the phonemic chart on page 6. Which sounds are difficult for you to distinguish or pronounce? Why?

b Listen to the recorded words and repeat.

c Listen again and write each word.
Put /t/, /dʒ/, /v/, /θ/, /ð/, /z/, /ʃ/, /ʒ/, /ŋ/, /h/, /r/, or /w/ above the appropriate consonants.

d Now say the following words aloud:

theory   therefore   whichever   barring   terms
casual   features   discretion   average
marriage   whose   quotation

2 Interview

Photograph

Work in pairs. Ask your partner to look at the picture, tell you about the people and say what they are doing.

Use the following types of expressions.

Nearest us there's . . .
The first thing that strikes you is . . .
In the background/distance there are . . .
The (man) standing behind/next to/near/in front of them is . . .
The (girl) to the left/right of (them) is . . .
I think the (very short guy) on the (far) left is . . .
The (long-haired young man) (in the centre) seems to be . . .

Give your partner marks for; *Pronunciation* of individual sounds, particularly of consonants; *vocabulary*, especially the use of adjectives to describe people.

Reading

Identifying the source of a passage enables us to form a clearer idea of the background. In the Examination you may be asked to say where a short text is taken from.

Match the passages below with the following sources:

a) a press report
b) a novel
c) a personal advertisement
d) a radio commentary
e) a police message

e 1 The man is described as about six feet tall and heavily built; of dark complexion and with brown wavy hair and blue eyes. When last seen, he was wearing a thick black overcoat.

c 2 Male, late twenties, average height, light brown hair, not unattractive, interested in the arts and politics, seeks good-looking, non-smoking, intelligent female companion.

b 3 She had straight shoulder-length black hair and enormous dark eyes set in perfectly rounded features; her warm smile showed off dazzlingly white teeth that contrasted delightfully with her complexion.

a 4 One of the neighbours said that a youth of about sixteen had pushed past her. He had cropped hair, a flag tattooed on his arm and was wearing a striped shirt, braces, jeans and heavy boots.

d 5 Poised, ready to strike the final blow, she waits for the serve. Tall, athletic, and today, with her fair hair tied back, she looks as if she could go on for another three sets.

REVIEW

1 Which sound?

a Listen, and put the words in the correct group. You will hear two words for each letter a)–h) below.

a)	**1** /s/	**2** /θ/
b)	**1** /ð/	**2** /z/
c)	**1** /w/	**2** /v/
d)	**1** /ŋg/	**2** /ŋ/
e)	**1** /ʒ/	**2** /dʒ/
f)	**1** /tʃ/	**2** /ʃ/
g)	**1** /h/ pronounced	**2** /h/ not pronounced
h)	**1** /r/ pronounced	**2** /r/ not pronounced

b Listen again and write down each word. Put the symbols above the appropriate consonants.

c Look back at the words in **1 Phonology – Consonants**, and at those you have written above. Make a note of the spellings which correspond to each consonant sound.

Example:
/r/ is often written *wr-*, *-r-*, or *-rr-*.

2 Quotation marks

In pairs, decide where you could place inverted commas in the following sentences. Explain any resulting change in meaning.

1 The President gave the freedom fighters his full support.
2 Born in the USA has always been the audience's favourite.
3 He said he wouldn't run for President.
4 The debate went into extra time.
5 He felt his honesty had been questioned.
6 A shareholder is someone who owns part of a company.
7 He could hardly be described as pretty.
8 The General gave instructions to his Parliament.
9 What is meant by better off on line 73?
10 The Chairman of the Party is seen as the Prime Minister's bodyguard.

3 Vocabulary

a Put the following expressions from this unit into **category a, b** or **c**. (See STUDY SKILLS on page 17.)

affluent interest group left-wing right-wing welfare features free market fit to pursue mandate complexion appoint to stress electioneering build (noun) to recap to sack expenditure deny opinion poll average to switch deprived resign native-born to regret lively

b Practise saying the **category a** words which contain consonant sounds you find hard to pronounce.

4 Oral descriptions

In groups, think of somebody who is currently in the news. Describe him or her to members of your group using some of the expressions in **3** on page 33. See who can identify the person you have chosen first.

5 Descriptive essay

In about 250 words, describe a ceremonial occasion in your country. You could use the following format:

PARAGRAPH 1
Introduction – the background: history, the public figures involved.

PARAGRAPH 2
The setting: the people waiting, any special arrangements.

PARAGRAPH 3
The scene: describe the event as it takes place.

PARAGRAPH 4
The public figures: physical appearance and clothes, what they are doing.

Where possible, use passive forms and **category a** words from this unit.

6 Now do the Progress Test for Unit 2 on page 179.

UNIT 3 PRIVATE LIVES MADE PUBLIC

READING

1 The topic

What kinds of newspapers are these? What sort of news do these types of newspapers usually contain?

2 Before reading

a Do you think public figures are given too much or too little exposure by the press, radio and television?

b Should the private lives of public figures be investigated by the media? Consider the cases of the following:

☐ Royalty/high society
☐ Rock stars
☐ Politicians
☐ Film/TV stars
☐ Sportsmen/women

3 While reading

a Read the text quickly and decide which of the following headings fit each paragraph:

Blame the press, not TV
A dream
Great – so long as it's not you
What ought to be done
Standards – ours and theirs

b Suggest a title for the whole text.

W hat cheap fun it is to sneer at the tabloids' excesses. How comforting, too, to read the alleged exposés of *other* people's lives – unless your name is on the growing list of public figures who have found themselves the utterly irrelevant victims of the tabloid ratpack of so-called investigative journalists. 5

'The Public's right to know'? – don't make me laugh. They are trading on the public's right to snigger, and exploiting our baser instincts for pro- 10 fit. Gossip is one thing; I have been Dempstered in my time and I suppose at that level it's fair game. But the introduction of the chequebook, private detectives, secret microphones, entrapment and the like have added a sordid, squalid 15 and, yes, obscene smear across our national life.

Television is accused by these 'papers' sometimes of contributing to the nation's moral decline. But no news programme on British television would have touched any of the recent 20 front-page exposés of public figures, nor would any responsible broadcaster condone the sort of tactics currently in vogue in the popular press. Perhaps some Tory back-bencher might now introduce a Private Member's Bill in the new Par- 25 liament to curb this ugly blot on our landscape. The tabloids are giving this country a bad name and it seems to me more urgent than yet another attempt to dilute the best of our television.

Much as my heart bleeds for the victims of 30 these tabloid assaults, I am not really in favour of the kind of censorial legislation it would take to end this kind of publishing. But I do have two possible solutions, the first admittedly just a fantasy: I'd like to head up a ratpack of my own to 35 'investigate' the private lives of the tabloid journalists and editors who write/invent this stuff. I would use the same tactics to give my stories 'the stink of authenticity'. I'd have a network of 'Sun insiders' to call on and 'exclusively reveal' any- 40 thing I could invent. If no one would publish my copy, I could start a newspaper.

The sensible antidote to all this poison is for television journalism to do its job and try to keep Fleet Street honest by making editors and re- 45 porters publicly accountable. Television has watchdog programmes about all kinds of consumer interests, not least television itself. Why not a programme calling newspapers to account?

4 Responding to the text

a Do you agree with the writer? Why/Why not?

b Do you think any of the following counter-arguments are valid?

1 Nobody is forced to become a public figure – less privacy is a small price to pay.
2 The famous can usually defend themselves – replying through the media, paying expensive lawyers, etc.
3 Some probably welcome the free publicity.
4 Those who gain most from revealing secrets are often relatives or friends.

What other arguments (for or against) can you think of?

5 Words from context

a Which part of speech is each of the following words?
Look for words or expressions in the text which have similar or related meanings.

1 *so-called* (6)   2 *trading on* (9)
3 *popular press* (23)   4 *Private Member* (25)
5 *this ugly blot on our landscape* (26)

b Do the following words have positive or negative connotations?

1 *sneer at* (1)   2 *ratpack* (6)   3 *snigger* (10)
4 *baser* (10)

6 The writer

a Is the writer's tone:
1 sad? 2 angry? 3 confused?
What is his aim? Does he succeed in convincing the reader? If so, how?

b Look at the writer's use of personal pronouns:
... unless **your** name ... (lines 3–4)
... don't make **me** laugh ... (lines 8–9)
... **I**'d like ... (35)
What does this tell you about the style of the text?

c Look at the adjectives which the writer uses. Is the article fact or opinion?

7 Pair work

Nigel Dempster writes about the private lives of the famous for a less sensationalist newspaper. The writer uses his name as a verb, *Dempstered* (11), to mean 'gossiped about in a newspaper'. Consider some contemporary public figures – could their names be used as verbs? What would they mean?

STUDY SKILLS   USING THE LIBRARY

a Where is your nearest English-language library?
Which of the following are available there?

Fiction	Non-fiction	Magazines
Newspapers	Cassettes	Videos
Computer software		

In addition, there will probably be a good selection of reference works:

English/English dictionaries
Bilingual dictionaries
Thesauruses/Synonym dictionaries
Dictionaries of abbreviations
Dictionaries of quotations
Biographical dictionaries
Atlases
Grammar books
Guides to appropriacy of language usage
Encyclopedias
The Guinness Book of Records
The Book of Lists, etc.

b In pairs, decide which book would contain the following information:

1 Which other words mean approximately the same as 'utterly'?
2 What does 'IOU' stand for?
3 What is the English word for 'sked'?
4 Who said, 'I never forget a face, but in your case I'll make an exception.'?
5 What are the modern names for: Siam, Abyssinia, New Amsterdam?
6 In which US state is there a town named Hell?
7 Why is this sentence incorrect: 'I have been on holiday last month'?
8 In which situations is it correct to use the vocative? eg. 'Waiter!', 'Can I help you, Madam?'
9 What is a 'palindrome'? e.g. 'A man, a plan, a canal – Panama.' (Election slogan)
10 What is the most money ever awarded for libel? What was the case?
11 David Cornwall is better known as
_ _ _ _ _ _ _ _ _ _ _
12 Why can we say 'the man's leg', 'the dog's leg' but not 'the chair's leg'?

Try to look up the answers for the next lesson.

Adapted from *Study Skills in English* by Michael J. Wallace. Published by Cambridge University Press.

PRACTICE

1 The third conditional

This form is often used to hypothesise about the past.

Example:
*If they had put a secret microphone in my house, I **would have waited** for them and ...*

a Tell your partner what you would have done in the situation described in the example above.
Notice the contractions used in less formal spoken English:

1 I would have	2 You would have
↓	↓
I would've	You would've
↓	↓
I'd've /aɪdəv/	you'd've /judəv/
3 He would have	4 I would not have
↓	↓
He would've	I wouldn't have
↓	↓
he'd've /hidəv/	I wouldn't've
	/aɪwʊdntəv/

b Tell your partner what life would have been like if you had been born:
1 in Britain or the USA.
2 a member of the opposite sex.

c Write sentences about six situations. They could be about potential disasters or things that you regret.

Examples:
*I was doing 120 kph on my motorbike when I saw the car. I **would have been killed if** I hadn't gone off the road.*
*I accused her of lying. **If I hadn't done** that, she **wouldn't have left** me.*

2 Reference words

Words like *it* and *this* often connect:
1 different parts of a sentence.
2 sentences.
3 paragraphs.
They usually refer backwards, but sometimes refer forwards. They occasionally do both.

a What do the following words from the READING text refer to?
1 *They* (9)   2 *our* (10)   3 *it's* (12)   4 *these* (17)
5 *it* (28)   6 *these* (31)   7 *this* (33)

b Look at the text below and fill in the gaps, using each of the following reference words at least once:
it   this   others   her   both   they
ones   its

The monarchy, as an institution, needs the interest of the public in the personalities of the Royal Family. And for the Press, public interest is ......(1) livelihood: a resource which ......(2) must mine, competitively, in order to survive. Public interest is an undulating, slippery, unstable substance. ......(3) is also ambivalent. A beautiful princess evokes different shades of emotion. There are the bright ......(4): admiration, loyalty, affection even love. And there are dark ......(5) lower down, beneath the surface of the ......(6): a desire to deface, to hurt, to humiliate.
......(7) sets of feelings are part of ......(8) same resource, known as public interest. And since ......(9) are part of ......(10), ...(11) are going to be tapped sooner or later at some level, by a free Press. There comes a time when a writer, or an editor, decides that adulation has had its day. People are tired of hearing ......(12) referred to as 'beautiful'. Time to give Envy an outing.

Now write down what each word refers to.

c In groups, use the reference words as clues to put the sentences below in the correct order. The first and last sentences are already in the right position.

'I went out on Wednesday and did something I haven't done for a long time.

a) These people, of course, thought he was there to rescue them.

b) But the 'Daily Express' man knew a trick worth two of that.

c) And addressed him with urgency.

d) Thus equipped, the reporter went in among the wreckage, and talked with survivors, people pinned under wheels and so on.

e) I bought a copy of the 'Daily Express'.

f) He liked to talk about his work, and he once told me a good story about how he beat the competition over the Harrow and Wealdstone rail disaster.

g) It makes a change from the 'Guardian'.

h) The survivors were trapped in this tunnel, you see, and the Press wasn't allowed in.

i) Also it brought back memories.

j) He paid one of the rescue workers to give him his gear, including the hat with the light on it.

k) A memory, among others, of a man I once knew who used to work for the 'Daily Express'.

. . . It made wonderful copy.'

3 Prepositions

Look at the diagrams below showing rules for prepositions of place:

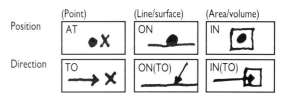

a Look at the following prepositions from the text on page 36. Say why the prepositions in brackets are not correct.

1 . . . **on** (in) *the growing list* (4)
2 . . . **on** (in) *British television* (lines 19–20)
3 . . . **in** (at) *the popular press* (23)
4 . . . **in** (on) *the new Parliament* (25)
5 . . . **on** (in) *our landscape* (26)

b Complete the sentences below with one of the following prepositions. Say why each preposition is correct.

at   on   in   to   on(to)   in(to)

Example:
They were spending the weekend *in* Italy. (*Position in area*)

1 The journalist followed them *in* the country.
2 They found a quiet place *on* the coast.
3 They dived *in* the sea.
4 He photographed them together *at* the beach.
5 He left and drove *to* the motorway.
6 He stopped *at* a service station to phone.
7 He raced *to* the airport.
8 He put the photos *on* the editor's desk.
9 The pictures appeared *in* the morning papers.

Now join up the story using narrative tense sequences and time links.

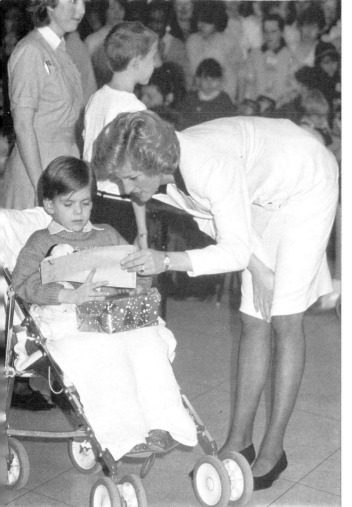

WRITING

1 Summary writing – 2

a The relevant points for a Proficiency summary are often in only part of the text. Look back at page 36. In pairs, choose the points below to include if the instructions are:

Summarise the writer's criticisms of tabloid exposés.

In this case, notice the key word 'criticisms'. Hopes, suggestions or wishes are not relevant.

1 Pointless personal attacks.
2 Unprincipled money-making.
3 Press coverage of the author's private life.
4 Unscrupulous methods.
5 Press attacks on television's standards.
6 Ethical standards are higher on TV than in the press.
7 They could be made illegal.
8 Harming Britain's reputation.
9 Against censorship imposed by law.
10 Exposing the secrets of the newspapers' staff.
11 False stories.
12 Television should publicise unethical press behaviour.

b Now use reference words to link the points you have chosen and form a paragraph:

Example:
Pointless personal attacks on the famous are increasing and they ...
Change the order of the points, if necessary.

2 The narrative/descriptive essay

a Look at the photographs. Do you recognise both of the women? What are their professions?

b Do you think their personalities are similar? Why/Why not?

c Now read the text and check your answers.

3 Text analysis

1 Which lines from the text are narrative, and which are descriptive?
2 What do you notice about the organisation of the text, ie where the narrative begins?
3 Which sentences describe a) Jackie's appearance? b) Jackie's character?
4 Which sentences contrast Jackie's character with Joan's?
5 Where do you think the text is from?
6 Is it sensationalist? If so, in what way?

JACKIE COLLINS was a child only in age. A tall girl with a striking figure and the family looks. At 14 she could look disturbingly adult. She was smoking, playing truant, and sneaking out of her bedroom at night to haunt Soho jazz clubs and date men. Back in the Fifties, the behaviour of Joan's sister was worrying the life out of Joe Collins and his wife Elsa.

'If you go on like this,' stormed Joe, 'you'll end up in juvenile court!' This was not at all a predictable family crisis in the Collins dynasty – even though Joan Collins was notorious as the ripe, teenage siren of British films, always portrayed as the Bad Girl, inspiring countless female clones to adopt her body-hugging sweaters and slim skirts to pose as Coffee Bar Jezabels. You'd think Mr and Mrs Collins could have expected much the same in private life. And you would be wrong ... because the Black Sheep wasn't Joan but her overly retiring, much-shadowed younger sister, Jackie Collins.

Intriguingly, Joe discloses that while Joan was belying her film image, revelling in the showbiz party circuit's froth and flashing cameras while staying timidly prim, sister Jackie was very different. 'Unknown to me, in her mid-teens Jackie was sneaking through her bedroom window and across the back yard, on her way to clubs and for dates with boys from the American School just down the road. Jackie went through a wayward phase long before Joan did ... though I did not learn till years later that Jackie had an early fling. As a young girl, despite her pigtails, Jackie looked older than her years and people did not realise there was about a five-years'

4 Essive organisation

A biographical composition may have the following format:

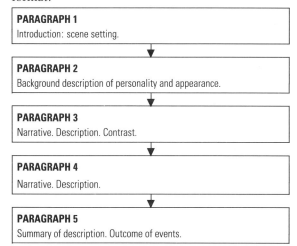

PARAGRAPH 1
Introduction: scene setting.

PARAGRAPH 2
Background description of personality and appearance.

PARAGRAPH 3
Narrative. Description. Contrast.

PARAGRAPH 4
Narrative. Description.

PARAGRAPH 5
Summary of description. Outcome of events.

In about 250 words, write an article about a real or imaginary person for a popular newspaper.

Try to base your topic sentences on 3 of the headlines for the **narrative**; imagine his or her personality and appearance at different ages for the **description**.

Think of a headline for the whole story.

MOTORCYCLIST INJURED

Love at First Sight

Examination Results

TEENAGERS ARRESTED

NEW CHAMPION!

Success Story!

EXAM SKILLS	ESSAY WRITING – WHICH APPROACH?

Essay topics sometimes allow a number of different approaches.
Consider the title *A Disastrous Day*.

You could choose to write about:
1 one terrible disaster.
2 a sequence of disasters.
3 one or more disasters and the consequences.
You could also choose to centre the story on yourself, someone else, or your country, the world, etc.

Your approach should let you:
1 follow the instructions and write the number of words specified.
2 make the best use of your knowledge of the topic.
3 use the widest possible range of structures and vocabulary.
4 write imaginatively and entertainingly.
5 write in a style (formal, humorous, etc.) that is appropriate.

In groups, look at the essay titles below.
Discuss the different approaches that are possible, and in each case consider the knowledge, grammar, vocabulary areas and style that will be needed.
Describe an event that changed your life.
Write a story entitled 'An awful Journey'.
What changes in society have taken place since you were a child?

age gap between her and Joan.

All the same, to me my younger daughter seemed a prim and proper girl – much quieter than her sister. 35
While Joan was so occupied with her outside interests, Jackie would help in the home, would always find time to play with her schoolboy brother Bill, and could even cook a meal if necessary. But at 15, Jackie dropped out of school – she hadn't just left but 40 had been expelled. "What are you going to do now?" I demanded. 'Jackie told me seriously she would like to go into journalism. Instead, knowing I had been wrong concerning Joan, I suggested Jackie should become an actress.' 45

In hindsight, Joe argues: 'Everything turned out well in the end. Though officially her profession was actress, really she was a trainee author. Her mind was always on writing. Jackie is always concerned with people around her and what makes them tick – 50 more so than most performers, whose over-riding interest is usually their own persona and career.' Joan took her to parties, where she met all the top stars: she dated Marlon Brando, young and slim in those days. Jackie was getting to know a cross-section of 55 the Los Angeles population, mixing with people who became characters in her books and earned her a fortune.

LISTENING

1 Pre-listening

a What investigative techniques might an unscrupulous journalist use?

b What do you think the journalist's 'victims' would feel about him?

2 While listening

a Listen, and write T (true), F (false) or NS (not stated) against each of the following statements:

F He only investigates politicians.

F He's ashamed of some of the methods that he's used.

NS He says he never uses violence.

NS He earns a huge salary.

NS He lives in fear of his life.

b Now listen again, and fill in the blanks in the table. Some of the information has already been filled in.

'Victim'	Method	Consequences
1 Sportsmen/pop stars	x	*couldn't sue*
2 Maltese vice ring	x	
3 Government Minister	*bug/ hidden camera*	
4 Westminster Models		x
5 Vice Madams		x
6 Silver Dollar	x	

3 Post-listening

a In pairs, look at each case in the table. Would you have been on the journalist's side or the victim's?

b Do you think the journalist's methods are immoral? Why?/Why not?
Are they justified by:
1 the 'public's right to know'?
2 the need to expose 'all vice, crime and corruption'?

c Look at the text on page 36. Compare the journalist's opinions in LISTENING with those of the writer in READING (the Controller of a TV channel). Who do you think is right?

4 Writing

Imagine your partner has been accused by the press of doing something illegal. You are convinced he/she is innocent because:
1 the description given of your partner is wrong.
2 he/she would not do something illegal.

Write an article for a newspaper defending him or her, using topic sentences that begin as follows:
1 The 'evidence' presented in a certain 'newspaper' claims . . . (Describe the article.)
2 The article refers to somebody who is . . . (Describe someone very different.)
3 This description does not fit him/her; he/she is . . . (Describe your partner's appearance.)
4 He/She would never have done anything like that because . . . (Describe his/her character.)
5 In fact, he/she often/never . . . (Give an example of his/her conduct – contrast it with the allegation in the first paragraph and conclude.)

Link your sentences with reference words.

FUNCTIONS

TALKING ABOUT THE PAST

1 Descriptive storytelling

a In pairs, look at the following expressions and decide which are used for:
1 the introduction.
2 background information.
3 narrative.
4 description.

a) **Then I saw** the most incredible/biggest ...
b) **The next thing I did was** try to get out of ...
c) **The first time** I went there was when ...
d) **There was this** (informal) bar in the middle of nowhere, ...
e) **It was one of those** misty Spring mornings, ...
f) **I'll never forget** going/the time I went ...
g) **I've never seen anything** so funny as the pair of them standing ...
h) **As soon as we** got to the village, I phoned ...
i) **I looked around and saw** I was being followed by a huge .../that house which ...
j) **It was so** dark **that** I couldn't see a thing.
k) **There were so many people** that the road was blocked.
l) **It wasn't until** I read the papers **that** I realised who she was.
m) **I used to think** that nothing ever happened to me.

b Invent a story to tell your partner, based on the scene in the picture. Use some of the expressions in bold above.

LANGUAGE NOTE
Used to + *infinitive* is used for habitual actions or states in the past. It has no present form; the simple present or 'usually' are the nearest equivalents. The most common interrogative and negative forms are 'Did you use to ...?' and 'I didn't use to ...' respectively.
Would + *infinitive* has a similar meaning, but not to start a story:

Example:
*I **used to wait** for the bus every morning and I **would see** him race past in his Ferrari.*

c Work in pairs.
Student A Your partner is a reporter. Tell him/her about something you are proud or ashamed of doing. Try to use expressions from **a**.
After the introduction, give some background information and then alternate between narrative and description.

Student B You are a reporter. Ask your partner about something that he/she is proud or ashamed of doing. Ask questions beginning:

What was it like ...?
Why didn't you ...?
Whereabouts ...?
What would you have done if ...?

Change roles when you have finished.

43

ORAL

1 Phonology – diphthongs

a Look at the diphthongs and example words in the phonemic chart on page 6. Which sounds are difficult for you to distinguish or pronounce? Why? Remember that in English the first half of a diphthong is the stronger.

b Listen to the recorded words and repeat.

c Listen again and write down each word. Put /ɪə/, /eɪ/, /ʊə/, /ɔɪ/, /əʊ/, /eə/, /aɪ/, or /aʊ/ above the appropriate diphthong.

d Now say the following words aloud:

assure	lying	sincere	condone
away	allow	lawyer	nowhere

2 Interview

Photograph

In the Examination, you may be asked to compare and talk about two photos. In pairs, look at the pictures below and describe one each.

Now compare and contrast the two scenes.

Give your partner marks for; *grammatical accuracy*, especially the correct use of verb tenses and prepositions; *pronunciation*, individual sounds, especially diphthongs.

Discussion

Work in pairs. Read the instruction below. Give each other marks for *fluency* and *interactive communication*.

Student A You are the Director of Television. You have decided to investigate a sensationalist reporter in the way the writer of the text on page 36 imagined. You have found out that:

☐ the politicians he/she investigates all tend to belong to the same party.
☐ an actress tried to commit suicide after false allegations about her private life.
☐ a 'white powder' has been found in his/her house and sent for chemical analysis.
☐ he/she has been bribed to keep quiet about corruption 'in high places'.

Interview the reporter.

Student B You are a reporter using the same tactics as the man interviewed in the LISTENING passage. You are investigating the Director of Television. You have the following information:

☐ He/She is married but has been seen with an attractive singer – you have bugged the car.
☐ A lot of money was paid into his/her bank account during the election campaign. TV coverage suddenly became pro-government.
☐ He/She has been paying his/her ex-companion a lot of money to keep quiet about aspects of their private life.
☐ He/She is also a director of a large multinational company. A documentary that criticised its treatment of workers never appeared on TV.

Interview the Director of Television.

REVIEW

1 Which sound?

a Listen, and put the words in the correct group. You will hear 2 words for each letter a)–f) below.

a) **1** /ɪə/   **2** /iː/
b) **1** /eɪ/   **2** /e/
c) **1** /ʊə/   **2** /ɔː/
d) **1** /ɔɪ/   **2** /aɪ/
e) **1** /əu/   **2** /au/
f) **1** /eə/   **2** /ɜː/

b Listen again and write down each word. Put the symbols above the appropriate diphthongs.

c Look back at the words in **1 Phonology – diphthongs** on the previous page, and at those you have written above which contain diphthongs. Make a note of the spellings which correspond to each diphthong sound.

Example:
/ɪə/ is often written *-ear*, *-eer*, *-ier* or *-ere*.

2 Prepositions

Write a paragraph about a journalist:
1 entering a celebrity's house.
2 placing a secret microphone.
3 leaving.

Use each of the following prepositions at least once:

to   onto   into   at   on   in

3 Vocabulary

a Put the following expressions from this unit into **category a**, **b** or **c**. (See STUDY SKILLS on page 17.)
tabloid   alleged   sneer   gossip
smear   stuff   network   accountable
so-called   fair game   libel   evoke
beneath the surface   sooner or later
wreckage   censorship   unethical
striking   sneak out   bribe   portrayed
disclose   showbiz   to revel in
wayward   hindsight   over-riding

b Practise saying the **category a** words which contain diphthongs you find hard to pronounce.

4 Past conditionals

Write a totally untrue headline for a newspaper about someone famous in your country. Give it to your partner and ask him or her to tell you what would have happened if it had been true, using expressions from the list above.

5 Narrative/descriptive essay

Choose one of the titles from EXAM SKILLS on page 41 and write the essay. Remember not to change your approach once you have started writing.

6 Now do the Progress Test for Unit 3 on page 180.

UNIT 4 GOING PLACES

READING

1 The topic

a In groups, look at the advertisement. Which of the countries would you most like to visit? Why?

b What would you do there?

2 Before reading

a Check the meanings of the following words:
disdain   contempt   condescension   rudeness

b Look at the title of the article. What reasons do you think the writer will give?

TREKKERS!

TIBET NEPAL LAOS THAILAND BURMA
INDIA SRI LANKA ZIMBABWE TANZANIA
YEMEN MONGOLIA MEXICO BRAZIL PERU
AUSTRALIA SWITZERLAND LAPPLAND
TURKEY GREECE USSR ALGERIA CHINA
plus many more!
For details of our 35 fantastic treks with experienced guides
and the most modern of equipment send for our full colour
brochure; Trekkers Tours, 45–47 Hartley Green, York

WHY TOURISTS DESERVE TO BE TREATED WITH DISDAIN

All tourists of whatever nationality are bad. I say this having just returned from being a tourist for three weeks. Do not imagine that my holiday was in any sense an embittering experience. On the contrary, I stayed in a rather fine hotel on a very beautiful island. The best thing was that there were not many tourists. But those there were (I will not exclude myself) on the whole behaved badly and were badly behaved to. Tourism corrupts everyone who has anything to do with it.

Travellers, as opposed to tourists, are all right. Many of us, I suspect, plan holidays with this distinction in mind. We may have an idealised picture of ourselves conversing competently with some ruddy-cheeked and innocent foreigner in his native language, the basics of which we have had the courtesy to learn. A thin though scholarly guide book nestles modestly in an inside pocket. We have just bought some rare and extremely inexpensive cheese known only to the very discerning. We are asking the way to a little gem of a church which is so off the beaten track that even the scholarly guide book omits to mention it.

For nearly all of us, the reality is very different. There is no slim but learned volume, only an over-priced pamphlet full of garish pictures of folk-dancers put about by the local tourist board. We have not bothered to learn even ten words of the foreigner's language and so address him in a kind of bellowing English. He regards one (as one regards a yattering Japanese tourist who stops one in the Mall) with appalled contempt, his only consideration being how much money he can squeeze out of this over-rich and ignorant interloper.

You are fortunate if you read these words in some unspoilt foreign clime where the locals still smile when they talk to you. But if you are on the beach of a popular foreign resort, ask yourself why it is that from the moment you arrived at your airport you may have been treated, if you are lucky, with long-suffering condescension, or, if you are less lucky, with downright rudeness. It is because the tourist knows nothing. He is thought by everyone but himself to be stupid. Stupidity is especially irritating to those who are much poorer than you but consider themselves (mistakenly, of course) to be your superior.

The taxi driver is rude, the waiter is rude, the policeman is rude – not because rudeness is wildly endemic in foreign parts, but because, however much they may depend on your financial patronage, they think that most tourists are fools. They are also rude, and sometimes bitter, because we, or tourists who came before us, have changed their world. Money is not complete compensation for the destruction of the scenes of one's childhood or the disintegration of small, united societies, to make way for hotels, discotheques and bars. The traveller leaves his own culture behind; the tourist is a kind of imperialist who takes his culture with him.

3 While Reading

Read the text quickly. Are the following statements true or false?

1 The writer is a traveller, not a tourist. *f*
2 Most people are tourists but think they are travellers. *f*
3 People in holiday towns are usually unfriendly to tourists.
4 Money from tourism has made local people happier. *f*

4 Responding to the text

a Is the text fact or opinion? How do you know?
b What is the writer's purpose? Is he successful?
c Why does the writer use the pronouns *we, us, you* and *one* when referring to tourists?

5 Words from context

Do the following words have positive or negative connotations?

1 *ruddy-cheeked* (18) *румяы*
2 *garish* (33) *ясрий ярох, ослепиость*
3 *bellowing* (38)
4 *yattering* (39)
5 *downright* (53) *явьен, отруненн / саньало / всен, отпрабон*

6 Reference words

What do the following words from the reading text refer to?

1 *those* (9)
2 *it* (12)
3 *this* (15)
4 *it* (29)
5 *us* (30)
6 *one* (38)
7 *it* (49)
8 *They* (64)

Answer the following questions:

1 *behaved* (10) Who did?
2 *were badly behaved to* (11) Who were?
3 *known* (25) What is?
4 *put about* (34) What is?
5 *address* (37) Who does?
6 *Ask yourself* (48) What?

7 Contrasts

The writer uses *on the contrary* (5) to build his argument by contrasting *an embittering experience* with *I stayed in a rather fine hotel on ...*
What is contrasted with the following expressions?

1 *Travellers* (13)
2 *conversing competently* (17)
3 *innocent foreigner* (18)
4 *a thin though scholarly guide book* (21)
5 *some unspoilt foreign clime* (45)
6 *those who are much poorer than you* (57)
7 *not because rudeness is wildly endemic in foreign parts* (61)

8 Discussion

Tell your partner about any experiences as a tourist/traveller/local inhabitant that were similar to the writer's.

1 Modals

May/might and can/could

Look at *may* (lines 16, 50 and 64) and *can* (line 42)
from the text on page 46 and at the following
diagram:

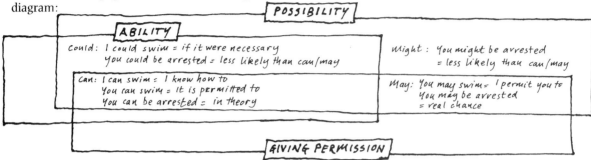

POSSIBILITY

ABILITY

Could: I could swim = if it were necessary
You could be arrested = less likely than can/may

Can: I can swim = I know how to
You can swim = It is permitted to
You can be arrested = in theory

Might : You might be arrested
= less likely than can/may

May: You may swim = I permit you to
You may be arrested
= real chance

GIVING PERMISSION

Must/have to/need to/should/ought to

Look back at the difference between *may* and *can*
when giving permission.
Now look at the difference between *must* and
have to:

'You must leave'. = 'You are obliged by me/us to
leave.' (internal)

'You have to leave.' = 'It is obligatory for you to leave.'
(external)

The arrow (→) denotes intensity:

must/have to (obligatory)

need to (necessary)

should, ought to (advisable)

---

a Imagine you are a very pessimistic tourist on
holiday with your partner. Look at the information
in the box below which tells you what a Consul can
and cannot do if you encounter problems when
travelling. Say what *may/might/could* happen.

Examples:
You may lose your passport!
You might need money from the Consul!

b Now imagine that things have gone wrong. You
have gone to the Consul for advice.
Write the dialogue with the Consul.

Example:
Can you advise me on this court case, please?
No, I'm sorry, I can only give you a list of lawyers.

A CONSUL CAN:

- issue emergency passports.
- at most posts (in an emergency) advance money
  against a cheque supported by a banker's card.
- contact relatives and friends and ask them to
  help you with money or tickets.
- as a last resort, and provided that certain strict
  criteria are met, make a repayable loan for
  repatriation. But there's no law that says the
  Consul must do this and he will need to be
  satisfied that there is absolutely no one else you
  know who can help.
- provide a list of local lawyers, interpreters and
  doctors.
- arrange for next of kin to be informed of an
  accident or a death and advise on procedures.
- contact citizens abroad who are arrested or in
  prison and, in certain circumstances, arrange for
  messages to be sent to relatives or friends.
- give some guidance on organisations
  experienced in tracing missing persons.

A CONSUL CANNOT:

- pay your hotel, medical or any other bills.
- pay for travel tickets for you except in very, very
  special circumstances.
- undertake work more properly done by travel
  representatives, airlines, banks or motoring
  organisations.
- get better treatment for you in hospital (or
  prison) than is provided for local nationals.
- give legal advice, instigate court proceedings on
  your behalf, or interfere in local judiciary
  procedures to get you out of prison.
- investigate a crime.
- obtain work or a work permit for you.

2 a In pairs look at the list of items for an adventure holiday. Tell your partner what to take using *must, have to, need to, should* and *ought*.

Now look at the differences in the negative:

mustn't/may not (formal)

shouldn't (not advisable)

don't have to/haven't got to/ don't need to/needn't (not necessary)

b Complete the following sentences:

Example:
You mustn't take any Scotch to Saudi Arabia because it's illegal.

1 ... take any wine to France; it's cheaper there.
2 ... take any beer with you; think of the weight!
3 ... take things through Customs for other people.
4 ... have malaria vaccinations for a trip to Sweden.
5 ... take photos near military installations.
6 ... ignore the laws of the country you're in.
7 ... spend too long in the sun.

3 Cause and result links

Look at the following sentences containing cause and result links:

Cause links
Examples:
*He can get free tickets **as** he works for the airline.*
***Knowing** the language, she soon **made** friends.*
***Having missed** the bus, he headed for the station.*

Others include: *because, since, as a result of, due to* (= caused by), *for* (formal), *owing to* (formal) and *on account of* (formal)

Look at lines 25–29 of the text on page 46. Here, *so* indicates that *off the beaten track* is the cause. What is the result?

Result links
Examples:
*He was **so** tired **that** he couldn't carry on.*
*It wasn't late **enough to** get a meal.*
*It closed at 12. **Consequently**, they slept in the station.*

Others include: *and, so, such ... that, too ... to, that is why, therefore, as a result, thus, hence* (formal), *so* less (formal).

Complete the following sentences:
1 Since it was our first visit to Rome ...
2 The Greek islands are so lovely that ...
3 So that I could fulfil my dream of going to Rio ...
4 The local people were too poor ...
5 On the German motorways, our old car wasn't fast enough ...

EXAM SKILLS   TRANSFORMATION – TYPE 1

In Paper 3 you will be asked to:
*Finish each of the following sentences in such a way that it is **as similar as possible in meaning** to the sentence printed before it.*

Example:
The water was too dirty to swim in.
*The water wasn't **clean enough to swim in**.*

Common mistakes include adding to, leaving out or changing part of the original meaning.

All the following sentences are correct, but some could be more similar in meaning.

a In groups decide which sentences do not follow the instructions in bold above, then re-write them.
  1 The plane was overbooked so we complained to the agency.
    *As **the plane was overbooked we complained to the agency**.*
  2 She spent all day on the beach and got badly sunburnt.
    *Having **got badly sunburnt, she regretted spending all day on the beach**.*
  3 We felt too exhausted to do anything.
    *We didn't **feel like doing anything**.*
  4 As there was a lot to do we stayed for another week.
    *There was such **a lot to do that we stayed for another week**.*

b Transform the sentences from lines 25–29 and 66–69 of the text on page 46:
  1 We are asking the way to a little gem of a church which even ...
  2 Also, we, or tourists who came before us, have ...

1 Contrast links

Look at the following examples of contrast links:
Although (***though*** – less formal) *the train takes much longer, you see far more than from the plane.*

We didn't go through the tunnel. ***Instead****, the weather being good, we took the mountain pass.*

In the heat of the day the town seemed deserted.

However*, as nightfall approached it came to life.*
OR *As nightfall approached,* ***however****, it came to life.*

While (***whereas*** – more formal) *the coast is mild, the interior is harsh.*
OR *The coast is mild* ***while/whereas*** *the interior is harsh.*
OR *The coast is mild.* ***In contrast/On the other hand*** *the interior is harsh.*

a Look at the two advertisements and write three sentences contrasting the holidays.

Example:
While *the Zanzibar trip only lasts two weeks, the Egyptian History Tour is up to three weeks long.*

b You would like to go on one of the holidays but find that they all have their disadvantages. Contrast them using *too* and *enough* and contrast links.

Example:
I think Greenland would be ***too*** *cold. On the other hand, Kenya would not be cool* ***enough****.*

2 Enumerating and Paragraph Building

When building an argument, writers often indicate the sequence of points at the beginning of each paragraph:

| **Firstly,** |
| **The first point . . ., To begin with, In the first place** |

↓

| **Secondly,** |
| **The next point . . ., To turn to . . ., As for . . .** |

↓

| **Finally,** |
| **The final point . . ., In conclusion, To sum up,** |

Example:
In the first place*, I would like to say that the tour was extremely well organised.*
This forms the topic sentence.
The writer may then justify the statement with a cause/result sentence.
Example:
The guide was ***so*** *professional* ***that*** *every single detail had been planned in advance.*

AFRICA
at your finger tips!

KENYA – the flamingoes of Lake Nakuru, the game of the Masai Mara and the coral reef at Watamu.   4 weeks
ALGERIA – mountain and desert, kasbahs and camels.   2 weeks
EGYPT – the Valley of the Kings and a cruise on the Nile.   4 weeks
ZANZIBAR – ancient spice markets and white sandy beaches.   1/2 weeks

for full details phone 0400 444555

VIKING RAIDERS!

see who your ancestors might be!
cruise in the Fjords, walk in the pine forests, bathe from sandy beaches, see hot springs and enjoy fresh seafood.

We visit Norway, Sweden, Denmark, Finland, Iceland, Gotland, Aaland, Greenland and the Faroe Islands.

Write to 'Norseman Holidays'
at 'The Gatehouse',
Stone Lane,
York

a Look at this extract from a report on campsites. Fill in the blanks with words that enumerate, justify or contrast.

> ..., slogans such as '10 minutes from the beach' are surely the product of somebody's vivid imagination. ... a 6-lane motorway separates campers from coastline a '30 minute run' might be nearer the mark. ... the brochure talks of 'the eternally blue sea', we found it obscured by the ever-present blue traffic fumes; and ... we listened out for 'the sound of crashing Atlantic rollers', it was totally drowned by incessant waves of 40 ton trucks.

b Look at the photograph and, using your imagination, complete the paragraphs.

To begin with, the town is ...
Since the mountains ...
Most towns near the Mediterranean ... but this ...
The next point is that the people are probably ...
They have had little contact with tourists so ...
Instead of the change of lifestyle experienced in the big resorts, ...

3 Discursive essay organisation

A plan of a composition asking for your opinion may look like this:

| **INTRODUCTION** |
| Enumerate. State your position. |

↓

| **ARGUMENT** |
| Enumerate. Topic sentence. Justify. Contrast/Examples. |

↓

| **ARGUMENT** |
| Enumerate. Topic sentence. Justify. Contrast/Examples. |

↓

| **ARGUMENT** |
| Enumerate. Topic sentence. Justify. Contrast/Examples. |

↓

| **CONCLUSION** |
| Enumerate. Summarise. Suggest. Justify. |

a Look back at the text on page 46. Which of these techniques does the writer use? On which lines?

b Write the following essay in about 250 words:
Mass tourism is one of the worst features of present-day society. How true do you think this is?

You can agree or disagree, but before deciding on your approach, consider other arguments such as:
☐ The jobs created by tourism.
☐ The income brought in.
☐ Pleasure for millions of ordinary people.
☐ Improved infrastructure in tourist areas.
☐ Discovery of the host country's culture.
☐ Spreading of new ideas.
☐ Contact between people from different countries.

LISTENING

1 Pre-listening

a Work in groups. Decide which country you would choose to live in if you ever moved abroad.

b Put these factors in order of importance when deciding which part of the country to live in.
- ☐ Scenery
- ☐ Local communications
- ☐ National/international communications
- ☐ Hospitals/university/schools/sports facilities etc.
- ☐ Local culture/language/history
- ☐ Near to big city – work/shopping/nightlife etc.
- ☐ Friendliness of the local people
- ☐ Climate

Why are these factors important to you?
Can you think of any more?

c Where and what are the 'Pyrenees'? Why might a person go to live there?

2 While listening

a Which of these reasons does the speaker actually give for living in the Pyrenees?
1 The nature of his work.
2 He thinks the Pyrenees are like Africa.
3 He enjoys living in Spain.
4 More relaxed way of life than in the north.

b A change in topic is often indicated by referring to a time, a place etc.

Example:
At that time . . . In Munich . . .
Listen again and answer these questions:
1 When did he finally face up to the fact . . .?
2 What belongs to the taxi driver?
3 What reminded them of Africa?
4 When is the valley home to him?
5 What has changed little with the years?
6 Who think it's a perversion of living?
7 To whom is a southerner a noisy, work-shy layabout?

3 Post-listening

a The speaker mentions *patches of yellow gorse – white briar – . . . new poplar leaves fluttering in the wind.*
Can you imagine the scene without understanding the precise meaning of every word?
What is: 1 *gorse* 2 *briar* 3 *a poplar*?
What sort of action is *fluttering*?

b Was the recording spontaneous or had the speaker prepared it? Why do you think so?

c How does the speaker *feel* about living there? Has he made *you* feel like living in the Pyrenees? Why/Why not?

STUDY SKILLS   EXTENSIVE LISTENING

The BBC World Service is one of many English-language radio stations you can tune in to. Look at the GMT programme times below.

```
1800 Newsdesk
  30 Multitrack 1: Top 20
1900 Outlook
  39 Stock Market Report
  45 Peebles' Choice
2000 World News
  09 Twenty-Four Hours
     News Summary
  30 Sports International
2100 News Summary
  15 Pressure Points
  30 The Chart Show
2200 World News
  09 The World Today
  25 Book Choice
  30 Financial News
  40 Reflections
  45 Sports Roundup
```

a At what times could people in Britain listen to the following programmes?
a) Multitrack 1
b) Sports International
c) Book Choice

b When could you hear them in your country?

c To check your progress, listen to the news and make notes.

Example:

WHO	WHAT	WHERE
US President	Meets Soviet Premier	Geneva

See if you've understood correctly by:
   1) Recording the programme on cassette.
OR 2) Checking the same news item in your first language.

You can obtain *London Calling*, the programme journal of the BBC World Service, by writing to:
BBC PO Box 76, Bush House, London WC2B 4PH

FUNCTIONS

1 Opinions

Asking for opinions

What do you think of camping holidays?
What's your opinion of motor-caravanning?
What do you feel about hitch-hiking?
What about (informal) package tours?
What are your feelings about luxury cruises?
How would you feel about moving abroad?

Expressing opinions

These can be used to answer the questions above:

In my opinion . . .   It would seem to me . . .
I reckon . . . (informal)   As I see it . . .
I don't really like . . .   To be honest . . .
Well, actually . . .   Well, I'm quite keen on . . .
I can't stand . . .   As far as I'm concerned . . .
I'd find that rather . . .   From what I've seen of
. . .   To tell the truth . . .   Personally, I don't fancy
. . . (informal)

a Use one of the phrases above in each of the following blanks:
1 _____ seeing other countries but_____ the idea of a move.
2 _____ living somewhere very different, though_____ you can get used to anything.
3 _____ I've never thought about it, but_____ Greece I might enjoy living there.
4 _____ I did live abroad for a while but_____ there's nowhere like home.
5 I don't know, but_____ that in many places foreigners aren't welcome.
6 _____ acquiring a new language and culture would be an enriching experience.
7 _____ the sooner I get out the better;_____ living here any longer.
8 _____ you'd end up neither one nor the other, and_____ alarming.

b Ask your partner the questions at the top of the page. He or she should respond using the expressions given.

Responding to opinions

These can be used to show agreement and disagreement.

Agreeing	Disagreeing
I see what you mean.	You must be joking!
That's just what I was thinking.	Come off it!
	You can't be serious!
Yeah.	I'm not sure I agree with you there.
Right.	
I couldn't agree more.	Do you really think so?

c In pairs, decide which are neutral, informal or very informal.

d Imagine you can choose any of the advertised trips below.

Discuss them with your partner.
1 Ask for opinion
2 Give opinion
3 Agree/disagree

Example:
A *What do you think of the flight to Rome?*
B *Well, actually it seems an awful lot of money for just six nights and I'd rather . . .*
A *I see what you mean; for that you could spend weeks . . .*
B *I'm not sure I agree with you there. It'd be . . .*

Dream Jet Breaks
fly away
to the place of your dreams . . .

First class jets complete with pilot are available for you to hire to fulfil your 'escape fantasy'. The ultimate 'get away from it all' experience is now waiting for you. Beginning your break from the executive lounge of Heathrow airport, we transport you in first class style into the deep blue beyond, with supreme cabin service and the finest cuisine. On arrival at your dream destination we provide the best of service in making all your personal arrangements.

Sydney Opera Experience November 12–30	£2350
Carnival time in Rio de Janeiro April 3–17	£2150
Fiesta in Seville March 27–April 2	£899
'Starlight Express' on Broadway December 19–23	£1595
Pacific Island Castaways January 25–February 12	£1985
Crusader Castles in Iraq March 4–18	£1850
Bangkok beaches and temples October 27–November 17	£1950
Elephant experience in Kenya December 1–12	£2235

Call us now at Dream Jet Breaks 0995–846728

e Imagine your partner is visiting your country. Ask for his/her opinions about it. You may choose to agree or disagree!

ORAL

1 Phonology — *Weak syllables*

Consonants:
/n/, /l/ and /r/ are often pronounced as syllabic consonants.
Examples:
carton = /kɑ:tn/   *channel* = /tʃænl/
fluttering = /flʌtriŋ/

a Listen to the recorded words and repeat.

b Listen again and write each word.
Put /n/, /l/ or /r/ above each syllabic consonant.

c Now say the following aloud:

castle	couples	eleven	local
murderous	battles	smuggling	national

Vowels

/ə/ is the most common vowel in English. /i/ is used to denote the sound between /i:/ and /ɪ/. Both /ə/ and /i/ are weak sounds.
Examples:
perform = /pəfɔ:m/   *valley* = /væli/

d Listen to the recorded words and repeat.

e Listen again and write each word.
Put /ə/ or /i/ where they occur.

2 Interview

a Look at the picture. Ask your partner to comment on:
1 the situation; its possible causes and probable results
2 possible solutions to the problem of football hooliganism
3 what could or should be done about badly-behaved tourists generally
4 the links between alcohol and bad behaviour.
The 'candidate' should use language from FUNCTIONS to give opinions. When he or she has finished you can agree or disagree.

Give marks as explained on page 7 paying particular attention to; *pronunciation of sounds* as practised above; *fluency* and *grammatical accuracy* when he/she is using modal verbs. Make a note of any mistakes which seriously impede communication and tell the 'candidate' after the interview.

REVIEW

1 Which sound?

a Listen, and put the words in the correct group:
   1 /iː/ **2** /i/ **3** /ɪ/
Listen, and put the words in the correct group:
   1 /ə/ **2** /ɜː/ **3** /ʌ/

b Listen, and write down each word.

2 Vocabulary

Put the following expressions from this unit into
category a, b or **c** (see STUDY SKILLS on page 17).
(The weak consonants and vowels are underlined.)

unspoilt   long-suffering   first aid kit
contempt   tracing   bother to
as a last resort   condescension   flattering
off the beaten track   squeeze out of
undertake   patronage   precarious
overbooked   stint   disdain
discerning   crucial   interloper
layabout   corrupt   a mixed blessing
outlying   disconcerted

Practise saying the **category a** words which
contain weak syllables.

3 Modals

a Look at all the modal verbs (*may, must*, etc.) used in
the leaflet opposite.
In groups, classify them into the following
categories:
1 ability
2 real possibility
3 unlikely possibility
4 theoretical possibility
5 permission given by the insurers
6 obligation imposed by the insurers
7 obligation not imposed by the insurers

b Imagine the others in your group are about to go
abroad on holiday. Choose one of the risks
mentioned in the leaflet, make notes and tell them
what they *should/ought to/need to* do in order to
avoid it. Sequence your points and justify your
opinions using cause/result links.

Example:
*Well . . . to start with, I think you should get vaccinated
before you go because . . .*

HOLIDAY INSURANCE

On holiday you hope everything will be plain
sailing but you might fall ill or have an accident
and need medical treatment; you could have your
money or luggage stolen; you might injure
someone, or damage their property and have to
pay costs; or your holiday could be cancelled or
cut short through accident or sickness. All these
risks and more can be met by a holiday insurance
package policy or by a selective holiday
insurance policy.

A standard package policy usually offers the
following cover, but remember, a small excess (or
first part of a claim which you pay) may apply to
sections of the policy.

Cancellation
You may claim for holiday costs which are not
recoverable if you have to cancel your holiday
because of accident, illness, quarantine,
pregnancy (unknown when policy taken out), jury
service or witness summons.

Medical Expenses
With some policies you must disclose full details of
any illness or condition of a permanent or
recurring nature.

4 Opinions

In groups, ask for and give opinions about six of the
following as tourists, using contrast links and
category a words from the list above.

Examples:
What's your opinion of the . . . ?
*Well, it seems to me that while the . . . are sociable, the
. . . tend to be more reserved.*
*Do you really think so? From what I've seen of the . . .
they're . . .*

Americans Brazilians British Dutch
French Germans Greeks Italians Japanese
Portuguese Scandinavians Spanish

5 Essay

'Travel broadens the mind.' Do you agree?
Write an essay of 250 words referring back to the
format in WRITING.

6 Now do the Progress Test for Unit 7 on page 181.

UNIT 5 UNIFORMS

READING

1 The topic

Can military intervention in the political system ever be justified? Under what circumstances?

2 Before reading

a Look at the text heading.
What do you think the connection is between the two men?
What kind of text do you think it is?

3 While reading

Here are the first sentences of each paragraph. Read the text and decide where they should go.

1 Political *naifs* are ill-advised to get mixed up in Latin American politics.
2 Greene's little book is fashionably timed.
3 Hence Greene's presumption of innocence for regimes which fly left-wing colours is wrong-headed, and often childish in its expression.
4 *Getting to Know the General* is an inapt title; we do not get to know him.
5 This thirst for comic-strip moral distinctions cannot be truthfully satisfied by the realities of Latin America.

Which of these are not topic sentences?

GRAHAM GREENE AND OMAR TORRIJOS
Paul Johnson

A I suspect, however, that he was not quite the paragon of political virtue Greene would have us believe. He tells us, for instance, that the General's only privilege as President 'was to have a reserved parking place for his car at the Hotel Panama'. But elsewhere we find the General using his presidential plane to fly to Bogota for a rendezvous at the airport with a girl he fancies; we learn that Castro 'kept him supplied with excellent Havana cigars, the bands printed with his name'; there are references, too, to the General's special bank account, presumably supplied from government funds, from which large sums in dollar notes are withdrawn for various purposes. He sounds like any other Latin American general to me.

B Greene is a romantic with a schoolboyish love of adventure-stories, which of course he writes very well. He needs to have heroes and villains, and though his set of values are no longer those of the *Boy's Own Paper* – rather the radical chic of *The New York Review of Books* or *Nouvelle Observateur* – Greene still demands very clean heroes and very deep-dyed villains.

C Inside every radical *caudillo* or successful student guerrilla there is a monster waiting to emerge; within most bloated dictators, bedizened with braid and stars, there is the residual husk of a former idealist or reformer. Castro's predecessor, Batista, started out as radical extremist, and Castro himself once had a few principles. Left- or right-wing ticketing makes depressingly little difference: what does it matter to a victim whether he is tortured in the name of Marx or some more conventional deity?

D He refuses to drink Chilean wine except from 'the Allende years'; he glowers at General Pinochet across a Washington reception. A wiser and better informed man might reflect that Allende's weakness and incompetence brought Chile to the brink of civil war, and that it was Pinochet who stopped the country falling over it. Most of the inhabitants of Latin America have to live there. They do not possess a return ticket to Antibes and they cannot afford the luxury of progressive *salon* opinions.

E But it does not address itself to the fundamental question of why these societies find it so extraordinarily difficult to devise forms of government which are both stable and reasonable. That is the kind of cultural question a good novelist has as much chance of answering as a political scientist, perhaps more. So it is a pity Greene falls into predictable sloganising when he has before him the splendid example of Joseph Conrad, whose *Nostromo* conveys more truth about the tragedy of Latin America than anything else I have read.

Getting to Know the General
By Graham Greene
Bodley Head £8.95

LIBRARY
BANK HOLIDAY CLOSING
— 1993 —

EASTER

 Friday 9 April
Saturday 10 April
Monday 12 April

MAYDAY

 Monday 3 May

SPRING

Saturday 29 May
Monday 31 May

SUMMER

 Saturday 28 August
Monday 30 August

CHRISTMAS

Friday 24 December
Saturday 25 December
Monday 27 December
Tuesday 28 December
Saturday 1 January 1994
Monday 3 January 1994

Hampshire
COUNTY COUNCIL

---

to read the book?

's political beliefs

of:

the following
of each word using

meaning
contrasts.
contrasts.
contrasts.
he context.
he context.
he hyponym *stars*.
nnotations does the
ve?
nnotation does the
ve?

ce on lines 24–28
reate difficulties even

d and *husk*, change
d see if the general

m Greene and you meet
Discuss the review.

iewer of Graham
im and discuss the

STUDY SKILLS EXTENSIVE RE

It is essential to read not only widely
wide a range of text types as possible
types of reading material on the left a
them with the sources, or means of c
them, on the right.

1	Public information leaflets	a)	Pen friends
2	Maps	b)	Computer dealers – head offices
3	Catalogues	c)	Newsstands in tourist areas, airports, stations etc
4	Timetables	d)	Domestic appliances sold by multinationals
5	Brochures	e)	Department stores (abroad)
6	Current affairs magazines	f)	Tourist Authorities in your country
7	Press	g)	Travel agents (abroad)
8	Operating instructions	h)	Political parties (abroad)
9	Professional magazines	i)	Subscriptions to *Newsweek, The Economist, Time,* etc.
10	What's on?	j)	Transport authorities (abroad)
11	Manifestos	k)	Government departments (abroad)
12	Personal letters	l)	Tourist offices (abroad)
13	Software	m)	Subscriptions to *New Scientist, National Geographic,* etc.

English-language libraries or consulates of
English-speaking countries can usually provide
the addresses of sources marked (abroad).

There are a number of bookshops which export
individual books: their addresses can be found in
publications specifically for English-speakers
abroad such as *The Guardian Weekly* and *The
International Herald Tribune*. (Both also available
on subscription).

1 Reported speech

Look at the Defence Minister's speech below, then look at the reported version in the newspapers the next morning.

a Identify the changes in tense that are made and fill in the table below the texts.

'There is no question of any troops being withdrawn until a cease-fire is agreed. The Foreign Minister has been in touch with the United Nations Secretary General and further talks will be taking place as soon as fresh proposals are made.

Sporadic attacks continued until eight o'clock this evening. According to senior officers I was speaking to just half an hour ago the best response would be an immediate offensive. They had expected a free hand in terms of strategy but feel that the new rules of engagement which have come into force today severely restrict their operational capacity.

Our coalition partners are deliberately obstructing attempts to settle the dispute quickly and this could bring about a military disaster. The country should unite behind the Government in a conflict which can, and must, be won.

Another press conference will be held here at ten o'clock tomorrow morning, although it may be brought forward if events move quickly.'

The Defence Minister, speaking in the press room, said there was no question of any troops being withdrawn until a cease-fire was agreed. He added that the Foreign Minister had been in touch with the United Nations Secretary General and that further talks would be taking place as soon as fresh proposals were made.

He pointed out that sporadic attacks had continued until eight o'clock yesterday evening and that according to senior officers he had been speaking to just half an hour earlier the best response would be an immediate offensive. They had expected a free hand in terms of strategy but felt that the new rules of engagement which came into force yesterday severely restricted their operational capacity.

He alleged that the Government's coalition partners were deliberately obstructing attempts to settle the dispute quickly and claimed that could bring about a military disaster. The country, he said, should unite behind the Government in a conflict which could, and must, be won.

The Minister closed by announcing that another press conference would be held there at ten o'clock this morning, although it might be brought forward if events moved quickly.

Direct speech	Example	Reported speech	Example
Present simple	*There is*	*Past simple*	*There was*
Present continuous			
Present perfect			
Past simple			
Past continuous			
Past perfect			
Future simple			
Future continuous			
Conditional			

b Have these expressions from the speech changed in the reported version? Write down the reported speech form for each one.

this evening   *ago*   *today*
tomorrow morning   *could*   *should*   *can*
must   *may*   *Our*   *this*   *here*

c What information has been added to the reported version? Why?

Make a list of the introductory verbs that are used.

Example:
said

Which of them indicate that:
1 the statements are true.
2 the statements are neutral.
3 the statements may or may not be true.

In pairs, look at the statements introduced by types 1 and 3 and decide why the reporter used these verbs.

d Now use the following notes to report the reply by the leader of another political party:

> Troops out now — ceasefire will take too long to negotiate.
>
> Talks at UN not serious — Minister wouldn't accept any proposals.
>
> No injuries in yesterday's attacks.
>
> Army wants fighting to go on — may be provoking incidents.
>
> Rules of engagement essential to reduce tension.
>
> PM needs a successful war to distract attention from economic situation.
>
> We'll comment again after the Minister's morning press conference

2 Wish/If only

Wish and *if only* (for stronger feelings) can be used to express the following three emotions:

1 Present wishes

Examples:
*He **wishes** he could be a pilot.*
***If only** I had a month's leave.*
*I **wish** I was/were sitting in the pub at home.*
***If only** they didn't give us such hideous uniforms!*

2 Past regrets

Examples:
***If only** they had listened to the pacifists.*
*I **wish** I hadn't joined the army.*

3 Dissatisfaction with the present, and future hopes

*I **wish** they would close that military base.*
***If only** those planes would stop taking off at night!*

a In pairs, match the following sentences with the categories above:
1 She doesn't like having foreign soldiers in her country.
2 He's a homesick soldier.
3 He's an air force mechanic.
4 War has broken out.
5 He's a soldier who desperately wants a holiday.
6 The noise wakes her up every hour.
7 He's very unhappy being a soldier.
8 They hate the clothes they have to wear.

b Re-write the following sentences using *wish* or *if only*.

Examples:
We're marching all day.
*I **wish** we weren't marching all day.*
We haven't got any artillery.
***If only** we had some artillery.*

1 We're not involved in the action.
2 We aren't winning.
3 That terrible war will never end.
4 Our biggest warship was sunk.
5 We didn't remain neutral.
6 These rifles keep jamming.

WRITING

THE FORMAL LETTER

1 Writing to the Editor

a Below are the names and addresses of people who wrote to the magazine following the review on page 56.

In groups, decide:
1 who wrote each letter.
2 which two letters were published first.
3 which two letters appeared in the next edition.
4 which was the last letter to the published.

Graham Greene, Antibes, France
Paul Johnson, Iver, England
Ronald White, Ontario, Canada
Richard D. Slater, Maryland, USA
J. Plested, Leigh-on-Sea, England

LETTERS TO THE EDITOR

1 SIR: It is sad Graham Greene could not restrain himself from replying petulantly to my far-from-severe review of his poor book, and the significance of his factual correction is so obscure as to be impenetrable.

J. Plested raises a more serious issue: the relative performance of Allende and Pinochet. But he misses my point. I knew Allende and found him an agreeable, well-intentioned gentleman, but he allowed himself to be stampeded by his followers into a social and economic revolution. The inevitable result was civil war, and whatever else Pinochet has done, he at least spared Chile from the fearful experience which overwhelmed Spain in 1936–1939. I deal with these events in detail in my *History of the Modern World*.

2 SIR: Paul Johnson's question as to why these societies find it difficult to devise democratic forms of government seems perfectly legitimate to me. There is such a thing as political culture, and while there is a consistent democratic strain to be found in that of Latin America, it seems to have been subordinated much of the time to the tradition of the *caudillo*, particularly in the countries just to the south of us. Whatever criticisms may be levelled at US policy in the region, now or in the past, the United States is not responsible for that tradition.

3 SIR: I can believe that Graham Greene may be politically naive (*vide The Lawless Roads* but not, perhaps, *The Quiet American*). I can also believe that Omar Torrijos may have been less than morally spotless. But anyone who thinks that Conrad's *Nostromo* conveys any 'truth' about Latin America should not be casting stones, let alone writing history books.

Behind Conrad's fantasy of the Goulds' silver mine lay the hideous reality of Potosí, in which at least a million Andean Indians have died over the past four centuries.

Perhaps Paul Johnson should look for a 'splendid example' there.

4 SIR: Mr Paul Johnson, in his review of *Getting to Know the General*, which I have no desire to defend except on points of fact, seems so bent on burying his perfectly honourable left-wing past that he has failed to read carefully the book he was given to criticise.

General Torrijos is described throughout his review as President of Panama. He was never President, and when I wrote that the only privilege of the President was a reserved parking space for his car I was, of course, not referring to Torrijos, as Mr Johnson assumes, but to the President of Panama. When Mr Johnson writes, 'He (Torrijos) sounds like any other Latin-American general to me', he is exposing his ignorance of Latin America. The words 'to me' sound a little over-confident and egotistic. Perhaps Mr Johnson should have travelled a little further than the safe haven of Mrs Thatcher before he ventured to write about the situation in Central America and the character of Latin-American generals.

5 SIR: In his right-wing polemic purporting to be a literary criticism of Graham Greene's *Getting to Know the General*, Paul Johnson would have us believe that President Allende was a total incompetent in economic affairs in comparison with the latter-day saint General Pinochet. Is that so? The massive debts owed by the Pinochet regime to the international banking system would suggest otherwise.

In seeking answers to the fundamental question of 'why these societies find it so extraordinarily difficult to devise forms of government', surely Paul Johnson should address that question to the White House.

b In 100–150 words, write in response to either the original review or one of the letters above using the following format:

> Say which text you are referring to. (See letters 4 and 5)

↓

> State the purpose of your letter in a topic sentence: attack or defence? (Letters 2 and 4)

↓

> Give opinions and/or new information. (All letters). Contrast examples. (Letters 1, 2, 3, and 5)

↓

> Conclusion (letter 2) and/or suggestion. (Letters 1, 3, 4 and 5)

2 Writing job applications

a An author has decided that he needs more background information on South America.

In groups, look at his advertisement, below, then place the items a)–k) in the correct position on the letter diagram opposite. The first one has been done for you.

> **Experienced and reliable research assistant needed for well-known author.**
> **English essential, knowledge of Portuguese and Spanish an advantage:**
> **PO Box 7043**
> **Brussels**

a) Yours faithfully,

b) I would be available for interview at any time and can supply sample work if required. I enclose my CV and look forward to hearing from you.

c) 9th July, 1990

d) I am writing to apply for the post of research assistant as advertised in the 'Herald Tribune'.

e) *Javier Ochoa*

f) 26, Park Rd.,
Rock Ferry. L57 6PQ

g) Javier Ochoa

h) Since then I have been working freelance for various organisations on the role of the military in Latin America. I am used to meeting short deadlines and have my own work station.

i) Dear Sir,

j) PO BOX 7043,
Brussels.

k) I think I would be suitable for the work because I have a good degree in history and obtained a grade 'B' in Cambridge Proficiency three years ago. My first language is Spanish and I spent several years in Brazil as a child.

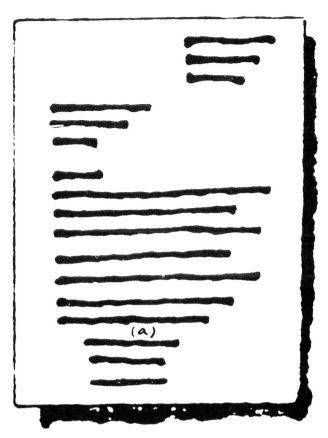

(a)

b Write the second half of this application:

> Dear Madam
> I would like to apply for the position advertized in the 'Financial Times' on the sixteenth of this month.
> The main reason I am applying is that I feel I have the drive, ambition and commitment you are looking for. In addition . . .

c Write the first half of this application:

> . . . Although I have no experience of this kind of work, I have always taken a great interest in people's problems and how to solve them.
> I can provide excellent references that will show I am at my best working as a member of a team and would be most grateful if you could give my application serious consideration.
>
> Yours sincerely,
> *Simone Martin*
>
> Simone Martin.

LISTENING

EXAM SKILLS LISTENING COMPREHENSION – PREDICTING

In the Examination, there will be a pause in each part between the instructions and the listening passage. You should use this time to predict the content by looking at the questions/statements. These often give clues to the situation or type of discourse. Graphics often indicate that you will have to listen for dates, names, figures, etc. Some you might be able to guess using your general knowledge.

But to form a more complete picture in your mind of what is to come, listen to the short introduction before the pause. This might only say *You will hear two people talking*, but there is usually more information. For example, from the sentence *You will hear a railway station announcement*, you can predict that the listening passage will be a public monologue and it may:

1 contain words and figures such as: place names, train times, platform numbers.
2 express functions such as:
   giving information – *The next train to arrive will be the . . .*
   requesting politely – *Would passengers please cross the line to platform 8.*
   apologising – *We regret to announce the cancellation of the 0825 to . . .*
3 use structures such as:
   The train **arriving** at platform 14 is the . . .
   The 1635 Intercity **will depart** *from platform 6.*
   There **has been** *a derailment on the main line between . . .*
4 be in a certain style: rather formal expressions with very few contractions –
   we regret to . . .
   depart
   restaurant facilities
5 have special features: repetition, poor sound quality – including echoes.

In groups, look at these introductions and make lists like the one above.
1 You will hear the weather forecast.
2 You will hear a dialogue between a policeman and a young motorcyclist.
3 You will hear a young couple getting to know each other at a party.
4 You will hear a group of football fans arguing.

If you practise this technqiue whenever you hear or read an introduction to a text, it will become a subconscious process.

1 Pre-listening

a Are the police in your country generally successful in controlling crime? Why?/Why not?
b Can any other organisations do police work more effectively? What are the advantages and disadvantages?
c In groups, make a list of the names of any illegal drugs that you know of (including slang words).

2 While listening

a Look at the list of people below. How do the different groups feel, in general, about 'The Angels'? Listen and make notes.
1 Property developers. 2 Restaurant owners. 3 The police. 4 Those who live in the area.

b Listen again, and fill in the blanks with one word.
   1 . . . they may just be _innocent_ groups . . .
   2 . . . members started _____ New York's subway . . .
   3 . . . frightening off _muggers_
   4 . . . a crack _dealer_ sail through the plate glass . . .
   5 Groups of Angels were _arrested_.
   6 . . . one Angel was _stabbed_ by an irate pusher . . .
   7 _____ , red-bereted youngsters . . .
   8 . . . and forcibly _searched_
   9 . . . even the _quietly_ have any vestige . . .
   10 . . . _____ trampled on.
   11 . . . ceremony for _____ . . .
   12 . . . _____ by any other name.
   13 . . . _____ have been brought.
   14 . . . in keeping _law_ and _order_?

3 Post-listening

a Do you think the Angels could be accused of being:
   1 elitist – only there to protect the well-off?
   2 provocative – likely to lead to organised counter-violence?
   3 untrained in the use of minimum force and accountable to no-one?

b In pairs, talk about any occasions when you might have been pleased to see the Angels in your town?

4 Role play

In groups of four, choose one of these roles each:
☐ Guardian Angel
☐ Policeman
☐ Drug pusher
☐ Innocent victim of the Angels

Defend your opinions and criticise those of others on the subject of the Angels.

COERCING [kɔː'ɜːsɪŋ] – zmuszenie

a People try to force others to do, or not to do, things by:

1 using their personal authority.

Example:

Don't *do that!* (informal)

2 using impersonal authority.

Example:

It is *absolutely* ***forbidden to*** *do that!* (formal)

3 using threats.

Example:

If you *do that* ***I'll*** *report you to the police!* (neutral)

(Compare 1 and 2 with *must* and *have to* on page 48).

In pairs, put the following expressions into each category and decide which are formal, neutral or informal.

a) **I want you to** deliver this immediately.

b) **Unless** your work improves, **you'll** be out.

c) **Keep away from** the wire.

d) **Either you** leave **or (else) I'll** call the police.

e) **Stop** firing!

f) **Don't you dare** break that!

g) **You are not allowed to** park here.

h) **Into** the water!

i) **If you** are late again, **we will have no alternative but to** dismiss you.

j) **Down** you get!

k) **Will you** leave at once.

l) **I wouldn't** point that at me **if I were you**.

m) **You** drive.

n) School **will** attend the match and cheer enthusiastically.

o) You **are to** be here at 0700 sharp.

p) **You are obliged to** notify us of any changes.

q) **You'd better not** move **or I'll** shoot.

r) **Do that again and I'll** flatten you.

s) **It is not allowed**.

t) **In** you go!

u) **Never** trust them!

b Work in pairs. Read the news item opposite and then roleplay the conversations between the man and:

1 the bank manager, when he is refused the loan.

2 a workmate who suspects what he is going to do.

3 the police officer who arrests him.

4 one of the magistrates, when he is in court.

Bulldozer revenge on bank
By David Rose

A Man refused a loan by his bank manager last week wreaked a terrible revenge. He demolished the bank with a bulldozer.

The man, aged 20, was said by his workmates at a quarry near Nottingham to have been 'upset' about his failure to obtain a loan and to have been 'brooding all night'.

At 6 am, he entered the quarry alone and drove away the bulldozer, a huge machine 80 ft long, with wheels 7 ft tall. He smashed through the locked gates of the quarry and drove on to Arnold, three miles away where he aimed it straight at the bank. The demolition done, he boarded a double-decker bus. But his actions had set off an alarm and he was arrested before it moved off.

A man later appeared before Nottingham magistrates, charged with taking a vehicle without the owner's consent and criminal damage. He was granted bail and remanded until October 26.

ORAL

1 Phonology – Word stress (1)

Simple words

Non compound words without prefixes or suffixes are knowns as 'simple'. They may be stressed.

Examples:
<u>fan</u>cy   sup<u>ply</u>

a Listen to the recorded words and repeat.

b Listen again and write each word, underlining the stressed syllable.

c Now say the following words aloud:
unite   stampede   villain   expose
prevent

Parts of speech

Some words are stressed according to whether they are acting as verbs, nouns or adjectives.

a Look at the following and work out the rule.
1 Customs have seized some <u>suspect</u> packages.
2 I am writing to pro<u>test</u> about the treatment of conscientious objectors.
3 There is a <u>con</u>trast between their attitude to defence spending and overseas aid.

b Write sentences using the following words:
<u>con</u>flict   <u>rebel</u>   <u>ad</u>dict   con<u>vict</u>
es<u>cort</u>   con<u>script</u>   de<u>sert</u>   <u>per</u>fect

2 Interview

Passage

a In pairs, look at the five paragraphs below and decide which source they are taken from.

b Now match each paragraph with the following purposes:
1 to criticise	4 to contrast
2 to suggest	5 to defend
3 to inform	

A	Whereas previous demonstrations have broken up without further serious incidents, on this occasion clashes continued until the small hours and several cars were set alight in order to form barricades across the narrow adjoining streets.
B	At the height of the confrontation there were some 2000 demonstrators facing over 500 police officers. 148 arrests were made – mainly for assault and possessing offensive weapons. 67 people were taken to hospital, some suffering from serious head injuries.
C	One lesson to be learnt is that the police should only fire plastic bullets as a last resort; hopefully greater control will be exerted over the use of these potentially lethal weapons.
D	The police were subjected to a barrage of missiles including bottles, darts and petrol bombs. It is hardly surprising, therefore, that the Superintendent ordered snatch squads into the crowd to arrest those identified as ringleaders.
E	The use of plastic bullets at very short range cannot be condoned. Instructions to the officers concerned state they are not to be fired at short range and must never be aimed at 'the upper part of the body'. TV film shows both regulations being contravened.

c Now put the paragraphs in the order they probably appeared.

Discussion

Work in pairs.
Student A Look at the list of countries below which do not have conscription. Without mentioning their names describe them to your partner by giving clues. (Do not look at your partner's list.)

Examples:
By population, it's the world's largest democracy.
It achieved independence in 1947, led by a famous pacifist.
It's to the south-west of China.
ANSWER: India

USA, Japan, New Zealand, Britain, Iceland.

Listen to your partner's clues and guess which countries he/she is describing.

Student B Look at the list of coutries below which do not have conscription. Without mentioning their names describe them to your partner by giving clues. (Do not look at your partner's list.)

Examples:
The official language is Spanish.
The capital is Montevideo, a big port on the River Plate.
It's located between two big neighbours.
ANSWER: Uruguay

Canada, Australia, The Philippines, Pakistan, Panama.

Listen to your partner's clues and guess which countries he/she is describing.

Give marks for; *interactive communication*; *pronunciation*, sentences, particularly word stress.

REVIEW

1 Word stress

a Listen, and put the words in the correct group by writing **a**) for a word where the stress is on the **first** syllable, **b**) for a word where the stress is on the **second** syllable.

b Listen again and write each word, underlining the stressed syllable.

c Look back at the words in **Simple words** in the Oral section and at those you have written above. Concentrate on the last syllable of each one:

1 Which contain long vowels (/iː/, /uː/, /ɜː/, /ɔː/, /aː/) or diphthongs? Which have more than one final consonant?

2 Which contain short vowels (/ɪ/, /e/, /ɒ/, /æ/, /ʌ/, /ə/ or /əʊ/)? Which have fewer than two final consonants?

3 What do you think the rules usually are?

Notes

1 These rules generally apply to verbs, nouns, adjectives, adverbs and prepositions (except for the consonant rule in the case of nouns).

2 Words of recent foreign origin are often exceptions.

2 Vocabulary

a Put the following expressions from this unit into **category a**, **b** or **c** (see STUDY SKILLS on page 17)

avail (oneself of)   inapt   glower
devise   dealer   restrain (oneself from)
maxim   stampede   fearful   to level
assume   haven   purport   hideous
dismiss   casual   shelter   exert
lethal   condone   revenge   quarry
remand   granted

b Underline the stressed syllables in the **category a** words and practise saying them.

3 Coercing/reported speech/*wish* and *if only*

a Ask your partner what he or she would say in one of the following situations, using some of the words from **2 Vocabulary** where possible.

Example:
You have been arrested for a crime you didn't commit.
I haven't done anything. I just happened to be there with some friends.

☐ You are caught by the police breaking into your own house after forgetting your key.

☐ On holiday an Immigration officer says you need an entry visa – you know you don't.

☐ Half an hour after taking your order, the waiter still hasn't brought the first course.

☐ The person sitting next to you in the library is listening to a personal stereo.

b Now write out the sentences in reported speech, using verbs such as *told, threatened, made, forced*.

Example:
She protested that she hadn't done anything. She said she just happened to be there with some friends.

4 The formal letter

a Write a letter of application for one of the jobs below:

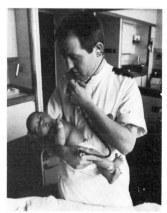

b Give your letter from *Writing to the Editor* to another student. He or she should write a letter responding to yours.

5 Now do the Progress Test for Unit 5 on page 182.

UNIT 6 WHAT NEXT?

READING

1 The topic

a Look at the picture. What advantages do you think computers have over people?

b How will people react as information technology becomes more and more sophisticated?

2 Before reading

a Look at the title of the text below. What reasons do you think the writer will give?

b Write down ten words you think will appear in the text.

3 While reading

The first sentences of six of the paragraphs have been mixed up. Which sentences are they? Which paragraphs should they begin?

Why the computer's days are numbered

The counter-revolution is coming, says

Richard Parlour

A A computer-based economy contains the seeds of its own destruction. That was the revelation that flashed upon me the other morning while I was depositing a cheque at my local building society. 5

B A transaction so banal is not, perhaps, the most likely occasion for an insight of such apocalyptic gravity. Indeed, when I walked into the society's office everything seemed normal to a fault. Miss A, as always, was 10 mooning over the *TV Times*; Mr B, as always, was plaintively asking whether it was time for coffee yet; Miss C, as always, was gazing into space with that terrifying vacancy usually seen only in the eyes of chronic users of personal 15 stereos. Even the sleepwalking languor with which Miss C eventually greeted me and slid my passbook into the printer was, for her, immaculately typical.

C Ultimately, I think, sabotage of computers 20 will become so common and so damaging as to make mass computerisation no longer ⮕ practicable. Before my cashier had even time to take my cheque from me, the printer gave an abrupt metallic retch and coughed out my 25 passbook. Miss C, eyebrows raised, wonderingly pushed it back in; the printer, with a gurgle of indignation, spat it decisively back out. Animation began to glimmer in Miss C's face like the flickering of a lighting- 30 tube which has just been switched on. She tapped at the keyboard, peered into the VDU and then beamed up at me with a smile of enormous, shining delight: 'It appears,' she said, 'that you no longer exist!' 35

D The ordinariness of all this only emphasised the extraordinariness of what happened next. It was electrifying. The *TV Times* was forgotten, the coffee postponed. Somnambulism became just an awkward word 40 in the dictionary. The various technological, financial and metaphysical aspects of my annihilation were debated with an excitement which soon became so intense as to demand physical expression as well as verbal. The 45 printer was gleefully torn apart into a room-wide, electromechanical chaos. Where all before had been melancholy, now all was joy. And that set me thinking.

E The prognosis is plain enough. But in practice 50 hadn't it more often intensified that drudgery? It certainly had – in some respects – in science: the modern researcher's struggles were less with the problems of the Universe than with those of the university's operating system. In 55 manufacturing, computerisation had degraded master craftsmen into nannies to Japanese robots. And what about my building society's poor Miss C? Formerly, she had filled my passbook with an exquisite, slow- 60 penned calligraphy that had made it a private work of art: now, like the misbehaving printer, she was just another computer peripheral.

F It seemed to me that wherever computers had 65 been imported into the world of work they had made it ever more stiflingly impersonal. In fact, computers had proved so radically hostile to the spirit that it was really as natural as springtime that their occasional failures 70

4 Responding to the text

a Have you ever seen, or experienced, similar reactions to computers?

b Do you think the writer's predictions will turn out to be correct? Why?/Why not?

5 Words from context

a What do the following expressions have in common?
mooning (11)   *gazing* (13)   *sleepwalking* (16)
langour (16)   *somnambulism* (40)

b Find synonyms for *insight* (7) and *electronic box of tricks* (104).

c Find antonyms for *joy* (48) and *mitigated* (94).

d Read on for clues to *beamed* (33) and *Luddism* (80).

6 Ignoring difficult words

It is sometimes possible to ignore difficult words (*gleefully* (46), *stiflingly* (67), *wilfully* (84)) and still understand the meaning of a phrase.
Explain the following phrases:

1 *The printer was torn apart . . .*
2 *. . . ever more impersonal.*
3 *. . . engineers on production lines sometimes neglect routine maintenance . . .*

7 Style

The writer uses several different kinds of *figurative* language.

a Metaphor

A metaphor is an expression which is not used in the literal sense.
Examples:
seeds (2)   *chronic* (15)   *electrifying* (38)
nannies (57)   *computer peripheral* (63)
What do they mean in the literal sense? What do they mean in the context?

b Simile

A simile is a comparison which describes a similarity between two things.
Examples:
*. . . **like** the flickering of a lighting-tube which has just been switched on.* (30)
*. . . **as** natural as springtime . . .* (69)
Discuss the examples with your partner. Why are they appropriate?

c Personification

Personification is when an object, or abstract idea, is represented as a person.
Examples:
retch, coughed (25)   *gurgle, spat* (28)
Which part of the body are they usually associated with? Why are they used about the printer?

Which words might be used in a similar way when referring to:
a mainframe computer?   a VDU?   software?

8 Text organisation

The article consists of four stages:

1 introduction.
2 anecdote: scene setting and action.
3 arguments: generalising, contrasting, comparing.
4 prediction: causes, effects and conclusion.
Which paragraphs correspond to each stage?

Example:
Paragraph A – Introduction.

---

should make spirits leap. And wouldn't it be quite natural if some people – however wrongly – were to try deliberately to bring such failures about?

G   What struck me about this discovery was not so much its significance for myself – instant bankruptcy, relegation to Orwellian unpersonality, confirmation of my belief in life after death – as the effect that it had upon the mood of the other two staff. Luddism motivated by boredom and frustration is already a fact of industrial life: analysts of the motor industry found long ago that engineers on production lines sometimes wilfully neglect routine maintenance in order to have the pleasure of coping with the challenge of a full-scale breakdown. From such passive vandalism to more active kinds is a very short step indeed, and hackers have long since shown that even the best protected mainframes are anything but disruption proof.

H   I knew, of course, that the introduction of computers into the workplace was supposed to have mitigated mechanical drudgery. As computer systems become ever more huge and more intimately interlinked, they will become ever more vulnerable too. And, as more and more people come to see computers as usurpers of their humanity, the wish to sabotage them will become ever more urgent and widespread.

I   The question was, and is, anything but fanciful. People will not be prepared simply to sit back and let an electronic box of tricks do all the interesting work for them. The same desire for creative self-expression that brought computers into being will ironically – but no less necessarily – reject them. And the computer revolution, like so many other revolutions, will turn out to have borne its own counter revolution within it.

PRACTICE

1 Prepositions

Here are some more diagrams for prepositions of place:

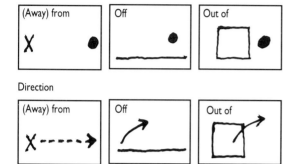

a Complete the following sentences with one of the prepositions opposite. Say why each preposition is correct.

> ## Compact Floppy Disc
> ### Precautions
> ☐ Keep heavy weights ＿＿ disc.
> ☐ Move ＿＿ any magnetic objects.
> ☐ Take disc ＿＿ drive before switching off.
> ☐ Keep ＿＿ dust and dirt.
> ☐ Do not leave ＿＿ plastic case.
> ☐ Keep ＿＿ direct sunlight.

b In pairs, imagine you have bought a new home computer system. Make a list of the precautions you would take.

2 Phrasal verbs

The second part of a phrasal verb sometimes gives a clue to its meaning.

Examples:

off

	General sense
Get *off* the grass.	– leaving a surface
He broke *off* a piece of chocolate.	– separating
The lights went *off*.	– disappearing/not happening

on

It fell *on* the floor.	– making contact with a surface
Switch *on* the lights.	– connecting
Read *on* to the end of the page.	– continuing

away

They are *away* on holiday.	– in another place
She ran *away* from home.	– from here to somewhere else
The laughter died *away*.	– disappearing gradually

Phrasal verbs tend to be more informal, and more commonly used than their one-word equivalents. Complete the table. The first one has been done as an example.

Phrasal verb	Meaning	General sense	Prompt	Example sentence
Get _on_	Mount	Making contact with a surface	Motorbike	He got on his motorbike
Take ＿＿	Rise from the ground		Aeroplane	
Pass ＿＿	Convey		Message	
Get ＿＿	Escape		Prisoner	
Cut ＿＿	Isolate		Radio contact	
Carry ＿＿	Persevere		Difficulties	
Call ＿＿	Cancel		Meeting	
Keep ＿＿	Not go near		Launch pad	

3 The future perfect

The future perfect is used for something which will be completed before a point in the future.

Example:
*They **will have flown** at Mach 5 **by** then.*

The future perfect progressive can be used if an action is not interrupted.

Example:
*They **will have been flying** at Mach 5 **for** years **by** then.*

a Look at the pictures. These ideas all looked very modern once. How will life have changed for you personally and for the world by the year 2010? In pairs write down a few ideas.

Using your imagination tell your partner how things will have changed using *by* and *in* and the future perfect.
Examples:
*By 2010 people **will have been living** on the moon for a few years.*
*In 20 years time **I'll probably have gone** grey!*

b For each year on the time line, write sentences about yourself using *probably/possibly, perhaps/maybe, might/may/should* + future perfect simple.

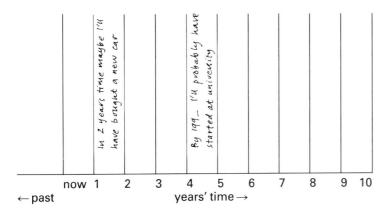

In 2 years time maybe I'll have bought a new car

By 199_ I'll probably have started at university

| now 1 | 2 | 3 | 4 | 5 | 6 | 7 | 8 | 9 | 10 |

← past   years' time →

c Now write sentences using the progressive form:

By then I might have been living abroad for a few years.

| now 1 | 2 | 3 | 4 | 5 | 6 | 7 | 8 | 9 | 10 |

← past   years' time →

WRITING

WRITING ABOUT THE FUTURE

1 What readers want to know

a If you indicate you are going to describe plans or make predictions for the future, your readers might ask themselves:

1 what difficulties there would be,
2 how serious they would be,
3 how they could be overcome.

In groups, look at the pre-text information below and ask the questions above.

b Now read the text and write down the proposed solutions to the following problems:
1 The kind of material for the road surface.
2 Shifting ice.
3 The cost of the material.
4 Political uncertainty.
5 How the material would be extracted.
6 The city's commercial viability.
7 Its food supplies.
8 Its source of energy.

Ice Highway to warm up trade traffic

A road across the North Pole could link Europe and Russia to North America. JOHN NEWELL looks at an oilman's plan.

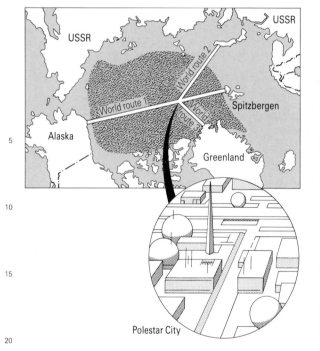

Polestar City

A HIGHWAY built of super-strong ice and running across the North Pole from Alaska to Spitzbergen is the fantastic dream of Harold Heinze, vice-president of the American oil company Arco.

Heinze wants to build a road named World [5] Route One across the Arctic ice cap with branches to Russia, Europe and Greenland. He would also build a trading city at the North Pole.

The road material, or 'asphalt' of World Route One would be granular ice, a material which has [10] already been used by oil companies to make artificial islands for oilrigs.

Granular ice is made simply by spraying water into very cold air. The water freezes into tiny ice particles which when compacted make a tough [15] but flexible material. This has valuable road-making properties; the movements of ice-packs under World Route One would strengthen the road rather than damage it.

Granulated ice is so cheap to make that the road [20] would cost only a few hundred thousand dollars a mile, cheap in view of its value for international trade. Even without Russian trading, World Route One could open up European markets to goods from northwestern Canada and Alaska. [25]

The highway would be built at the rate of a metre an hour by a machine which would move along the road as it built it, drawing on a reservoir of water pumped up from beneath the ice cap. The advancing machine would be fed with water by a [30] pipeline or aqueduct built behind it from more granulated ice.

Roadrunning trailers able to withstand Arctic weather conditions would be used to carry commerce over the roof of the world. [35]

A trading city named Polestar could grow up at a road junction at the North Pole. Heinze envisages Polestar living off trade and being fed mainly by food processed from shrimps and fish which are abundant in the oceans beneath the Arctic ice cap. [40]

'200 metres down in the Arctic the temperature is the same as it is in the ocean anywhere,' says Heinze.

Heinze thinks power for Polestar could be somehow tapped from the Earth's magnetic field, [45] the lines of which curve up and outwards from the magnetic North Pole not far from the geographical pole. He points to the Aurora Borealis, the northern lights, as evidence of the vast amount of magnetic and electrical power available, if means can be [50] found to tap it.

c A writer can convince sceptical readers that his/her vision of the future is practicable by:

1 considering all the possible objections to it while planning the essay.

2 writing at least one counter-argument to each objection.

In pairs, look back at the *proposed solutions* you noted down in **b**. Which of them do you find convincing/unconvincing? Why? Are there any alternative ways of dealing with the problems?

d Can you think of any objections to the scheme that have not been considered in the text? Ask other students for ways of dealing with them.

2 Future or conditional?

a *Will* indicates a more definite prediction than *would*. Compare the text opposite with the last two paragraphs of the article on page 67. What reasons do you think there are for each writer's choice of tense?

b In groups, look at the different types of writing below. Which probably use the future and which the conditional? Why?

☐ An election manifesto.
☐ A report on the design for a silent plane.
☐ A job application – your intentions if appointed.
☐ A football manager quoted in the press.
☐ A plan to put an end to all traffic jams.

Make lists of other kinds of writing which use *will* or *would*.

3 Seeing into the future

The verbs *envisage, foresee* and *prophesy* tend to be used for speculative ideas about the future; *predict* and *forecast* are preferred if the basis is more factual.

a Look at line 37 of the text opposite. Why do you think the writer uses the word *envisages* here?

b Using one of the verbs above, write a sentence about each of the following.
Examples:
*They **foresee** a world in which nobody has to study.*
*Geologists **predict** a major earthquake within five years.*

1 Tomorrow's weather.
2 The use of robots in the home.
3 Fashions in the next century.
4 Share prices on the stock exchange.
5 The next prime minister.
6 The world's biggest city by the year 2000.
7 The country of the future.
8 The winner of the next World Cup.

Show the sentences to your partner and see if he or she agrees with your ideas and choice of verbs.

4 Tense sequences

The present tense is used for the future with time links.

Example:
*Before excavation **begins**, careful studies will have to be carried out.*

The present perfect is used to emphasise the future completion of actions.

Example:
*As soon as mass production **has started**, the price will fall.*

The present perfect is also used in this way with *the first time*, etc. but not with *the last time*.

Example:
*It will be **the first time** they **have tried** to launch it.*
Join the following sentences using the link in brackets.

1 The bridge will be built.
Trade patterns will change. (once)
2 The motorway network will expand.
Traffic volume will increase. (as)
3 A centralised air traffic control system will be introduced.
There will be long delays. (until)
4 The tunnel will be finished.
A second one will be needed. (by the time)
5 The new space plane will come into service in 2001.
It will fly from Europe to Latin America in one hour. (when)
6 The train will travel at 600 kph.
This will be a record. (the first time)
7 The 150,000 ton 'floating city' will be under construction.
Thousands of local people will be employed. (while)
8 Tickets for the space shuttle will go on sale.
The organisers will be bombarded with applications. (immediately)

5 Text organisation

Look at the text opposite. Where does the writer give an overall picture of the scheme? Do the ideas become more realistic or more speculative as the article progresses?

In about 300 words, describe:
EITHER The plans for a new transportation system in your country.
OR   Your vision of city life in twenty years' time.

Use a variety of tenses, but do not change from *will* to *would* or from *would* to *will*.

LISTENING

1 Pre-listening

In groups, make notes on everything you know about the moon. Consider:

- □ where it is.
- □ its history.
- □ its properties compared to Earth.
- □ astronauts who have been there.
- □ its possible future uses.

2 While listening

a Listen to the introduction and make notes. Write down what you expect to hear in terms of:
- □ vocabulary and numbers.
- □ functions expressed.
- □ structures (especially verb tenses).
- □ style and register (specialist language).
- □ special features (speed, accents, etc.).

b Listen to the rest of the recording and put the speakers in order from the most to least convinced about the practicality of living on the moon.

c Look at the chart below. Listen again and put a tick in column A next to the predictions that are made in the recording. Write the speaker's initials (P.M., J.N. or G.B.) in column B. One of them has been done as an example.

	A	B
1 Out on the moon's surface, spacesuits will always have to be worn	✓	P.M.
2 People who live on the moon will be accustomed to artificial conditions	✓	J.N.
3 Those who live in coastal areas will be good space travellers	✓	J.N
4 Those who are used to living on the moon will be good space travellers		
5 The Earth's deserts and polar regions will be fully explored		G.B.
6 We will not learn anything from a dead, inert mass like the moon		
7 To the next generations, the moon will seem quite near to the Earth	✓	G.B.
8 The colonisation of Mars will have started by the year 2100	✓	G B
9 A lot of people will be keen to live on the moon	✓	J.N.
10 The quality of life on Earth is going to get worse and worse		

3 Post-listening

a Burns predicts that man will have visited Mars within two generations. In groups, decide when the other predictions made by the speakers will probably come true.

b Newton uses a historical parallel with the Vikings and Phoenicians to support a prediction; Burns does so by comparing Mars in the future with North America in the past.

Compare the following situations with historical examples:

- □ having to take supplies to be able to live somewhere.
- □ people living in an artificial environment.
- □ overgeneralising after visiting only a few places.
- □ using a place as a 'stepping stone' to explore further afield.
- □ people emigrating to an inhospitable place.

4 Role play

Work in pairs.
Student A You are one of the speakers from LISTENING. Make more predictions about the moon.
Student B You are the interviewer. Argue against the predictions.
Change roles when you have finished.

FUNCTIONS

PREDICTING

1 Making predictions

In pairs, put the following expressions in order, from the most likely to the least likely:

a) There'll definitely be ...
b) There certainly won't be ...
c) Perhaps there'll be ...
d) I don't imagine there'll be ...
e) There's no chance there'll be ...
f) I wouldn't be surprised if there were ...
g) I suppose there might be ...
h) I expect there'll be ...
i) There's bound to be ...
j) I'm sure there'll be ...
k) There might possibly be ...
l) It's likely there'll be ...

2 Reacting to predictions

The listener may or may not be convinced. Put the following expressions in order, from the most convinced to the most sceptical:

a) It's out of the question.
b) Very likely.
c) What a load of rubbish!
d) I'm sure there will.
e) It's not impossible.
f) It could happen.
g) I doubt it.
h) Almost certainly.
i) I'll believe it when I see it.
j) You must be joking!

Which of the expressions above are: neutral, informal or very informal?

3 Practice

a In pairs, discuss the innovations below.

Example:
Perhaps there'll be no need for dentists by 2010.
It could happen.

1 Long-range electric cars.
2 The perfect painkiller.
3 Weather control.
4 A cure for drug addiction.
5 Agriculture on other planets.
6 Robot surgeons.
7 100% accurate machine translations.
8 A cure for the common cold.

b Make and react to more predictions in the fields of technology, science, medicine, space exploration, sports, leisure and music.

STUDY SKILLS   PERSONAL AIMS

In what ways do you think English will be useful to you in the future? In groups, look at the situations 1–13 and decide which:

☐ you are likely to want to do.
☐ you are likely to need to do.
☐ you feel capable of doing now.
☐ you should be able to do when you have passed Proficiency.
☐ the Proficiency Literature and/or Translation optional additional papers would help prepare you for.

1 Travel abroad for pleasure.
2 Meet people from other countries.
3 Talk/Write to friends.
4 Study in an English-speaking country.
5 Read text-books in English.
6 Listen to/watch/read foreign radio/TV/press.
7 Study the culture of English-speaking countries.
8 Study languages at university.
9 Teach English.
10 Work as a translator or interpreter.
11 Travel abroad on business.
12 Work with high technology.
13 Use English at work:
   a) in your own country.
   b) in a country where it is the first language.
   c) in a country where it is a *lingua franca*.

Which language areas should you concentrate on in order to achieve your long-term aims?

ORAL

1 Phonology – Word Stress (2)

Words with suffixes

An addition to a word may change the stress.

Example:
magnet → *magnetic*

a Listen to the recorded words and repeat.

b Look at the words in the table and underline the stressed syllables.

c Listen to the recorded words again, write them down in the table and underline the stressed syllables.

equip		absent	
industry		fancy	
courage		break	
strength		convince	
value		engine	

Compound words

The first part of a compound word may be an adjective, as in **wide**spread, or a noun, as in **pipe**line.

a Listen to the recorded words and repeat.

b Listen again and write down each word, underlining the stressed syllable.

EXAM SKILLS ANTICIPATING THE QUESTIONS

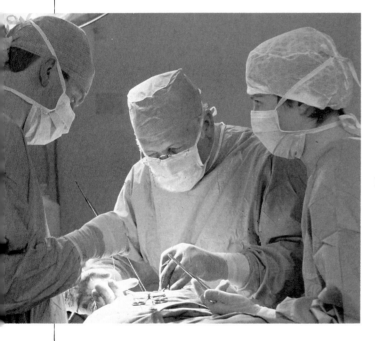

In the Interview, you will have a little time to study the photograph before the Examiner asks you about it. Forming an idea of the likely questions should help you to feel more confident and relaxed and to predict the kinds of vocabulary, grammar and functions you will need.

a Look at the photograph.

The conversation often begins in quite general terms.

Examples:
What can you see/is happening in the picture?
Could you describe the scene, please?
Where/When was this photograph probably taken? How do you know?
What is most striking about the picture?

Which do you think is the most likely question in this case? How would you answer?

b Questions may then focus on particular aspects.

Examples:
What is the man doing?
What sort of person does he look like?
What is he wearing?
Do you think he enjoys his work?
What is going on in the background?

Which might be asked about this picture? How would you answer?

Work in pairs. Considering the picture, discuss related topics.

For example:
What medical breakthroughs do you anticipate in the next twenty years?

Student A Take the part of the Examiner.
Student B Take the part of the Candidate.
Give marks for; *interactive communication*, paying particular attention to the Candidate's ability to deal with questions about more abstract subjects; and *pronunciation* – sentences, especially correct word stress.

REVIEW

1 Word stress

a Say the following words aloud, write in the form without the suffix and underline the stressed syllables in both.

ordinariness		lifelike	
plaintively		viability	
discovery		terrify	
regardless		Chinese	
sceptical		apocalyptic	

b Look back at the words in *Words with suffixes* on the opposite page and those above. Put them into three groups according to the effect the suffixes have on the stress. What are the general rules?

Example:
Equipment – *the suffix -ment usually has no effect on stress.*

c Say the following words aloud and underline the stressed syllables.

springtime   seaboard   high-powered   spaceship
craftsmen   long-term   overcome   white-hot
outdated   oilrig

d Look back at the words in **Compound words** on the previous page and those above.
What is the usual rule for:
1 those beginning with an adjectival form?
2 those beginning with a noun?

2 Vocabulary

a Complete the phrasal verbs in the following sentences:
1 The protective covering was burnt ___ in seconds.
2 We'll keep ___ looking for the fault.
3 They've added ___ a complete new section.
4 The UFO flew ___ from the Solar System.
5 They landed ___ Mars.
6 All germs are killed ___ by this new spray.
7 I'm staying ___ until I'm sure the area is safe.
8 The new trains don't actually run ___ the rails.
9 At that surface temperature, any water would eventually boil ___.

b Put the following expressions from this unit into **category a, b** or **c**. (See STUDY SKILLS on page 17.)

to leap   to bring about   immaculately
mood   practicable   to cope with
to slide   wonderingly   to tap
electrifying   to peer   annihilation
out in the open   to beam   wrongly
plain   breakdown   box of tricks
self-expression   to bear   launchpad
tough   reachable   at a/the rate of
somewhat   earthly   withstand

c Practise saying the **category a** words of more than one syllable.

3 Predicting

a In pairs, imagine what people predicted – or foresaw – twenty years ago. Use the simple or progressive forms of the future perfect, the simple present or the present perfect.
Examples:
'In twenty years' time, home computers will have become common.'
'Well, maybe.'

'When people realise how dangerous it really is, millions will give up smoking'
'I'm certain they will.'

'By the time the next generation has grown up, students will be right-wing.'
'You can't be serious!'

b Use some of the expressions from **2 Vocabulary** to discuss:
1 East-West relations
2 Organ transplants from animals
3 Changes in the weather patterns
4 Supersonic civilian aircraft
5 A healthier diet
6 Holograms

4 Writing about the future

a In groups, decide what people would be sceptical about if you planned:
1 free air travel.
2 a cure for phobias.
3 an underwater city.
4 a rain forest in the Sahara.
5 a fixed link across the Atlantic.
6 a 100% safe car.

b Choose one of the ideas above and write an essay of about 300 words.

5 Now do the Progress Test for Unit 6 on page 183.

UNIT 7 TAKING PART

READING

1 The topic

Look at the picture. Write down all the expressions you can think of concerning the Olympic Games.

Examples:
marathon
exhaustion
gold medal

2 Before reading

In groups, discuss the following statements:
1 Olympic athletes should be amateurs.
2 The Games have become politicised.
3 There is too much emphasis on national achievement.
4 The use of drugs is widespread.
5 Athletes are pushing their bodies beyond 'natural' limits.
6 Some of the sports should not be included.

3 While reading

Read the text quickly and decide which of the following is the correct title:

1 **TOWARDS OLYMPIC WAR GAMES**

2 **OLYMPIC SEX DISCRIMINATION**

3 **NATIONALISM – ENEMY OF THE OLYMPIC IDEAL**

4 **KEEP POLITICS OUT OF SPORT**

The organizers of international athletics meetings, however loudly they may reject 'political interference', have long organized such games on an overtly political basis by construing them *not* as a competition between free individuals, but between representatives of nation states.

In principle there is no reason why international athletic events should not involve multinational teams of Methodists, divorcees, employees of General Motors, monks, lawyers, freemasons or homosexuals – but they do not. People are only allowed to run, throw or jump for a State with a flag, a national anthem and the other paraphernalia of a *political* territorial unit. This is hardly surprising, since the skills on display are of no value except to the military establishment of the State, who still respect these archaic military techniques and virtues.

An athlete who throws a javelin must have in mind that it is designed to skewer, impale and disembowel an enemy soldier. Otherwise no adult could ever take seriously the childish antics of javelin throwers, fencers, shot-putters or sprinters, which would otherwise be on a par with egg-and-spoon and sack races.

The main value of these anachronistic military tasks is that they indirectly indoctrinate the male youth of a country with the vital martial virtues of patriotism, blind obedience and loyalty, and the physical courage to commit aggression.

In a world where disputes between nations are settled by force of arms, male participation in athletics is a regrettable necessity, but female athletes are merely a grotesque parody of their masculine counterparts. We should regard female hurdlers or caber-tossers with the same horror we feel at the idea of women being employed as combat troops.

In the days before rigorous sex tests were applied, there were few sights more repellent than that of the Eastern bloc on the sports tracks of the world; some of these unfortunate ladies were on occasions even force-fed with male hormone pills to assist muscular development. If feminists had any sense, they should be protesting against this callous forcing of women into a male mould. Instead, they are likely to demand government funding to try and produce women who will run, throw, hop-skip-and-jump as well as men.

The flaw in their case is that true equality demands unisex events where women compete directly with men. It is true that the women would hardly ever win, but that is just too bad. We do not have separate and special events for nations whose people are naturally short, slender or feeble – there is no special low high jump for pygmies or Welshmen, no separate balsa-wood caber-tossing for Glaswegians, no 10 yard start for heavy-calved white men running in the 100 metres.

We rightly reject the very idea as racist. Why then are there separate and very much second-class events for women? Why are women debarred from events such as boxing and wrestling? The answer is not one that will please the egalitarians, for it resides in the fact that women are specifically designed for bearing children.

The athlete, then, is either a potential soldier or an actual clown, and only the dignity of the former role can rescue him – and I mean him – from the obloquy reserved for the latter. Fortunately the periodic fuss and farce over the Olympic Games has suggested a solution, for it has made everyone conscious of the essentially military and political nature of sport.

The time has come to make this explicit by replacing traditional athletics with overtly military exercises and abolishing female participation altogether. What is needed instead is some form of minimally-lethal ritual clash between each nation's elite military or police units – the SAS against the Spetnatz, the US Marine Corps versus Les Paras, the Alpini versus the Gurkhas, the Guardia Civil against the Gárda Síochana.

I am sure it is not beyond the wit of the world's military staff colleges to design active and competitive Kriegspielen that would be of value to them, no more dangerous than boxing or motor racing and thoroughly good television. We can make a start right away by transforming our Minister of Sport into a Junior Minister at the Ministry of Defence.

4 Reading for detail

Make a list of the Olympic sports or sportspersons mentioned in the text.

5 Responding to the text

a In groups, list all the different groups of people who could be offended by the content.

b What would you say to the writer about his views if you met him?

6 Reference words

What do the following words refer to?
1 such   (4)
2 they   (16)
3 this   (21)
4 their   (50)
5 it   (75)
6 the former   (99)
7 the latter   (102)
8 it   (105)
9 this   (108)
10 them   (125)

7 Text organisation

Newspaper articles are often made up of very short paragraphs. Divide the text into only four paragraphs. Complete the line references for the four paragraphs in the following diagram.

PARAGRAPH 1
Introduction and political arguments. Lines: 1–____

↓

PARAGRAPH 2
Military arguments. Lines: ____

↓

PARAGRAPH 3
Male-only arguments. Lines: ____

↓

PARAGRAPH 4
Suggestions and conclusion. Lines: ____–131

8 The writer

In groups, discuss these questions:
1 Do you think the writer's aim is to:
   a) suggest?
   b) provoke?
   c) inform?
   d) amuse?
   e) do more than one of these?
   Is he successful?
2 He is probably:
   a) an army officer
   b) a sociology professor.
   c) a sportsman.
   d) a conservative politician.
   Why do you think so?

PRACTICE

1 Omission of relative pronouns

a As long as *that*, *which* or *whom* is the object of the clause, it may be left out in defining clauses.

Example:
*... with the same horror (**which/that**) we feel ...* (52)

If it is the subject it must be included.

Example:
*... **which** would otherwise be ...* (34)

In a non-defining clause, which is always enclosed in commas, the relative must be used.

Complete the following sentences, if necessary, with relative pronouns. In each case, say why omission is or is not possible.
1 The original Olympics, _____ included music and literature competitions, began in 776 BC.
2 The first modified revival _____ took place was in Athens in 1896.
3 Greece, _____ of course is where they began, has been suggested as a permanent site for the Games.
4 Throwing the discus is one of the sports _____ we call 'field events'.
5 The 1500 metres final is perhaps the event _____ spectators most look forward to.

b Both the subject relative pronouns *that*, *which* or *who* and the verb *to be* can often be left out in defining or non-defining clauses.

Examples:
*The steeplechase is a track event (**which is**) run over 3000 metres.*
*Ice hockey, (**which is**) a physical contact sport, can sometimes get violent.*
In pairs, make similar sentences about these sports:
long jump   hurdles   pole vault   relay
triple jump   decathlon   high jump
marathon

2 Past modals

To speculate about the past, the form *modal + have + past participle* can be used.

Example:
*They **must have won** the match because the home fans are looking happy.*
Look at the diagrams below. The arrows denote decreasing certainty.

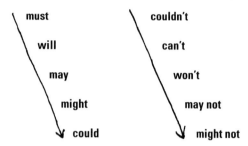

Note: while the form 'needn't have done' refers to an unnecessary past action, 'didn't need to' often indicates that the action probably did not take place.

a Complete these sentences using *because*, *but* or *although*.

Example:
*They **must have made** millions from sponsorship, **but** they are still borrowing money.*
1 He may not have felt like playing ...
2 They'll have finished training by now ...
3 They might not have known the rules ...
4 The leaders won't have reached the stadium yet ...
5 He may have used steroids. ...
6 She couldn't have broken the record ...
7 He might have missed his last chance to win the title ...
8 They can't have scored ...
9 He could have caused a terrible pile-up driving like that ...
10 She needn't have looked round when she reached the finishing line ...

b Look at the pictures. In groups list all the things that *must, couldn't,* etc. *have* happened.

In Paper 3 you are instructed:
*For each of the sentences below, write a new sentence **as similar as possible in meaning to the original sentence**, but using the word given. This word must **not be altered** in any way.*

EXAMPLE: The crash happened because a wheel suddenly came off.
caused

ANSWER: The crash was caused by a wheel suddenly coming off.

a In pairs, decide which of the following do not follow the instructions in **bold type** above, say why not, then re-write them correctly.

1 The match was highly tedious as both teams were afraid to lose.
fear
The match was highly tedious owing to both teams' fear.

2 He's one of the most competitive players in the league.
few
There are few players in the league as competitive as him.

3 He missed the gold medal because he made a very bad turn.
result
He made a bad turn, resulting in his missing the gold medal.

4 There will be seats instead of terraces.
replaced
The terraces will be replaced and there will be seats.

5 She protested against the decision and walked off the court.
protesting
She walked off the court protesting against the decision.

b Transform the sentences from the text on page 76 which begin:
1 . . . male participation in athletics is a regrettable necessity. (lines 47–48)
need
2 Why are women debarred from events such as boxing or wrestling? (lines 90–92)
allowed

WRITING

THE DISCURSIVE ESSAY (BALANCED)

1 Predicting

a Look at the title and the first paragraph. What is *screening*?

b What do you think the arguments will be on each side?

2 While reading

Now read the rest of the text and see if you were right.

MARATHON MENTALITY –
THE RISKS SPORTSMEN RUN

Some doctors take the view that middle-aged sportsmen should be warned of the health risks they are running, so that they might moderate their sporting activities. A debate has begun about the merits of screening potential heart-attack victims who   5
take part in sports such as marathons or squash.

In the blue corner, the pro-screening lobby is led by two Glasgow doctors, Dr Robin Northcote and Dr David Ballantyne of the cardiology department at Glasgow's Victoria Infirmary. They studied 30 recent   10
deaths on the squash court and found that a third of the victims had medical records which showed that they had suffered from high blood pressure on two or more occasions. But only one had received any treatment for it. The two doctors are now screening   15
200 squash players in Glasgow, all of them over the age of 40, in the hope of identifying those with obvious heart disease and warning them of the risks they run.

In the red corner, Dr Dan Tunstall-Pedoe, medical   20
adviser to the London Marathon, opposes mass screening on the grounds of both effectiveness and expense. Of the four deaths in marathons and half-marathons in the last year in Britain, some of the victims knew they were at risk of heart failure, he   25
claims. Mass screening would not have deterred them, he says; it would simply have frightened a great many people who were not at risk. The squash lobby argues much the same way. If only 20 people over the age of 40 die of heart failure on the squash courts every year,   30
they say, that is a small risk compared with the 150,000 who play on without suffering adverse consequences.

Perhaps the answer is a compromise. Instead of mass screening, why not give marathon runners or   35
squash players the choice of cheap individual screening, paid for by themselves or their clubs? Then at least sportsmen are making informed choices.

---

3 Text organisation

Find the appropriate expressions from the article to complete the notes below.

INTRODUCTION

Introducing the topic: *Some doctors* _____

Opinions differ: _____

ARGUMENTS FOR

Who? _____

Where? _____

Which sport? _____

Statistics: _____

Present action: _____

ARGUMENTS AGAINST

Who? _____

Where? _____

Which sports? _____

Statistics _____

Opinions _____

ENDING

Conclusion _____

Suggestions _____

Jusitification _____

4 Introductory expressions

a Why does the writer use *In the blue corner . . .* (line 7) and *In the red corner . . .* (line 20) to introduce the two sets of arguments?

b Which of the following phrases would be used to introduce the first set of arguments and which the second?

  1 Some would say that . . .
  2 Conversely . . .
  3 On the other hand . . .
  4 Others might argue that . . .
  5 On the one hand . . .
  6 It can also be argued that . . .
  7 It is often claimed that . . .
  8 Those on the left, however, would say . . .
  9 It has often been said that . . .
  10 It is claimed by those on the right that . . .

5 Balance

The key to writing a good balanced essay is to include as many arguments you disagree with as those you agree with. They should be noted impartially, although in your conclusion you can say why you find one side more convincing than the other.

a Look at the notes which follow the essay title below. In groups, decide which you agree/disagree with and add more points.

'Sport is of no benefit to humanity.' Discuss.

FOR
☐ drugs
☐ spectator/on-field violence
☐ political manipulation
☐ commercialisation
☐ extreme nationalism
☐ danger e.g. motor sports
☐ overtraining
☐ young people's education suffers
☐ win-at-all-cost mentality
☐ resources wasted on expensive stadiums, etc, especially in poor countries

AGAINST
☐ Health/fitness
☐ entertainment
☐ jobs created
☐ team spirit encouraged
☐ peaceful outlet for aggression
☐ helps medical research
☐ can bring young people of all nations together
☐ rich and poor people compete on equal terms
☐ sense of personal achievement
☐ small countries can beat big ones.

b List the arguments for and against each of the following statements:
1 Violence at football matches is inevitable.
2 Politics and sport should always be kept separate.
3 Any sportsperson found to have used drugs should be banned for life.
4 There is too much sport on TV.

c Choose one of the statements and write an essay of about 300 words.

STUDY SKILLS LOOKING FOR MISTAKES

a Work in pairs. Find, underline and correct the 22 mistakes in the essay below. Use the following code to write notes in the margin:
V = Vocabulary   P = Punctuation
WO = Word Order   Sp = Spelling
G = Grammar   St = Style

'Political interference in sport is a new phenomenon.' Discuss.

Throughout this century there has been political interests involved in sport, beginning with the try in 1908 by Russia to stop Finland to use its own flag in the Olympics.

After both world wars the countries on the losing side were not let to compete in the Games, and of course the 1936 Olympics famous for Jesse Owens' gold medals were used for propaganda purposes. The Cold War also brought about rivalry between the USA and the USSR in sport. Winning more medals than the other superpower, they hoped, would 'show' the superiority of their system. There athletes were really profesionals paid to do 'degrees' in swimming, weightlifting, the long jump and so on.

In the 1960s, a student demonstration in Mexico against the big expense of the Games ended with hundreds of killed, while there was a political storm in America over two sprinters who made a Black Power salute. South Africa was kicked out of the Olympics owing to its politic of Apartheid. Then, in the 1970s, many African countries boycotted the Games on account of the presence of countries which have recently played in South Africa. The 1980 Western boycott of the Moscow Olympics was due to the Soviet intervention in Afghanistan the Russians retaliated by refusing to go to Los Angeles. North Korea was accused of trying to jeopardise the Seoul Games.

Some might argue, however, that the recent news stories about governments putting pressure in certain sportspersons not to speak to the foreign media is something new. It appears that those who do not share Ministers' political views have been told they would not represent their country if they would criticise its goverment abroad. This must have happened many times in totalitarian countries but it surely is the first time it occurs in a democratic society.

To sum up, the statement is obviously a load of rubbish as there has been continuous political interference in sport, particularly by the big powers.

b Make notes on the organisation of the essay above, like those in **3** opposite. How could the organisation be improved?

c Look at the title again. What other major criticism can be made of the essay? What would you add or leave out?

LISTENING

1 Pre-listening

a What is the most popular way of keeping fit in your country?

b Look at the keep-fit activities in the pictures. Compare them in terms of:
- [ ] time
- [ ] cost
- [ ] effectiveness
- [ ] effort
- [ ] convenience
- [ ] risk

c What do you think of the activities below? Fill in the table.

ACTIVITY	ADVANTAGES	DISADVANTAGES
Jogging		
Squash		
Weight training		
No exercise in particular		

2 While listening

a The first time you listen to the recording, tick the points you have written opposite when you hear any of the speakers mention them.

b Now listen again and add, in note form, any other points the speakers make.

3 Post-listening

a In groups, decide which of the speakers was the most convincing. Give reasons for your choice.

b Compare the speakers' arguments you noted down. Which are the most convincing?

TALKING ABOUT LIKES AND DISLIKES

1 Expressing likes and dislikes

a In groups, write down all the verbs you know which have similar meanings to *like* or *dislike*.

b Write a sentence about an activity with each verb.

Examples:
I don't mind DIY.
I loathe hunting.

c The following express similar ideas:

You can't beat (informal) riding a powerful motorbike.
Windsurfing **is really** exhilarating.
What I like best is playing chess.
There's nothing I love more than hang-gliding.
What I most enjoy is (formal) gardening.

I'm not crazy about (informal) badminton.
The thing I don't like about skiing **is** queuing for the lifts.
There's nothing I like less than walking all day.
I don't think much of card games.
Cycling **doesn't appeal** to me at all. (formal)

In pairs, look at the picture below and discuss the activities that are available.

2 Asking about likes and dislikes

Which of the following expressions are informal?

What do you like doing in your spare time?
How do you spend your free time?
Don't you find watching TV boring?
Canoeing's **great, isn't it!**
Do you like reading?
Isn't sky-diving incredible!
Do you go fishing?
Do you paint?

3 Responding

a Match the expressions 1–10 below with the functions a)–d).

a) Agreeing with likes
b) Agreeing with dislikes
c) Disagreeing with likes
d) Disagreeing with dislikes

1 Neither do I.
2 Don't you? I quite enjoy it myself, actually.
3 Yeah, it's a waste of time, isn't it?
4 I'm not so keen myself.
5 Yes, I do too.
6 So do I, actually.
7 Yes, it's amazing, isn't it!
8 No, I don't either.
9 Oh, do you? I don't, really.
10 Doesn't it? I'd love to try it myself.

Which are informal or direct?

b Ask your partner about his or her leisure activities and respond as above.

ORAL

1 Phonology – stressed words

Words that convey information are stressed, while those that have a grammatical function are usually unstressed.

Examples:
the end of the game
We can easily settle the argument.

a Listen to the recording and repeat.

b Listen again and underline the stressed words.

1 a new guide for stamp collectors
2 Because of the virus, she fell ill.
3 a thoroughly awful weekend
4 We can try again but I think we'll need help.
5 Let's compromise and take it in turns.
6 Bird watching doesn't appeal to me at all.

c Now say the following sentences aloud and underline the stressed words.

1 They aren't on a par with the best.
2 It was a regrettable mistake.
3 It's often said that gardening is relaxing.

2 Interview

Passage

a Read the following text and decide what its source and purpose probably is.

The best news for the world's slobs since the invention of the TV remote controller may come from a Health Science Centre in Texas. Dr Roger McCarter, a specialist in ageing research at the University of Texas in San Antonio, is working on the theory that exercise may actually shorten your life. McCarter has begun research into the 'rate of living' theory that every human being is genetically allocated a limited number of calories to burn during his or her lifetime. 'If you use those calories quickly by having a high metabolic rate, such as one has while exercising, then it could shorten your life-span,' he warns.

b In pairs, discuss the content. Is it convincing?
Examples:
McCarter is obviously well qualified, but the writer cautiously uses the word 'may' twice.
The human body could eventually wear out, like a machine. On the other hand, it can break down prematurely if it is functioning inefficiently.

c Now do the same with this passage:

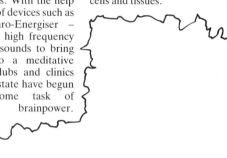

Throughout the Golden State, young Californians are taking to 'brain building' with the same enthusiasm that they took to aerobics and body-building in the 1980s. With the help of a series of devices such as the Synchro-Energiser – which uses high frequency lights and sounds to bring clients into a meditative trance – clubs and clinics across the state have begun the awesome task of enhancing brainpower. Among the benefits claimed by all those involved are deeper relaxation, improved memory, lesser drug use, increased intelligence, and even expansion of brain cells and tissues.

Give your partner marks for *pronunciation* and correct *word stress* in sentences.

Discussion

Tell your group about your favourite hobby in a talk lasting about two minutes. Before you begin, briefly note down:

1 what it consists of.
2 how you became interested in it.
3 why it gives you pleasure.
4 any disadvantages it may have.
5 how you deal with them.
6 your future plans.

When you have finished, answer questions from the others.

Listen to another student and give marks for; *fluency* during the talk; *interactive communication* when answering questions.

REVIEW

1 Stressed words

a Listen, and underline the stressed words:
1 . . . tonight's clash between the top two teams.
2 They're making such a terrible fuss!
3 He collapsed within sight of the summit.

b Now underline the stressed words in the following:
1 They made a feeble excuse for playing so badly.
2 They always take part in the regatta.
3 . . . the best match I've seen recently.

c Look at the words you underlined above and in ORAL **1c**. Which four of the following categories do they belong to?

Prepositions   Verbs   Nouns
Pronouns   Adverbs   Conjunctions
Adjectives   Articles

Note: Where there is a corrected misunderstanding or a contrast, any class of word can be stressed.

Examples:
'No, it's not your free-kick, it's theirs.'
SPEAKER A: *We spent the day on the river.*
SPEAKER B: *We spent most of it in the river.*

2 Vocabulary

Put the following expressions from this unit into **category a**, **b** or **c**. (See STUDY SKILLS on page 17.)

overtly   to construe   national anthem
on display   antics   feeble   slender
debarred   callous   mould   funding
flaw   unisex   rightly   fuss   clash
right away   thoroughly   record-holder
pile-up   to deter   fitness   outlet
to ban   retaliate   media   to bribe.

3 Past modals

Make excuses for the following situations.

Example:
Your team has lost the Cup Final.
The referee could've been bribed!

Use some of the expressions from **2 Vocabulary**. (They are usually stressed.)

1 The judges weren't impressed by your skating.
2 Your country's top athlete came last in the Olympic final.
3 Your new sports car wouldn't start when you left the disco.
4 Your girlfriend or boyfriend has been seen dancing with someone else.
5 The video didn't record the match your friends have come round specially to see.

4 Omission of relatives

In groups, write twelve questions about sports and leisure activities. See how many of them other groups can guess correctly.

Examples:
It's a team game, usually associated with the USA, which is played in the summer.
It's a board game played by up to six people which tests general knowledge.
It's an outdoor activity some people call the opposite of mountaineering.

5 Essay

a In about 300 words, write a balanced composition entitled:
'The ideal lifestyle would consist purely of sport and leisure.' Discuss.

b When you have finished make notes on the organisation like those in question **3** on page 80.

6 Now do the Progress Test for Unit 7 on page 184.

UNIT 8 SHARING IT OUT

READING

1 The topic

a What is the most striking thing about the map?

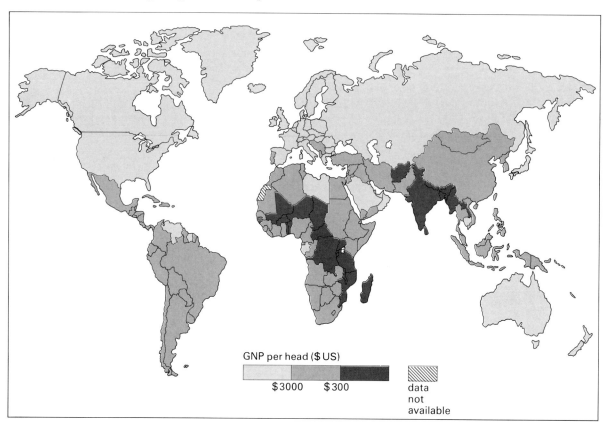

GNP per head ($US)

$3000 $300   data
                       not
                       available

b In groups, decide which of these factors best explains the differences in wealth:
   □ Climate   □ Geographical situation
   □ Imperialism   □ Political system
   □ Overpopulation   □ Social structure
   Can you think of any others?

2 Before reading

a Look at the text heading and write down twelve words you think will be used in the text.

b Find Ethiopia on the map. How important are the factors in **1b**?

3 While reading

Read the text on the opposite page. Does the writer feel:

1 angry?   2 frustrated?   3 bored?   4 hopeful?

4 Reading for detail

Which of the following are reasons for the famine victims not receiving aid?
   1 Donkeys are used as transport.
   2 Religion.
   3 Road transport can be difficult.
   4 Air transport is expensive.
   5 Armed conflict.
   6 The food is still at the ports.
   7 Politics.
   8 $3 million.
   9 British officials.
   10 A TV programme.

Hugh Herbert on the return of Bob Geldof, and famine, to Ethiopia

Labours with a Hercules

MAYBE the saddest thing about *Geldof: Back to Ethiopia* (Central TV) is the feeling that the most deluding mirage on the parched roads is that they lead somewhere. The first shot is of Geldof riding in on a donkey, like a fourth Wise Man who somehow missed the trail a couple of thousand years back. But this is only partly an ironic reference to Christmas Year Zero, the reference is less to holy matters than to haulage.

As Geldof tells the Ethiopian Relief Commissioner, 'If one of the problems becomes *trucking* after all the money they've sent, it's going to disenchant people'. The next saddest thing is that this should surprise anyone. In every famine – at least back to the great Sahelian disasters of the Seventies – no matter how much the world's heart bleeds, or how many tons of aid pile up at the ports, if you can't distribute the food you might as well send coffins.

Trucks? Fine, as long as you have them; they are built like tanks, and there are no flash floods. Aircraft? Fine, but what you spend on them swallows money for long-term development. Civil strife? Well, yes, in Ethiopia there's that too. 'Their top priority is the war,' the US Chargé d'Affaires tells the Boomtown Rat in a straw hat, 'That's not uncommon in the West.'

So if you could stop the rebels rocketing the UN protected trucks, or get a few more Hercules flying the stuff into the interior, would all be solved? Well, yes, if there were stocks at the ports. And are there big stocks at the ports? Er, not exactly, because you remember all those pledges, well they were *pledges*.

Still, the US Government chipped in $1 billion over several years for emergency aid. It steadfastly refuses long-term development aid, as it has for years because of Ethiopia's Marxist orientation and because Congress won't cough up any more cash till Ethiopia redeems its $3 million debt on an earlier deal. And as we also know from every earlier famine, handouts are no long-term substitute for wells and irrigation schemes and food growing in the fields.

It was, of course, the measly $3 million that did it. 'I'd give it you meself – Band-Aid would give it you,' Geldof burst out, only to be told that even if that embargo were lifted, the political objections would still stand. But you have to hand it to American officials, they didn't wrap it up. I mean, can you imagine the kind of diplomatic gobbledegook British officials would use to tell Geldof that?

Charles Stewart and Malcolm Hirst have been filming this story on and off for five years, and their first documentary *Seeds of Disaster* came months before the shattering and famous Michael Buerk report that had such a remarkable impact on public opinion. The latest UN estimate of possible famine victims is creeping up from 5 million people towards maybe 8 million. Some people would get cynical. Geldof said: 'If you see those pictures again, don't come and say you hadn't been warned.'

5 Responding to the text

With your partner discuss the problems of famine relief. What do you think should be done?

6 Connecting ideas

1 *. . . they lead somewhere . . .* (3)
   What do?
2 *. . . all the money they've sent . . .* (12)
   Who have?
3 *'Their top priority is the war,' . . .* (24)
   Whose is?
4 *'That's not uncommon in the West.'* (26)
   What isn't?
5 *. . . to tell Geldof that?* (51)
   To tell him what?
6 *'If you see those pictures again . . .'* (60)
   Which pictures?

7 Vocabulary

Look at the following expressions from the text. Which of the two alternatives best fits the context?

1 *you might as well* (informal) (18)
   a) it would be just as useful to
   b) you could also
2 *pledges* (33)
   a) ships
   b) promises
3 *did it* (informal) (44)
   a) made Geldof react emotionally
   b) showed us what to do
4 *only to be told* (46)
   a) but then was told
   b) was told nothing except

8 Style

a Why does the text contain informal expressions such as *Well, yes, . . .* (30) and *Er . . .* (32)?

b Match the informal expressions on the left with the neutral expressions on the right.

1 *maybe* (1)   a) ridiculously inadequate
2 *stuff* (30)   b) give reluctantly
3 *chipped in* (34)   c) until
4 *cough up* (38)   d) material
5 *till* (39)   e) pompous, meaningless
                          language
6 *measly* (44)   f) added (their share)
7 *I mean* (49)   g) perhaps
8 *gobbledegook* (50) h) that is to say

c What are the two nonstandard expressions in the sentence beginning *'I'd give . . .'* in line 45?

PRACTICE

1 Contrast links – 2

Look at the links *But* (informal) (line 6) and *Still* (line 34) of the text on page 87. They could be replaced by: *Even so, Nevertheless, (And) Yet* or *All the same* (informal).

The two sentences on lines 4–9 could be linked using *Even though* or *In spite of the fact that*:
Even though/In spite of the fact that the first shot is of Geldof riding in on a donkey, like a fourth Wise Man who somehow missed the trail a couple of thousand years back, *this* is . . .

The following two sentences could also be joined using the more formal structures . . . *as/though* . . . *are* . . . or *much as*:
The contributions are greatly appreciated. Even so, more money is needed.

Example:

Greatly appreciated *as/though* the contributions *are*, more money is needed. *Much as* the contributions are appreciated, more money is needed.
(Note *Much as* is only used with verbs of emotion.)

Complete the following sentences with a suitable word or phrase.
1 ____ international trade is booming, Third World countries are becoming poorer and poorer.
2 ____ some children will survive, many will starve.
3 There are signs of economic recovery. ____ it will come too late for many.
4 Pessimistic ____ everyone is, relief work must go on.
5 Millions will die of hunger every year, ____ the world spends $2 billion on arms every day.

2 Phrasal verbs – 2

Look at the general sense of the second part of the following verbs:

round	General sense
They sat *round* the wood fire.	– circle/encircle
She walked *round* the corner.	– move in a semi-circle or curve
Come *round* after you finish work.	– visit someone
We drove *round* the country.	– go to a number of places

out	
He took *out* a pistol.	– move from the inside
They handed *out* the blankets.	– distribute
The drinking water has run *out*.	– no longer exist/ eliminate
She called *out* to the men in the field.	– be clear or loud

up	
They picked *up* their few possessions.	– move to a higher position
The government promised to step *up* aid.	– increase
He came *up* to me and asked for food.	– move towards
We've used *up* all our medical supplies.	– do something completely
They split *up* at the village.	– separate into smaller units
The rebel groups joined *up* for the offensive.	– come together

a Work in pairs and complete the following table. The first one has been done as an example.

PHRASAL VERB	EQUIVALENT	GENERAL SENSE	EXAMPLE SENTENCE
Stand _round_	Surround	_encircle_	_The hungry people stood round the relief lorry._
Break ____	Disintegrate		
Throw ____	Expel		
Go ____	Go and see someone		
Climb ____	Ascend		
Travel ____	Tour		
Sum ____	Summarise		
Stand ____	Be conspicuous		
Wipe ____	Annihilate		
Tidy ____	Put everything in order		
Turn ____	Face the opposite way		
Speed ____	Go faster		
Share ____	Apportion		
Go ____ to	Approach		

b What is the general sense of the following verbs from the text on page 87?

1 _pile up_ (17)   2 _burst out_ (46)   3 _creeping up_ (58)

3 Mixed conditionals

_If_ sentences do not always fall into the categories of first, second and third conditionals.

Modal verbs can be used instead of _will_ or _would_. The imperative can be used instead of the future.

Look at these forms from the text on page 87:
'_. . . **if** you **can't** distribute the food you **might** as well send coffins._' (17)
'**If** you **see** those pictures again, **don't** come and **say** you hadn't been warned.' (60–61)

If the actions or states are recurrent, the meaning of _if_ is _when_ or _whenever_.

Examples:
If the sky **is** clear, night temperatures in the desert **are** often below zero.
Until ten years ago, grain **was** exported **if** there **was** a good crop.

In the following sentence, the past condition is linked to the present:
If it **had rained**, there **would be** a good harvest by now.

Here, it is linked to both the present and the future:
If the supplies **have arrived**, we'**ll collect** them.

a Give the form of each verb in the following sentences:

1 If you're going by car take plenty of water.
2 If we hadn't run out of diesel, we'd be back at camp by now.
3 If there's going to be a sandstorm, we were right not to go on.
4 If there's been flooding, the roads will have been blocked.
5 If they left at six they must have got there by now.
6 If lorries were arriving all morning, there should be enough food by now.
7 If we needed anything, people always did their best to help.
8 If you don't like hot weather, you would've had a terrible time in Chad.

b Now write your own endings to the conditionals in 1–8.

Example:
1 _If you're going by car **stay on the main roads**._

WRITING

Summary writing – 3

1 Reading for gist

Read the text quickly and suggest a title.

An adequate intake of calories is the most common and the most important measure of adequate nourishment. The minimum calorie intake regarded as adequate by the World Health Organisation differs from state to state; taking into account climatic conditions, patterns of work, the average weight of inhabitants, and other relevant factors.

Figures for deficit countries inevitably understate the nutritional deficiency suffered by many inhabitants, as figures for surplus countries mask altogether the existence of any such deficiency, for the figures apply to average calorie intake, and average intake can obscure extremes of self-indulgence and deprivation. There are inhabitants of surplus states who do not have enough to eat, and inhabitants of deficit states who eat as abundantly as do the rich and powerful elsewhere.

Far from being relieved in the last few years, the horror of mass starvation would seem only to have spread and strengthened its hold. But if the vagaries of the weather contribute to visitations of famine, they are far from accounting for nutritional deficiencies over much of the world. Food production per head in Africa fell in general throughout the 1970s and 1980s.

The pressures of population growth might have been relieved by appropriate social policies and economic development. Instead, a rapid urbanization has drained human and material resources from the countryside. The new urban elites have acquired a taste for foods, such as wheat and rice, which are not traditional crops and have had to be imported in increasing volume at increasing cost. Shortages of foreign exchange, in part arising from the cost of providing the elites with the foreign consumer goods they demand, have promoted government concentration on encouraging the growth of non-nutritional cash crops for export. And policies to keep food cheap for the appeasement of the urban populace deprive farmers of resources and accelerate the drain of population from the countryside. Not least, warfare – whether waged by discontented peoples against the artificial unifications of the state, as in Ethiopia, or promoted by foreign intervention, as in Angola and Mozambique – has devasted vast areas of once richly productive agriculture.

But the mounting plight of Africa is only an extreme example of preoccupations and policies so distorted and distorting across the world of states that many hundreds of millions are permanently undernourished, while certain governments are agitated by the problem of what to do with their accumulated surplus stocks of food. There seems little doubt that the world is perfectly capable of feeding decently all its inhabitants. That it is so conspicuously not doing so at present is the product not of human necessity but of choice.

2 Relevance

Look at the following summary of the text. The instructions are:

In a paragraph of 70–90 words, summarise the reasons why hunger in Africa is getting worse.

Which of the expressions in **bold** is:

1 an unnecessary example?
2 a superfluous detail?
3 a subjective comment?
4 an evaluation, not a reason?
5 adding little, or nothing, to the meaning?

The situation is often worse than is shown by the statistics, and climatic factors on their own do not account for declining agricultural output over recent decades. As a result of the failure to plan **in any way** for demographic changes, resources have been transferred to the cities, whose richer inhabitants now demand low farm prices – as well as imports of expensive food, **like wheat and rice**, and other items. Partly in order to make up for the cost of imports, crops **which are** of no food value are being cultivated for export, thus reducing the rural population even more. Civil wars, **in which people have fought to maintain the independence of their territory**, and invasions have laid waste prime farming lands. In spite of the fact that enough food is available in global terms, there is an apparent unwillingness, **and this is particularly true of the USA and EC**, to get rid of hunger **once and for all**.

3 Economy with words

Even after cutting out the irrelevant or superfluous expressions the summary is still 23 words too long.

In pairs, bring the number below 90 by replacing 12 expressions in the text with:

although	without	eliminate	to
explain	ruined	owing to	alone
worldwide	this	offset	further

Now re-write the summary and compare it with the original text.

Other ways of reducing the word-count include:
- □ removing unnecessary adverbs and adjectives, especially intensifiers like *very*.
- □ replacing the passive form of verbs with the active.
- □ avoiding repetition by the use of ellipsis (the use of 'has' on line 36 of the READING text).
- □ using nouns as adjectives: *food prices* instead of *the price of food*.

EXAM SKILLS TIMING

In the Examination, you will have to write two essays of up to 350 words in two hours: it is vital that you finish them both.

Of the hour available for each, you should spend 5 – 10 minutes planning the composition, and another 10 minutes checking it for mistakes. With only about 40 minutes of writing time, you cannot afford to waste time counting the individual words.

Look at as many samples as possible of your written work in English (preferably those done with a time limit), and work out the average number of words per line on A4-size paper. Then, when writing an essay, count the number of lines you have written.

a In pairs, look at this title and the suggested plan which follows:

In approximately 300 words, write about:
EITHER *a) a region of your country which is poorer than the rest.*
OR *b) a country which is poorer than yours.*
You have one hour.

Paragraph	Content	Minutes	Words
1	Introduction: location, main geographical features	5	30–50
2	History and culture.	10	60–80
3	Current problems and consequences.	10	60–80
4	Contrast: positive aspects.	10	60–80
5	Conclusion: prediction and/or suggestion.	5	30–50

Now choose option a) or b) and write the essay. Do not choose the same option as your partner.

b Count the number of lines you wrote. To save more time, you could work out how many words you tend to use in blocks of 3 or 5 lines. Then, count the blocks.

c Now change papers with your partner.
  1 Correct any mistakes.
  2 In 70–90 words, summarise the reasons why the country or region chosen is poor. You have 15 minutes.

LISTENING

1 Pre-listening

a Which countries would you identify as the leaders in world trade? Were these countries also world leaders fifty years ago?

b Which countries, do you think, are increasing/decreasing their share? Why?

c You are going to hear about patterns of international trade. Which expressions do you think:
1. you're certain to hear?
2. you're likely to hear?
3. you're unlikely to hear?

2 While listening

a The first time you listen, note down answers to these questions:
1. Why do the West European countries apparently dominate world trade?
2. Which two countries have much larger economies than their trade suggests?
3. What has happened to oil exports?
4. Apart from falling metal prices, which other factor has been significant?
5. Which part of the world has had the highest growth in its share?

b Listen again, and tick the percentage change in each country's share of world trade.

| | 10 year period – percentage change in share | | | | | | |
| | RISE | | | | FALL | | |
More than:	100	50	25	5	5	25	50
USA							
Iran							
Saudi Arabia							
Iraq							
Poland							
Japan							
Zambia							
South Korea							
Taiwan							
Singapore							

3 Post-listening

Can you think of any other changes that could happen to world trade?

4 Role play

Work in pairs.

Student A You are a radio interviewer. You are interviewing an expert on your country's trade. Ask the following questions:
- What are our country's main imports and exports?
- Which countries do we buy them from and sell them to?
- What recent events have affected them?
- What factors might affect them in the future?
- What new products could we sell abroad?

Student B You are an expert on your country's trade. Answer the radio interviewer's questions.

Change roles when you have finished.

FUNCTIONS

COMMUNICATION STRATEGIES

Both speakers' and listeners' confidence is greatly improved if they know when there is a risk of communication breaking down – and how to avoid it.

Communicating

a Look at the following expressions.

The Speaker
Checking:
Is everything clear so far?
Are you with me?
Do you see what I mean?
Right/OK?
Does that make sense?

Clarifying:
Well, what I mean is . . .
In other words . . .
Maybe I should rephrase that . . .
Well, the point I'm making is . . .
That's to say . . .

The Listener
Confirming:
Yes, I've got that.
Right/OK/Yeah.
Yes, that's quite clear.
I see.

Asking for clarification:
I'm sorry but I didn't quite catch . . .
Sorry/Pardon?
I'm sorry, what was the word after . . .?
What was that again?

Which of the above expressions would you use in the following situations?

1 Talking to your host family abroad.
2 Being interviewed for a job.
3 Telling a close friend a joke.
4 Getting to know someone at a party.
5 Asking the teacher for clarification.
6 Speaking to a stranger in the street.

b Work in pairs. Imagine an economic inversion in which Southern Europe, Latin America, Africa and the south of Asia started to become the richest areas in the world. Discuss what the effect would be on: politics, languages, religions, fashion, music, sports, art and the way of life in general. How would the South treat the newly poor North? Speak fairly quickly, but check your partner's understanding and clarify when necessary.

STUDY SKILLS   SELF ASSESSMENT

You are now about halfway through the course. In future units, assess your progress by completing a table similar to the one below.

READING & LISTENING
How much have you understood of the texts in this unit:
a) gist and all details
b) gist and some details
c) gist only
d) part of the gist
e) none of the gist

SPEAKING
How fluent are you when you are avoiding a communication breakdown? Tick the appropriate box.
very fluent ☐   quite fluent ☐   average ☐   rather hesitant ☐

WRITING
Check your essay on page 91 against the criteria on page 11. What mark out of 20 would you give it?

Ask your partner to suggest improvements.

GRAMMAR
How confident do you feel about your ability to use these forms?
highly confident
quite confident
fairly confident
rather unsure

a) contrast links	
b) mixed conditionals	

VOCABULARY
Without looking at your notes, write down all the words and phrases you have learnt in the last week. Compare the number and their usefulness with other students' lists.

YOUR FEELINGS
Which of these activities have you enjoyed most or least recently? Number the boxes in order and then find out which are the most/least popular among other students, and why.

reading ☐   practice ☐   writing ☐   listening ☐
functions ☐   phonology ☐   interview ☐
study skills ☐   exam skills ☐   review ☐

Discuss your self-assessment with others in your group, and compare it with the marks you get from your teacher in the test on page 185 and in *The Complete Proficiency Practice Test Book*.

Do you under-estimate or over-estimate your knowledge and skills? Keep a record of your own estimates and the marks you receive. Make a list of your weak points and update it at the end of each unit.

ORAL

1 Phonology – weak forms

Apart from contractions (*I'd, he's, she would've*, etc.) certain words have a weak form of pronunciation.

Examples:
wells and /ən/ irrigation   *conditions can /kən/ vary*

a Listen to the recorded phrases and repeat.

b Listen again. Write down the middle word of each phrase then match it with the correct transcription from the list below:

Example:
*Might **as** well*
ANSWER 11 /əz/

1 /ə/   2 /i/   3 /kəd/   4 /ðət/   5 /əv/   6 /də/
7 /jər/   8 /ðə/   9 /wəz/   10 /əm/   11 /əz/
12 /tə/   13 /frəm/   14 /ɪz/   15 /ðən/

These forms are not used:
1 if the word is emphasised.
2 if it begins with *h* and is the first word.
3 in most cases, at the end of a sentence.

2 Interview

Photograph

a In pairs, look at the photograph and describe:
1 the setting.
2 the people's appearances.
3 their facial expressions.
4 what the people are doing.

b Referring back to Contrast Links in the PRACTICE section on page 88 expand six of the arguments below.

Example:
*People say it isn't our country **even though** many of us were born here.*

For
☐ Many of us were born here.
☐ Our parents' countries were colonised.
☐ We were invited here to work in industry.
☐ We've a right to live where we want.
☐ We've escaped from poverty and oppression.
☐ Ethnic diversity enriches the culture.
☐ Immigrants work harder in order to survive.
☐ We do essential jobs no one else will do.

Against
☐ They've taken all the jobs.
☐ There aren't any houses for us.
☐ They've got different customs.
☐ It isn't their country.
☐ They don't try to integrate.
☐ They over-use social services.
☐ Schools are now multilingual.
☐ They're involved in crime.

Which side do you find more convincing? Why? Can you think of any other arguments?

c Now discuss the issue of immigration in your country.

Give your partner marks for; *grammatical accuracy*; *pronunciation*, individual sounds, especially weak forms.

REVIEW

1 Which sounds?

a Listen and repeat.

b Listen again and write down the middle word. Then write the phonetic transcription of each word.

c Look back at the words you wrote in **1 Phonology – weak forms** and those above. What kinds of words are they?

2 Vocabulary

a Form an imperative phrasal verb with the word in brackets. What would you say to someone who:
1. asks for directions to a mountain village? (round)
2. should not be in a place? (out)
3. doesn't know how much he's spent? (up)
4. has a dirty and untidy room? (out)
5. you want to invite to your house? (round)
6. is speaking too quietly? (up)
7. you can't hear because she's in a crowd? (out)
8. is too shy to talk to strangers? (up)
9. wants to see the southern continents? (round)
10. is still in bed at 10 a.m.? (up)
11. has all the papers? (out)
12. is taking too long over his meal? (up)
13. wants to find out the local people's opinions? (round)
14. is behaving very childishly? (up)

b Put the following expressions from this unit into **category a**, **b** or **c**. (See STUDY SKILLS on page 17.)

famine   mirage   parched
to chip in with   steadfastly   to cough up
handouts   measly   gobbledegook
shattering   cynical   intake
nourishment   understate   surplus
self-indulgence   deprivation   elsewhere
starvation   to account for   to drain
crops   shortages   appeasement
plight   to lay waste   raw materials

3 Mixed conditionals

Imagine you are travelling round a poor country. Tell your partner about your reactions to the situations below using conditionals and weak forms where appropriate.

Example:
You didn't learn any of the local language before you came.
If I'd gone for a couple of lessons when I was at home, I'd be able to understand a little.

Use expressions from **2 Vocabulary** where possible.

1. It appears there's been a guerrilla attack near a big town you hope to go to.
2. Your friend wants to go into the desert alone.
3. It seems the Government isn't going to allow any more foreigners into the country.
4. You think you've lost your passport.
5. Someone says it was raining in the east at dawn.
6. You've heard there was a locust swarm approaching rich farming land.
7. You arrive home, and speak to a friend who is allergic to malaria injections.
8. In every village you went to you saw hungry people.

4 Summary writing

Look back at the text on page 87.
In a paragraph of 70–90 words, summarise the reasons why the people of Ethiopia are not receiving enough aid.

5 Now do the Progress Test for Unit 8 on page 185.

UNIT 9 CLEANING UP

READING

1 The Topic

a Look at the two pictures. Which do you think damages the environment more?

b Make a list of ecological disasters. Which are naturally occurring and which are man-made?

2 Before reading

a Check the meanings of the following words:
dreadful   thoughtless   greedy   misdeeds   bullies
What do they have in common?

b Look at the title of the article. How do you think the writer will justify this statement?

3 While reading

Fill in each of the blanks with one of these expressions:
Turning to the animal kingdom,
In a sense,
Of course, as a geologist,
It follows, then,
Think of
Throughout the country,

Pollution? it's only Natural

Our concern for the environment includes a large measure of self-interest and hypocrisy, says geologist Derek Ager.

I often wonder how many forests have been cut down to provide all the paper about the environment that arrives on my desk. The word 'environment' provokes a hostile reaction in me. Perhaps concern for the subject is last year's bandwagon, 5 but the wagon is still rolling fast and there are lots of people on board.

____ there are numerous university departments and schools of 'environmental science' and 'environmental studies'. There's even 'environ- 10 mental geology', though no one seems to know what this term means. I wonder what all these departments are doing, what happens to their graduates? Personally, if I had a problem with my environment, I would want a chemist or a geol- 15 ogist to solve it for me.

The biggest joke is the government's Department of the Environment, which covers every-thing from poll tax to rats. Presumably it exists only for its title. After all, no one could possibly 20 be *against* the environment, could they?

____ I'm on the side of the angels, but haven't we overdone it? And are we not shutting our eyes to the facts of geological history?

____ environmental science is a negative sort of 25 subject, comparable to gemmology in that it is a supposed science founded on humanity's dis-honesty and misbehaviour. If there were no fake precious stones, there would be no need for gem-mologists. If the world were not ill treated by 30 man, there would be no need for environmental science. Or would there? What about natural pol-lutants and natural disasters?

Most of our oil and gas reserves must have escaped into the environment millions of years 35 before the D'Arcy Exploration Company, Paul Getty and the Torrey Canyon. I have a strong sus-picion that many of the things we see in the geo-logical record, such as blank bituminous shales with accompanying mass extinctions, may be 40 blamed on naturally leaking hydrocarbon reservoirs.

What is a pollutant anyway? Was not oxygen a pollutant in the early atmosphere, produced by all those dreadful organisms not caring about the 45 environment in which they found themselves? What about the salts in the sea? It has been sug-gested by Reiner Jordan that the massive de-position of various salts during the Permian and Triassic periods may in turn have affected the 50 contemporary seas and their faunas. As M. M. Roeber said in *Geotimes* ten years ago: 'Mother Nature is the Earth's biggest polluter, far out-distancing man's feeble acts of desecration . . . Pollution . . . is an ongoing and intimate part of the overall evolution process.' 55

____ all the land environments that were de-stroyed every time we had a marine trans-gression; all the shallow marine environments that were lost every time there was a regression. 60 Both of these phenomena have occurred many times in the Earth's history, and correlate far bet-ter with mass extinctions of life than do supposed cosmic collisions.

____ what about all those early worms turning 65 over the surface layers of the lithosphere to cover the land with that dirty stuff called soil? Or those early birds devouring all those early worms so vo-raciously, without a thought of endangered spe-cies? What happened to all those beautiful 70 ammonites and belemnites? Were they not brought to extinction by the thoughtless, greedy marine reptiles and marine mammals? It's as good a theory as most.

____ that when we turn to man and his mis- 75 deeds the logic is not all that convincing. Is not man just one more species 'doing his thing', like the millions of species that went before him? Is he not following the age-old Darwinian principle of 'my species right or wrong'? Like all his prede- 80 cessors, man is making the most of his ecological opportunities, he has occupied every possible ecological niche from the Greenland icecap to Pacific atolls and, like all the bullies before him, he makes use of any other species that serves his 85 purpose, and destroys any species that gets in his way. By all means let us preserve our fleeting environments for future generations if it suits us, but let us also be honest about it and admit that our attitudes include a large measure of self- 90 interest, hypocrisy, sentimentality and nostalgia. And nostalgia, as they say, is not what it was.

4 Responding to the text

The writer uses several rhetorical questions to construct his argument.

Examples:
Or would there? (32)
What is a pollutant anyway? (43)
What about the salts in the sea? (47)

Why do you think the writer has used this technique? How effective is it?

5 Register

a Few native speakers would know the exact meaning of geological terms, e.g. *bituminous shales* (39) and *hydrocarbon* (41) but they would get the gist by using contextual clues:

1 Look for a synonym of *hydrocarbon* in the same paragraph.
2 Imagine a *geological record*. What kind of material are *bituminous shales* likely to be?
3 Being formed by *hydrocarbons*, what would *bituminous shales* look like?

b Using contextual clues, work out the approximate meanings of the following terms:

1 *Permian and Triassic* (49)
2 *lithosphere* (66)
3 *transgression/regression* (58–60)
4 *ammonites/belemnites* (71)

6 Idioms

Common phrases are often modified to give a humorous, vivid or less clichéd effect. Look at the modified versions in the text of the expressions below. What extra meaning have the changes given to each expression? Use the clues to help you.

To get on the bandwagon.
= To join a fashionable movement
Is the movement new? How popular is it? (5)

The early bird catches the worm.
= People who get up early are successful
What other meaning of *early* is implied? (68)

My country right or wrong.
= Whatever my country does, I will support it
What did Darwin say about competition among different species? (80)

7 Personification

a In line 45, the writer describes the *organisms* as if they were capable of human emotions (*not caring*) and morally reprehensible (*dreadful*).

What is he comparing them with? Why?

b Which words are used in a similar way:
1 in the sentence on lines 52–56?
2 in the paragraph on lines 65–74?

8 Inferring

Ideas that are important to the meaning of the text may not be explicitly stated but implied. Which lines in the text support the following statements?
1 The study of environmentalism has few practical applications.
2 Geologists tend to be environmentalists.
3 A certain person has been blamed for causing oil pollution.

PRACTICE

1 Dependent prepositions

Look at the expression *founded on* (line 27 of the text on page 96). The preposition *on* can mean *supported by*.

With can be used for relations with other people.
Example:
*I was disappointed **with** the council when they took no action.*

About can mean *concerning*.
Example:
*We are sorry **about** the harm done to local wildlife.*

At is sometimes used for ability to do something.
Example:
*Friends of the Earth are good **at** exposing official indifference.*

From can indicate separation or difference.
Example:
*They claim the contaminants are completely isolated **from** the environment.*

Complete the following sentences with *on*, *with*, *about*, *at* or *from*.

1 Observers are doubtful ____ the effectiveness of the measures.
2 They are quite distinct ____ the European Green Parties.
3 The report is based ____ information from Greenpeace.
4 The Environmental Protection Officer must be very poor ____ his job.
5 Local people are annoyed ____ the demonstrators.
6 We are quite pleased ____ the new Health Inspector.
7 Climatic factors had an influence ____ the siting of the power station.
8 Nobody is sure ____ the cause of the poisoning outbreak.
9 They're very clever ____ playing down the damage done.
10 The controversy is far ____ over.

2 The gerund

Some verbs are always followed by the *-ing* form if there is a second verb.

Examples:
*I can't imagine liv**ing** in a lifeless world.*
*I can't stand listen**ing** to gloomy ecologists.*

a Read the following text quickly and suggest a title.

The end of the Human Race cannot be put before the interests of aerosol manufacturers. This important decision was reached by the top brains of 24 countries in Montreal last September.

It was an historic decision, because – for the first time – governments from all over the world put aside political and national differences to ensure that the threat of global pollution does not bring disaster on the multinational companies who are causing it.

In 1985 a hole the size of the United States appeared in the ozone layer above the Antarctic. Without the ozone layer, more UV-8 rays from the sun penetrate the atmosphere with various inconvenient results, such as: a massive increase in skin cancers, reduced crop productivity, depletion of fish stocks, and climate changes resulting in floods and famine and, for all I know, another Republican Senate.

The scientists rushed to the conclusion, over the following few years, that the depletion of the ozone layer was due to chemicals known as chlorofluorocarbons or CFCs, which are used in such things as aerosols, hamburger packaging and refrigerators.

The cooler heads of such companies as ICI, DuPont, Hoechst and Antochem (who, incidentally, make CFCs), advised caution, until it could be proved beyond all reasonable doubt that global extinction was at hand and they had developed a cheaper alternative. But moderation, I'm afraid, lost the day. Hence the Montreal conference.

Most scientists agree that a reduction of 85% in CFC emissions is needed immediately – just to stabilize conditions. In Montreal, however, the top brains from 24 countries (aided, I suppose, by advisers from ICI, DuPont, Hoescht and Antochem) decided on a reduction of only 50% and then not until 1998.

Moreover, they were only talking about *consumption* of CFCs. If you read the fine print, you'll find that they've actually agreed to let the big companies increase their *production* of CFCs for another 3 years.

Ultimately a decrease is to be achieved by 1999, but then only by 35% – not 50%. Meanwhile, exports to the Third World are to be stepped up, presumably on the principle that if the ozone layer does finally go, at least we can blame it on people with unpronounceable names.

b Refer to the text and complete each of the following sentences using a gerund.

Example:
*They are not going to risk **damaging the manufacturers' interests**.*
1 Manufacturers apparently do not mind . . .
2 If the ozone layer carries on . . .
3 Scientists said that protecting the layer entails . . .
4 The manufacturers would not admit . . .
5 They wanted to put off . . .
6 The scientists recommend . . .
7 The advisers probably suggested . . .
8 The top brains decided to postpone . . .
9 The decision involves . . .
10 We can then avoid . . .

c The gerund is always used after prepositions. Where *to* forms part of the infinitive, it is not a preposition. To check, imagine a noun following it; if the *to* + noun combination is impossible, it is not a preposition and the gerund cannot be used.

Examples:
We hope to *succeed*. (success)
The noun *success* is not possible so the gerund *succeeding* cannot be used.
How will they react to *failing*? (failure)
The noun *failure* is possible, so the gerund *failing* can be used.

Use the nouns in brackets to decide on the correct forms of the verbs.
1 We are planning to ___ . (expansion)
2 People will get used to ___. (adaptation)
3 We have offered to ___. (assistance)
4 It doesn't apply to ___. (publications)
5 Everyone seems to ___. (agreement)
6 We are attempting to ___. (diversification)
7 They resorted to ___. (lies)
8 The deal amounts to ___. (victory)
9 They haven't promised to ___ production. (reductions)
10 The company objects to ___ profits. (cuts)
11 They refuse to ___ the matter. (discussions)
12 People will have to learn to ___ their use. (limitations)
13 We look forward to ___ mutual understanding. (improvements)
14 They prefer ___ to ___. (consumption) (conservation)

3 Conditionals

The sentence on line 14–16 of the text on page 96 could be written:
*If I **were to** have a problem with my environment, I would want a . . .*
This formal expression makes the event even less likely.

Probability can also be reduced by using the forms *should, happen to* and *should happen to.*

Examples:
*If that **should** (formal) occur, the effects would be devastating.*
*If you **should** find one, send it for analysis.*
*If you **happen to** see one, take a photo of it.*
*If you **should happen to** meet the writer, tell him I disagree.*

Use one of the constructions above to begin each of the following sentences in your own words:
1 . . . call the fire brigade.
2 . . . there would be a clean atmosphere.
3 . . . don't touch anything.
4 . . . thousands of species would disappear.
5 . . . watch the sea freeze over.
6 . . . there would be no need to burn oil or gas.
7 . . . all the world's coastal regions would be flooded.
8 . . . take the lorry's number and report it.
9 . . . there would be virtually no noise in the cities.
10 . . . don't say I didn't warn you.

WRITING

1 The directed writing task

Question 4 of the Composition Paper requires a response to structured information, which is often in tabular or graphic form. This entails formal or informal letter-writing, giving explanations, writing reports or advertisements etc, in an appropriate style and/or register.

a You work for a 'serious' newspaper and this map was sent by a correspondent in the USSR. Your sub-editor told you to write a news item in about 250 words.

What did you leave out of the news item opposite?

Sea turning into desert

Soviet scientists fear that the world's greatest man-made ecological disaster is now brewing in Central Asia, where the damage to the Aral Sea has been declared quite irreversible. The Aral Sea has lost a barely credible 60 per cent of its water in the past 30 years. The sea level has fallen by almost 40 feet since large irrigation projects steadily diverted the flow from the two great rivers of Central Asia, the Amu-Darya and the Sir-Darya. In places, the lake has receded by 62.5 miles. In the 1960s, the lake's surface area was more than 25,800 square miles. It is now down to barely 15,500 square miles.

A new salt desert formed on the sea's bed is advancing, and its vast dust storms are swirling more than 50 million tons of salt-sand into the air each year, dropping up to half a ton of this crop-killing substance onto each hectare of cultivated land in the main Uzbek farming region.

SEA TURNING INTO DESERT

Dust storms erode 50m tons salt-sand, and drop up to ½ ton/hectare on land producing:
- 95% cotton
- 40% rice
- 35% fruit
of USSR total.

Scientists say damage is permanent. Since 1960s, sea has:
- lost 60% of water.
- fallen 39.5 ft.
- shrunk from 25,800 to 15,510 sq ml.

KAZAKHSTAN

SIR-DARYA Water taken for irrigation.

ARAL SEA

Up to 62½ml

MUINAK (formerly fishing port)

←New salt desert.

UZBEKISTAN

MOSCOW

USSR

Salt lake appears.

Black Sea

Caspian Sea

AMU-DARYA (OXUS) Water taken for irrigation.

150 miles

b Re-write the news item so that it follows the instructions exactly.

100

In essay titles, certain expressions tell you exactly what is required.

a In this example, the key words are in **bold print**:

*Write the **dialogue** between two motorists who **have just** been involved in a **minor** accident.*

In pairs, decide which of the following points you would include in the essay:
☐ The passengers' comments
☐ Whose fault it was
☐ What the witnesses said
☐ Exchanging insurance details
☐ The garages' estimates for repairs
☐ The conversation in the ambulance
Would the style of language be formal, neutral or informal?

b Identify the key words in the following titles. Choose the relevant points and say which style you would use.

1 Write a letter of complaint to the Director of the Airport Authority about the introduction of night flights.
☐ Insomnia
☐ Danger of crashes
☐ Increase in burglaries
☐ Gardening no longer enjoyable
☐ Vibration causes damage to property
☐ Recent improvements in noise level

2 Describe an invention of your own which will improve the quality of life.
☐ How it works
☐ Expected results
☐ Money-saving
☐ First thought of twenty years ago
☐ Already a great success
☐ What it looks like

3 Write an article for a serious foreign magazine about the environmental problems of your town.
☐ Noise
☐ Climate
☐ Towns that are worse
☐ Development of town
☐ Location of industry
☐ Local politicians

4 Write a descriptive advertisement for your house so that it would appeal to the environmentally-conscious buyer.
☐ Rising damp
☐ Handy for MacDonald's
☐ Oil-fired central heating
☐ Solar panels
☐ Organic garden
☐ Nearby nuclear power station perfectly landscaped

LISTENING

1 Pre-listening

a Make a list of unusual weather conditions you have heard of lately.

b What theories claim to explain them? Which do you believe/disbelieve? Why?

c What would the consequences be for your country if these theories proved correct?

2 While listening

a The first time you listen, tick the reasons the speaker gives for potential disasters.
1 Part of Antarctica floating north.
2 The effect of heat on water.
3 Short, very hot periods.
4 Equatorial temperatures rising fastest.
5 A more humid atmosphere.

b Look at the map below. Listen again, and write the appropriate letter next to the place where each is expected to occur. In some cases more than one answer is possible. C has been done as an example.
A Immigrants   B More rain   C Ice melts
D Forest fires   E Shipping lanes   F Hunger
G Floods   H Desert

3 Post-listening

The meaning of expressions can often be inferred from the context. Look for key words which give clues.

What is probably missing from the following sentences?
1 Both short-term and ____ planning are needed.
2 Neither naturally-occurring plenomena nor ____ can stop the process.
3 Let's move on from the general picture to ____.
4 This will affect not only the Third World but also ____.

Discussion

Compare the following theory with that of the speaker in LISTENING. Which do you find more convincing?

> 'If the earth gets hotter, there will be more evaporation from the sea, which will mean more clouds. It is possible that these clouds will protect the earth from the incoming sunlight, as well as precipitating in the form of snow over the poles. If this happened, then the earth would probably cool down again.'

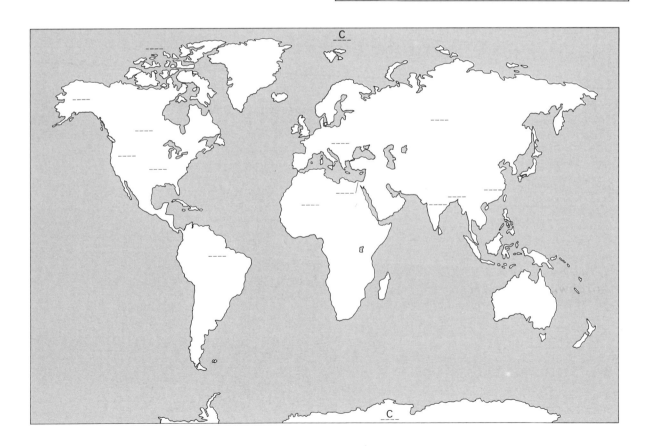

FUNCTIONS

PREFERENCE

In pairs, decide whether each of the following expressions in A, B or C is formal, neutral, informal or very informal:

A Asking about preference

1 Would you prefer to/rather ... or ...?
2 Which appeals to you more, ... or ...?
3 Which would you rather ..., ... or ...?

B Expressing preference

1 I think I'd rather ..., because ....
2 I tend to prefer ....
3 I'd much sooner ... than ....
4 Rather than see ... happen, I'd ....
5 If I had to choose, I'd ....
6 Perhaps the best thing would be to ....

C Expressing indifference

1 I couldn't care less.
2 I really don't mind/care.
3 It's all the same to me.
4 I don't give a damn.

Practice

a Work in pairs. Which alternatives are suggested by the cartoon? Ask your partner which he/she would prefer. Discuss similar present-day dilemmas.

b Match the alternatives suggested in these headlines and ask your partner questions.

Example:
5% GROWTH THIS YEAR/CONSERVATION TOP PRIORITY
Which would you rather see, better conservation or higher growth?
If I had to choose, I'd go for conservation because ...

MOTORWAY NETWORK PLAN
FEWER MOUTHS TO FEED
NUCLEAR POWER CLEAN
MEDICAL RESEARCH VITAL
5% GROWTH THIS YEAR
GREEN BELT 'SACROSANCT'
CONSERVATION TOP PRIORITY
OIL, GAS AND COAL SAFE
BABY BOOM
CHEMICAL-FREE FOOD
ANIMAL PROTECTION
FOOD PRICES DOWN

STUDY SKILLS REVIEWING TO REMEMBER

If you follow this review procedure you will find it easier to remember what you have learnt:
1 After each lesson, tidy up your notes and spend ten minutes studying them.
2 A day later, note down everything you remember about the lesson. Now compare what you have written to your original notes and modify it accordingly.
3 Repeat stage 2 a week later, after a month and shortly before the Examination.

Can you answer these questions from memory alone?
1 *Hitherto* means:
   a) everywhere.   b) until now.
   c) this way.   d) all the time.
2 What do the abbreviations *NB, aka, nr* mean?
3 Write down four common spellings of the sound /eɪ/.
4 Which of the following expressions is informal?
   As I see it ... Well actually ... In my opinion ... I reckon ...
5 Mark the stress on these words:
   conflict (noun)   perfect (verb)
   rebel (noun)   desert (verb)
6 Fill in the blank with a preposition:
   Drive ____ as far as the barrier.
7 Why is this sentence incorrect:
   The oil slick, threatened the beaches, was one mile long.
8 *Offset* means:
   a) compensate for.   b) leave.
   c) change places.   d) explode.
If you didn't get all of them right, start reviewing today.

1 Phonology – intonation

The most common tones in English are: falls ($\searrow$) rises ($\nearrow$) fall-rises ($\vee$)

a Listen and repeat.

b Listen again and mark the tones.
The first two have been done as examples.

1 There'll be floods, (↗) fires, (↗) and drought. (↘)

2 As it heats up, (∨) the icecaps get smaller. (↘)

3 They resorted to sabotage. ( )

4 Don't be so thoughtless. ( )

5 When was the leak detected? ( )

6 Is it based on fact ( ) or speculation? ( )

c Now say the following sentences aloud and mark the tones.

1 Tell us the truth. ( )

2 The accident was blamed on human error. ( )

3 Why is government action so feeble? ( )

4 Apart from the noise, ( ) there'll be the mess. ( )

5 Will production be stepped up ( ) or cut back? ( )

6 They're selfish, ( ) greedy ( ) and destructive. ( )

GREENPEACE

LOST DOLPHINS

Britain has lost many of her coastal dolphins and porpoises. Pollution, over-fishing and incidental catches are likely to be to blame for this decline.

To stem the decline and protect remaining dolphins and porpoises, Greenpeace is working to establish Marine Nature Reserves in areas where they are still to be found.

This summer, the Greenpeace ship Moby Dick is working in Cardigan Bay and The Moray Firth for the establishment of protection zones in these areas.

THANK GOD SOMEONE'S MAKING WAVES

2 Interview

Reading passage

In pairs, discuss the source, purpose and content of this text.

> Vast areas of Central American rain forest are being burnt down to convert the land to pasture. The few cattle the poor soil can support are mainly destined for the US hamburger and pet food markets, while the lack of expensive fertilisers is gradually turning the land into semi-desert.

The text is always linked to the theme of the interview. Which of these ideas connect the passage to the topic *Environment*?

1 US fast food   2 absorbing CO_2
3 desertification   4 forest fires   5 animal conservation   6 climatic changes   7 chemicals in farming

Give your partner marks for *pronunciation* of sentences, especially intonation.

Discussion

What do you know about Greenpeace?
What methods do they use to achieve their aims?
What is the usual purpose of their advertisements?
In pairs, study the advertisement. Consider:

☐ the effectiveness of the heading, picture and slogans.
☐ the seriousness of the dangers being faced.
☐ what action they have already taken.
☐ how your money might be spent.

Give your partner marks for *interactive communication* and *vocabulary*.

GREENPEACE URGENTLY NEEDS YOUR SUPPORT.
Please send a personal donation of £12 or a family donation of £17.50. Or more. In return you will receive our quarterly newsletter and campaign updates. Remember, the more you can afford to send us, the more we can do to protect the natural world.

Please accept my donation of: ☐ £12 single ☐ £17.50 Family ☐ Other £____

☐ I enclose cheque/P.O. for £_____ payable to Greenpeace Ltd.

☐ Please charge my Visa/Access a/c no:

Signature: ____   Date: ____

Name: Mr/Mrs/Ms ____

Address: ____

Postcode: ____

Please return to: Greenpeace, FREEPOST, 30-31 Islington Green, London N1 8BR.

1 Intonation

a Listen, repeat and mark the tones.

1 Our overall impression was ( ) negative.

2 What will the incoming government do? ( )

3 Work hard, ( ) but don't overdo it. ( )

4 Does it amount to ( ) victory or defeat? ( )

5 I'd sooner go by train than face hold-ups, ( ) radar ( ) traps and black ice. ( )

6 If the 'urgent measures' are going to be put off, ( ) we'd better act now. ( )

b Look at the sentences in **1 Phonology – intonation** on the opposite page and at those above.
What kind of tone is usually associated with the following?
1 lists   2 *'or'* questions   3 imperatives
4 pauses before commas   5 statements
6 *Wh* questions
Which tones indicate the speaker has not finished?

2 The gerund

Think of a suitable noun to classify *to*, then complete the sentences with the correct form of a verb.
1 They resolved to ＿＿ the problem.
2 Industry is committed to ＿＿ effluent by 50%.
3 Scientists are close to ＿＿ the virus.
4 We've managed to ＿＿ the worst excesses.
5 One government has threatened to ＿＿ the factories.
6 We'll get accustomed to ＿＿ on public transport.

3 Vocabulary

Put the following expressions from this unit into **category a**, **b** or **c**. (See STUDY SKILLS on page 17.)

on the side of the angels   fake   to leak
to out-distance   ongoing   to correlate with
to become extinct   endangered species
misdeeds   age-old   fleeting
to make the most of   to brew   to suit
to play down   to divert   wasteland
greenhouse effect   to the detriment of
marsh   to lobby   wilderness

4 Conditionals

Look at the following press announcement.

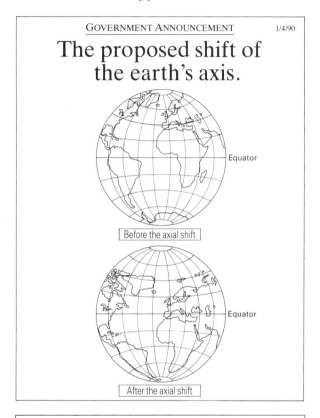

GOVERNMENT ANNOUNCEMENT   1/4/90

The proposed shift of the earth's axis.

Equator

Before the axial shift

Equator

After the axial shift

The proposed repositioning of the earth's axis will be achieved by a series of three electromagnetic charges.

Three five hundred megaton electromagnets have been launched into the earth's orbit and are now circling the earth at a velocity of two orbits per hour.

Ask your partner questions using *should* and *were to*.
Example:
What would happen if the shift should take place?
Europe would become tropical.
Use expressions from **3 Vocabulary** and decide which are the appropriate tones before you speak (refer to the six types of question or answer in **1 Intonation**).

5 Essay

In about 250 words, write a report for your Government on the announcement above. Say what you think would happen to your country's climate.

6 Now do the Progress Test for Unit 9 on page 186.

UNIT 10 INTERACTING

READING

1 The topic

a How far have women achieved equality of opportunity and treatment in your country?

b How have men reacted to the changes?

2 Before reading

This is the introductory paragraph of the text:

> A quarter of a century since American men bowed to the onset of feminism, they are standing up for their rights. Things have, in the opinion of many US males, gone too far in favour of women.

What examples and arguments do you think will be used in the text?

3 While reading

Read the text quickly. Which of the following do you think is its title?

> **HOW MILITANT AMERICAN MALES FINISHED OFF FEMINISM**

> **AMERICAN WOMEN BEAT OFF MALE COUNTER-OFFENSIVE**

> **ANGRY AMERICAN MEN UNITE IN ANTI-FEMINIST CRUSADE**

> **BRUISED AMERICAN MALES FIGHT THE FEMINIST TIDE**

It is not as if women had taken power; there are no women presidential candidates, no female bosses of the big corporations, and only one woman Supreme Court justice. In fact, the feminist movement has over the past two years beaten a tactical retreat with the demise of the sexual revolution, the return to conservative values, and the realization that combining childbearing with a successful career is difficult.

But more than two decades of female assertiveness have left the American male bruised and defensive, a victim of what spokesmen for the emerging men's movement call 'reverse sexism'. Their creed is that women cannot have it both ways.

'There is a revolution brewing,' says Mr William Farrell, author of the successful book *Why Men Are the Way They Are*. 'It is spreading slowly among men who are getting the courage to say, "I've been attacked long enough. I need to tell women that I have hurts and hang-ups, too".'

Men are weary of the derision heaped on them in magazines and a spate of best-sellers, the latest of which is Shere Hite's *Women and Love*. Sales of that book have fallen since Miss Hite was accused by (male) sociologists of using false data and pseudo-science to support her ideology.

Such man-bashing works usually assign unflattering stereotypes to the gender such as 'poodles, wolves, turkeys, sharks and worms', as one recent book listed them.

Mr Sidney Siller, a New York divorce lawyer who has founded the National Organization for Men, says men have been politically threatened. 'Men have been wimpified. They are intimidated by what amounts to a female party.'

Mr Siller and like-thinkers are enraged by Supreme Court decisions that effectively give priority to women's rights over individual liberties. In the most celebrated ruling, the court last March upheld the principle of 'affirmative action', the

4 Responding to the text

Agree or disagree with these ideas from the text. Give reasons for your opinions.

1 *Things have . . . gone too far in favour of women.*
2 Feminists are in *retreat.*
3 *female assertiveness*
4 *defensive* men
5 *stereotypes* in *man-bashing* publications
6 Men are *politically threatened* and *intimidated.*
7 *affirmative action* is fair
8 *the state has no right to interfere*
9 Evidence of *sexual harrassment of men.*
10 Women see men as *success objects.*

5 Vocabulary

a Synonyms

How many words can you find that are used to mean *men*?

---

practice enforced in some states under which female employees are promoted over better-qualified males to rectify past injustices to women.

The organization this month filed lawsuits in New York against two exclusive women's clubs, the *Colony* and the *Cosmopolitan*, because they rejected male members. This was a response to court rulings this year that have forced celebrated men-only establishments, such as the *Century* in New York and the *Bohemian* in San Francisco, to open their doors to women. Men's advocates say the state has no right to interfere with privacy and free association.

On another legal front so far dominated by women, men's organizations say they are gathering evidence of sexual harrassment of men at work by female colleagues.

Mr Farrell, a psychologist who has undergone a conversion since serving as an officer of the trail-blazing *National Organization of Women*, says women must face up to some of their own shortcomings.

Among these, he says, is a tendency to view men as 'success objects', just as men have treated women as sex-objects. Popular fiction, television soap operas and films show that, despite all the propaganda about sensitive, caring males, women still prize strong, successful and sometimes violent men – the knight with the black Porsche.

Women still do not want vulnerable bumblers like Clark Kent; they want his bulletproof alter ego, Superman. A successful career woman wants her man to be even more successful and strong, says Mr Farrell.

(line numbers: 50, 55, 60, 65, 70, 75, 80)

b Word formation

Match the prefixes and suffixes 1–8 with their meanings a)–h).

Example:
1–e

1 -friendly   a) main, chief or worst
2 fore-   b) protected against
3 -proof   c) helpful to
4 -ese   d) not genuine
5 mock-   e) language variety
6 -ish   f) in advance
7 -ship   g) typical of / fairly
8 arch-   h) skill / position of being

c

The compound word *best-sellers* (27) can be explained as *(books) that sell best.*
Explain the following compound words:
1 *man-bashing* (32)
2 *like-thinkers* (41)
3 *trail-blazing* (66)

d

Prepositions which form part of compounds can give clues to the meaning. Which is the probable meaning, a) or b)?

onset (2)   a) start   b) end
hangups (25)   a) anxieties   b) pleasures
upheld (45)   a) rejected   b) confirmed
undergone (64) a) enjoyed   b) experienced

6 Reference words

What do the following words refer to?

1 *It* (22)   2 *Such* (32)   3 *which* (46)   4 *the* (50)
5 *they* (52)   6 *this* (53)   7 *these* (69)

7 Transformation

Complete each of the following so that it is as similar as possible in meaning to the sentence in the text.

Example:
Lines 36–38
The National Organization for Men . . .
The National Organization for Men has been founded by Mr Sidney Siller, a New York divorce lawyer who says men have been politically threatened.
1 Lines 41–43
Supreme Court decisions . . .
2 Lines 50–53
Two exclusive women's clubs, the *Colony* and the *Cosmopolitan*, rejected male members, so . . .
3 Lines 71–76
Popular fiction, television soap operas and films show that, even though . . .

PRACTICE

1 Phrasal verbs

back	General sense
She never came back	To original person/ position
Sit back and relax	Away from the front
I'll ring you back later	In return
Think back to your childhood	To an earlier time

down	
The noise died down	Higher to lower level
We break down barriers	Destroy
I turned down the offer	Reject
Note down what he says	In writing

over	
We flew over Italy	From one side to the other
They talked it over	From start to finish
Hand over the tapes	From one person to another
The crisis blew over	Finish

Decide what the general sense of each of the following is.

Example:
Put your name down for the sub-committee.
= *In writing*

1 Think it over for a few days.
2 They moved back to their home town.
3 We crossed over the bridge.
4 Keep back! He's got a knife.
5 They're pulling down the old theatre.
6 I'll give it back to you when I've read it.
7 He'll get over her in time.
8 She toned down her criticism.
9 He took over the firm when the share price fell.
10 The tradition dates back to the Middle Ages.
11 He looks down on anyone poorer than himself.

Now write another example sentence for each of them.

2 Hypothetical forms

Past tenses are often used in hypothetical forms to refer to the present or the future.

Extend the following sentences to explain the meaning:

Example:
He'd sooner we met inthe pub, as . . .
He'd sooner we met in the pub as he doesn't want me to meet his mother.

1 He'd sooner we met in the pub, as . . .
2 It's high time you left him for good, because . . .
3 They're talking as if she weren't here, but . . .
4 It's not as though you didn't mean it; in fact . . .
5 We'd rather you didn't talk like that here, because . . .
6 It really is time he stopped being so unfriendly, as . . .
7 They're behaving as if they lived here, yet . . .
8 It isn't as though we needed advice; on the contrary . . .
9 She'd rather he'd mentioned it in private, because . . .
10 Isn't it about time you learnt to listen, instead of . . .?
11 He looked as if he was about to walk out, although . . .
12 It wasn't as though she hadn't been warned; indeed . . .

3 Inversion

a In literary style, subject and intransitive verb may be inverted after a place adverbial. The examples on this page and in **b** are taken from *The Man who loved Islands*, one of the *Selected Tales* by D.H. Lawrence.

Examples:
*But **over his face was** that gossamy look of having dropped out of the race of progress.*
***From far off came** the mutter of the unsatisfied thunder.*

Use the sentences below to write a description of a scene, involving a famous person of your choice. Change the sentences into a more colloquial style and link the points to form a paragraph.

Example:
In the crystal-clear night shone a full moon.
While a full moon shone in the crystal-clear night . . .

☐ High above hovered a helicopter.
☐ As far as the eye could see were people of all kinds.
☐ Through the darkness cut laser beams.
☐ Over the public address system came an announcement.
☐ From all sides came cheers.
☐ Into the sky raced hundreds of fireworks.
☐ Onto the stage walked . . .

b The literary or formal inversion of subject and auxiliary verb is required after adverbial expressions with a negative sense.

Examples:

*He felt that **only** with her will **had she wanted** him.*
*And **not until** the shock had undermined him and left him disembodied, **did he realize** that the black heads were the heads of seals swimming in.*

Match the beginnings of the sentences on the left with the correct endings below.

1 Not often do
2 So lively was
3 On no account must
4 Hardly ever have
5 In no way are
6 By no means was
7 Little did
8 Hardly had he begun
9 No longer, by law, will
10 Rarely on his travels has
11 Not till all agree will
12 No sooner had they met

a) he suspect where his wife was.
b) the secret be revealed.
c) he encountered such hostility.
d) when he was shouted down.
e) we seen such co-operation.
f) they be a persecuted minority.
g) than they became inseparable.
h) this meeting close.
i) they exchanged a polite word.
j) she unaware of the situation.
k) we to blame for the breakdown.
l) the debate that no-one left.

In Paper 3 of the Examination, you are instructed:

Fill in each of the blanks with a suitable word or phrase.

The key word is 'suitable', so clues must be found in the sentence(s). Look at this example of a single sentence and at the clues below:

I'd rather you _____ anyone about this tonight.

I'd	– contraction, so not formal
I'd rather you	– a past tense required
anyone	– verb will probably be negative
about	– verb will probably be tell/say/talk/speak, etc.
tonight	– future idea, so verb not in past perfect

Possible answers: *didn't tell/didn't talk to*, etc.

Sometimes there is another short sentence which provides the background:

Sadly, she is retiring this month.
Seldom _____ so hard for the Association.

retiring	– clue to meaning of verb
this month	– time period not finished: clue to tense
Seldom	– subject/auxiliary inversion, formal style
hard	– further clue to meaning of verb
Association	– clue to meaning of subject

Fill in the blank with a suitable phrase.

a Decide what each of the expressions in **bold** type tells you about the missing word or phrase, then complete the sentence.

1 **I'**ll **regret that** for ever. **If __** so impatient!
2 **Nowadays we** don't have time, **but __ every** weekend.
3 **They**'ve got a very stable **relationship. By** the summer __ **together for** two years.
4 **If** it **hadn't been** for you, __ **at all**.
5 'Do you think she **left** with him?' 'Well, she __, **but I doubt it**.'

b Some of the following answers are not suitable. Decide which they are and correct them, underlining the clue in each one.

1 So you've met him. Don't *you find* him an interesting person?
2 I'm going to see her *although* he tries to stop me. I don't care what happens.
3 I can't stand *to listen* to these endless arguments.
4 As far *as I know*, the sooner she leaves him the better.
5 At last we saw them. They apologised for *keeping us* waiting so long.

1 Dialogue

Incorporating conversation into narrative essays gives a more vivid effect than using reported speech.

a Look at this extract from *Hotel du Lac* by Anita Brookner and answer the following questions.

1 Is the style formal or informal?
2 Which 'reporting verbs' are used?
3 Which structure can be used with them? In which cases?
4 What background details does the writer give?

Mr Neville, noting the minute alteration in her attention to him, leaned over the table.

'You are wrong to think that you cannot live without love, Edith.'

'No, I am not wrong,' she said slowly. 'I cannot live without it. Oh, I do not mean that I go into a decline, develop odd symptoms, become a caricature. I mean something far more serious than that. I mean that I cannot live *well* without it. I cannot think or act or speak or write or even dream with any kind of energy in the absence of love. I feel excluded from the living world. I become cold, fish-like, immobile. I implode. My idea of absolute happiness is to sit in a hot garden all day, reading, or writing, utterly safe in the knowledge that the person I love will come home to me in the evening. Every evening.'

'You are a romantic, Edith,' repeated Mr Neville, with a smile.

'It is you who are wrong,' she replied. 'I have been listening to that particular accusation for most of my life. I am not a romantic. I am a domestic animal. I do not sigh or yearn for extravagant displays of passion, for the grand affair, the world well lost for love. I know all that, and know that it leaves you lonely. No, what I crave is the simplicity of routine. An evening walk, arm in arm, in fine weather. A game of cards. Time for idle talk. Preparing a meal together.'

'Putting the cat out?' suggested Mr Neville.

Edith gave him a glance of pure dislike.

'That's better,' he said.

---

b Read the following account of a job interview involving Wright, the personnel director, and Lomax, a candidate for the job. Fill in the blanks using verbs from the text in **1a** or from the list below. The first one has been done as an example.

boasted	agreed	answered	asked
commented	complained	argued	enquired
explained	insisted	confessed	observed
ordered	promised	objected	threatened
warned	went on	remarked	admitted

[W] Wright looked thoughtful. 'So you moved progressively from research into sales into line management. Are you satisfied that this was a good sequence?' *he asked.*

[L] 'Ideal,' ____, 'I didn't plunge too early into line management. I wouldn't have been mature enough. But coming to it after spells in two very different systems jobs, I found it fascinating to have to deal with a far less predictable resource. ie. people.'

[W] Wright seemed surprised. 'Interesting, so you treat people as no more than a resource?'

[L] 'Yes,' ____ 'isn't that what they are?'

[W] Wright considered for a moment. 'I suppose you're right – strictly speaking. Didn't you mention earlier certain difficulties with superiors, colleagues and clients? I would like to hear a bit more about why you think people have been uncooperative.'

[L] 'Frankly,' ____, 'I think people are too often slow on the uptake. I do my best to explain what I want, but they seem unwilling to think through the problem.'

[W] 'Don't you think this may be a natural tendency for people to oppose change?' ____.

[L] 'Yes, I know all about that, but this is what's wrong with the country, we don't seem able to shift from our old ways.'

[W] 'Mmm – well, it's a point of view.' ____. 'Let's change the subject and talk about your outside interests.'

Do you think Lomax got the job? Why / Why not?

c In everyday situations we often make 'mistakes' when speaking. These include false starts, hesitation, repetition, unfinished words or sentences, ungrammatical forms, etc. We also use 'connecting words', such as *I mean*, to maintain fluency.

Underline the examples of the above, in the following discussion. At which points do you think there was laughter?

SUE: 'I think clothes give um I think clothes like give you an immediate reaction about somebody . . . if you see them and, you know, you don't like what they're wearing I think that immediately slightly puts you off them . . .'

LIZ: 'I think their shoes . . .'

PAT: 'If they're wearing a suit with padded shoulders and stuff . . .

ANN: 'Shoes?' 10

LIZ: 'I think you can always tell somebody's personality through his shoes, I really do! It's always something, if I ever go out at night and somebody tries to chat me up I always look at their shoes and I think "Oh no". 15

SUE: 'I'm obviously looking at them the wrong way up here . . .'

LIZ: 'I don't know, well if you try it next time you're talking to somebody you'll see whether their shoes do um in fact represent 20 personality.'

SUE: 'Well don't you think their shoes usually go with their clothes, so their clothes are probably awful as well . . .'

LIZ: 'Oh yes, I know but the easiest first 25 indication to me . . .'

ANN: 'You look at the shoes first.'

LIZ: 'Yeah.'

PAT: 'That's 'cos she's smaller, so she's down . . .' 30

SUE: 'She's nearer the floor than we are, I suppose.'

ANN: 'So what's the first thing you notice, then, other than shoes? And if you walked into a wine bar or a pub and you saw somebody and 35 you thought "hmmm"! I mean what would you notice?'

SUE: 'Their face, their eyes and their expression.'

ANN: 'Yeah, I think for me it would be eyes.' 40

SUE: 'Hmmm, smiling eyes.'

PAT: 'I'd notice their height and the build first: sort of whether he was tall, broad, skinny, fat . . .'

ANN: 'Like a general impression?' 45

PAT: 'Right.'

LIZ: 'Yeah the the thing is though I find that er I think personality becomes more important to me, I think initially than looks and the way people are and whether they're tall, but I do 50 think that um personality is definitely what makes it for me once I get to know somebody . . .'

PAT: 'You never find the ideal guy, though, I don't think and if you do they're probably so 55 interested in their own image . . .'

SUE: 'I don't like it when they spend more time in front of the mirror than I do.'

ANN: 'So generally posey men are out?'

SUE: 'Hm . . . I mean I like them to take a bit of 60 effort, but when it comes to the extreme of them looking in every mirror they come to . . . you know. . . then forget it.'

ANN: 'Anything else?'

SUE: 'Well I don't like it if they've got sort of 65 like thin lips, you know, like, you know they've got to have a sort of . . . you know, when they're talking you sort of see their mouth and if it's really thin lips I think that's not very nice.' 70

ANN: 'So it's a mixture of the physical and the character to make things?'

SUE: 'Yes – I suppose character wins overall though.'

PAT: 'Yeah definitely.' 75

LIZ: 'In the end, yeah.'

d Here are some more connectors:

actually   at any rate   or rather
kind of   but er   well   yes/no
you see   the   at least

Imagine you and your partner had joined in the discussion above and talked about what makes either men or women attractive.

Write a report on the continuation of the dialogue in about 350 words.

1 Pre-listening

Look at the data from a recent survey of social attitudes in Britain.

Qualities that parents should try to teach children

	Quality	%
☐	Honesty	86
☐	Good manners	72
☑	Respect for other people	67
☐	Cleanness and neatness	42
☐	To act responsibly	35
☑	Independence	24
☑	Hard work	24
☐	Unselfishness	23
☐	Loyalty	22
☐	Being careful with money	22
☐	Determination and perseverence	20
☐	Self-control	19
☐	Obedience	12
☐	Religious faith	9
☐	Patience	8
☐	Imagination	6
☐	Leadership	2

a In groups, discuss the following questions:
1 Which other qualities could be included?
2 What might the order and percentages be in your country?

b You are going to hear a recording of two young people discussing the qualities they would like a new working colleague to have. Do you think there will be any significant differences from the results of the survey above? Why/Why not?

2 While listening

a Listen and tick the boxes next to the qualities in the table above which the speakers mention.

b Now consider the speakers **themselves**.
Listen to one speaker only. Decide with your partner who will listen to the man, and who will listen to the woman.
Look at the boxes 1–6 and tick A, B, C or D in each case. For boxes 1 and 2 try to use your imagination.

1

POSSIBLE AGE	
A Under 18	☐
B 18 – 20	☐
C 20 – 25	☐
D Over 25	☐

2

SOCIAL CLASS	
A Upper middle	☐
B Lower middle	☐
C Skilled working	☐
D Unskilled working	☐

3

LANGUAGE	
A formal	☐
B neutral	☐
C informal	☐
D very informal	☐

4

CHARACTER	
A Outgoing	☐
B Cynical	☐
C Untruthful	☐
D Introverted	☐

5

ATTITUDE TO TOPIC	
A Excited	☐
B Interested	☐
C Uninterested	☐
D Totally bored	☐

6

ATTITUDE TO OTHER SPEAKER	
A Intimidated	☐
B Patronising	☐
C Relaxed	☐
D Understanding	☐

3 Post-listening

Compare notes with your partner.
In what ways are the speakers similar/different?

HANDLING CONVERSATION

1 Classifying

a In groups, put the expressions into the following categories:
1 involving others
2 changing the topic
3 hesitating

a) By the way ...
b) Isn't that right, Sue?
c) My mind's gone blank; ...
d) That reminds me, ...
e) Incidentally, ...
f) I can't really say ...
g) Before I forget, ...
h) (Well) let me think, ...
i) What's your opinion, Paul?
j) Let me see (now), ...
k) If I may digress for a moment, (formal) ...
l) It's on the tip of my tongue; ...
m) Joe'll agree with me when I say ...
n) I'll think of it in a minute; ...
o) I don't know what Ann thinks, but ...

2 Practice

Discuss the implications of the following three news items **A–C**, and related topics.

A

DRUGS OPEN A GENERATION GAP

Scared kids are beginning to turn their parents in.

The parents were 'solid citizens' who taught their children not to smoke or drink. But last week two Silver City, New Mexico, youths called sheriff's deputies and said they had something to show them. They took the officers to their parents' bedroom and displayed a small box of marijuana. Their parents smoked pot on Saturday nights, the children said, and they were worried. In the wake of a much-publicized California case this month, experts are bracing themselves for more children turning their drug-using parents in to authorities. In part the conflict stems from a reverse generation gap growing between baby-boom parents with 1960s attitudes and their children coming of age amid far more conservative values.

B

Teacher fails in appeal over marriage rules

The Court of Appeal dismissed an appeal by Stephen Staerck, 37, a social studies teacher, against a divorce decree granted to his wife Janet, 31, a teacher, last March.

He denied claims by his wife that during their seven-year marriage, he drew up a contract which stipulated that:
• She must not mention the names of her parents or brother and sister-in-law in the house;
• She could only visit her parents twice a month, the cost to be met from the household budget, and would be home in time to prepare his evening meal;
• Her parents could visit her once a month while he was out. If he was at the house, an alternative venue had to be found;
• Mrs Staerck would be allowed £2-a-week personal spending money from the family budget;
• In the event of bereavement in the family, she would be allowed two days away from home and could spend up to five days a year away in the event of family illness;
• No presents for her parents were to be paid for from the housekeeping.

C

FOIL OR FAIL

A MAN has recently fallen foul of the law, much to his own surprise, for implementing what he thought was an absolutely brilliant idea. He hired himself out as a fake thug, striking up a deal with any man who had it in mind to impress a girlfriend. The fake thug would, by agreement, sit at the next table in a restaurant and make cheeky or disparaging remarks to the girl; the wimp who had hired him would tell him to shut up. He would get more truculent, and the wimp would end up slinging him into the street. At which point the girlfriend, presumably, was to collapse into a heap of grateful admiration. It only went wrong because the police decided that phoney fights were as much of a nuisance as real ones.

Phonology – intonation

a Listen and repeat.

b Which phrases sound friendly and which unfriendly?

c Listen again and mark the tones: ($\nearrow$) or ($\searrow$).

1 with everybody else ( )
2 as far as I'm concerned ( )
3 part of my life ( )
4 it can't be part of business ( )
5 I know what you're saying ( )
6 is this what you're saying? ( )
7 I can't say I agree with you there ( )
8 Would you like a coffee? ( )

STUDY SKILLS PRACTISING WITH PEOPLE

Knowing how to initiate and develop conversation makes it easy to practise and develop oral skills. Consider the examples 1–8 below:

Which do you use in your first language?

1 Begin with a statement – comment on the surroundings, then ask for advice, information, help or opinions.
Example:
They're so slow here. When do they stop serving?

2 Use statements as indirect questions – they may put people more at their ease.
Example:
It must be great travelling for a living.

3 Experiment with both personal and impersonal questions – people may or may not want to talk about themselves.
Examples:
What do you do?/What's the speciality here?

4 Try questions people can answer as they like, as well as those that invite a *yes* or *no*.
Examples:
Where else have you been here?
Do you like your job?

5 Ask questions about what people tell you – it helps them talk and shows you are following what they say.
Example:
Which one did you like best?

6 Give a short summary of what they say at natural pauses to show interest.
Example:
So it's not quite what you expected.

7 It may be appropriate to agree or disagree, but you can also give a non-committal answer or change the subject to a related topic.
Examples:
Right./Do you really think so?/Could be.

8 'Listen between the lines' to infer information that is not stated. Voice your conclusions.
Example:
You mean you weren't too impressed.

Interview

Discussion

Sit next to a student you don't know very well.

Student A
Your partner is a visitor to your country. Answer his or her questions and use any of these topics to develop the conversation:
☐ which sights to see ☐ transport
☐ music ☐ radio
☐ films ☐ what to avoid
☐ newspaper

Student B
You are a foreign visitor in your partner's country. Ask questions using any of the topics below and let him or her introduce others.
☐ where to stay ☐ TV
☐ theatre ☐ shopping
☐ visual arts ☐ what to do in
☐ where to meet people emergencies

Give marks for; *interactive communication*; *pronunciation*, sentences especially intonation.

REVIEW

1 Intonation

Mark the tones in this dialogue and then practise it. What happens when the 'bouncer' becomes more friendly?

A   Members only.   ( )

B   I'm sorry?   ( )

A   You need membership cards to come in.   ( )

B   But there's only two of us.   ( )

A   Guests before 10 pm only.   ( )

B   Well, can we join then?   ( )

A   If you can get two members' signatures.   ( )

B   I only know one member: Mr Stevens.   ( ) ( )

A   Mr Stevens? What's your name?   ( ) ( )

B   Paul Dimitri.   ( )

A   Paul! You should have said; please come in. ( ) ( )
    Sorry about that.

2 Phrasal verbs

Match parts 1–8 with a)–h) below:
   1 Stand back
   2 Look over
   3 Copy down
   4 They've cut back
   5 It's easy to knock down
   6 Pay me back
   7 She put him down
   8 Don't look back:

   a) think about the future.
   b) arguments like that.
   c) your work when you've done it.
   d) and let them through.
   e) spending on community centres.
   f) the address and phone number.
   g) when things are going better.
   h) with one sharp comment.

3 Hypothetical forms

How might you respond to these statements and questions? Try to use a friendly tone at the end of each response.
   1 'I had my 21st birthday last week – I do feel old.'
   2 'Don't sit there, that's my place.'
   3 'Wasn't the meeting supposed to begin at nine?'
   4 'I know you've given up but do you mind if I smoke?'

5 'He says he'll never be able to live without her.'
6 'Is it OK if I call round at five in the morning?'
7 'I've been here ages but still don't know anyone.'
8 'If I fail in June, when can I retake the exam?'

4 Inversion

In this interview, complete the politician's answers in the spaces provided.

A Your remarks earlier were, I take it, off the record?

B Not a word ____ must be reported.

A And are the convicted terrorists to be released soon?

B In no circumstances ____ be set free.

A Why pass emergency legislation at this stage?

B Only by ____ will we succeed.

A Why did you tell the press that no action was needed?

B At no time ____ such a thing.

A When did you decide to do something, then?

B No sooner was ____ than plans were made.

A Why do we need to borrow even more money from the IMF?

B Such ____ that there is no alternative.

A What brought about this financial mess?

B Scarcely had we ____ when a wave of strikes began.

A You once spoke of resigning over this issue.

B In none of my speeches ____ of such a thing.

A Abroad they say that such savage cuts are unnecessary.

B In no other country ____ such grave problems.

A Have you always been so incredibly pompous?

B Never ____ such a rude manner!

5 Vocabulary

Put the following expressions from this unit into **category a**, **b** or **c**. (See STUDY SKILLS on page 17.)
demise   weary   to have it both ways
spate   unflattering   to face up to
wimp   enraged   to lean over
caring (adj)   harrassment   to yearn for
to crave   shortcomings   slow on the uptake
thug   phoney   in the wake of
to stem from   to come of age   to fall foul of

6 Essay

In about 350 words, tell the story of a frightening or amusing incident which took place when you were with a friend. Describe the conversation as it happened, using expressions from **5 Vocabulary**.

7 Now do the Progress Test for Unit 10 on page 187.

UNIT 11 TIME OUT

READING

1 The topic

Which of the following kinds of music do you like most? Which do you like least? Why?

Blues   Jazz
Classical Opera
Folk   Pop/Rock

Do you prefer music from your own country or from abroad? Who are your favourite composers/songwriters/performers?

3 While reading

Which sentence best summarises the contents of the text?

1 How to become a pop star
2 Learning about rock music.
3 Do you want to make a fortune from music?
4 The story of *Wham!*

2 Before reading

Look at the by-line of the text.
Which aspects of pop music would you like to study?

Giles Smith reports on how the music business is being offered as a vocation by schools and colleges.

At school, the surest way to flummox any visting Careers Advisor was to inform him or her that you intended to become a pop star or, failing that, an astronaut. This would usually be enough to make the most efficiently-oiled system of career charts and computer read-outs freeze and jam. For pop stars and astronauts alike, it seemed, there was nothing you could call a recognisable career plan.

But now, here's pop, shaping up nicely as an educationally endorsed vocation. The GCSE course in Media Studies, available to secondary school students, offers a chance to study the music business with a view, perhaps, to seeking a career in it at some later date. The teaching materials for this course are still amassing and developing, but a fertile contribution has been made by the British Film Institute, who recently published a pop education pack. Teaching packs commonly centre on things like Indonesian rainfall levels, or *The Canterbury Tales*. The BFI's took as its subject Wham!.

'They were', says Christine James, who helped edit it, 'the perfect act to pick up on – from the dole queue to multi-millionaires in four years. And also their career came to a definite close with the farewell concert in June 1986, so the case study rounds off properly.'

Wham! Wrapping – Teaching the Music Industry is a thick file of worksheets and project cards (two and a half years of research), analysing the career of the tanned ones from three separate angles – 'Product', 'Promotion', and 'Consumption'. The idea is to encourage critical reactions at every level by turning the music industry's edifice inside out, exposing the plumbing, revealing the drains.

4 Responding to the text

In pairs, make a list of all the careers associated with rock music that you can think of.
Which of them might you be interested in?
What kind(s) of training would be needed?

5 Connecting ideas

1 This (4)	What would?
2 offers (11)	What does?
3 took (18)	What did?
4 came (23)	What did?
5 encourages (35)	What does?
6 which (41)	Which what?
7 sent off (55)	What is?
8 in control (79)	Who is?

6 Contrasts

What is contrasted with the following expressions?

Example:
multi-millionaires   the dole queue (20–21)

1 *Wham!* (25)
2 a different *idol called George* (40)
3 *jobs outlined in the file's 'Career Sheets'* (45)
4 *classical instruments* (60)
5 *management deals 'very confusing area . . . . no two are like'* (68)
6 *a degree of musical competence* (74)
7 *the cheerfully manipulable slob of old* (81)

7 Style

a A metaphor refers to one thing as if it were something else.

Example: *a **fertile** contribution* (15)
Here, the contribution is described as if it were particularly productive land.

In the following phrases, what would you normally associate with the words in **bold** type?
1 the student gets **let loose on** a miniature version (50)
2 and **firing off** a demo tape (58)
3 more **hallowed** rock and roll career practices (70)

b If a metaphor is extended, it must be consistent.

Example:
The music begins with a little phrase on the piano, just two bars long, which constitutes the seed from which the entire work germinates.
The music develops (*germinates*) from the two piano bars (*the seed*) as if it were a plant (*the entire work*).

Now consider the following example of a mixed metaphor quoted by George Orwell. Here, the writer was not thinking about the images created:
The Fascist octopus has sung its swan song.

Are the following metaphors from the text consistent? Why?/Why not?
1 . . . enough to make the most **efficiently-oiled** system of career charts and computer read-outs **freeze** and **jam**
2 . . . turning the industry's **edifice** inside out, exposing **the plumbing**, revealing **the drains**.

For instance, the file guides the class in the intense and sophisticated scrutiny of promotional videos and encourages reflection on the influence of television ⁣35 coverage on record sales ('From your graph and research, in your own words describe the progress of *Wake Me Up Before You Go Go* through the charts'). And it peers hard at the role of the fan ('Some of these letters were written in 1963 to a *different* idol called ⁣40 George. Decide which were written in 1963 and which in 1987').

Although *Wham! Wrapping* is probably set on encouraging not so much tomorrow's Andrew Ridgeleys as those likely to compete for the low kudos jobs outlined ⁣45 in the file's 'Career Sheets' (Display Manager, Project Manager, Radio 1 DJ), elsewhere it is specifically musicians who are being readied in a practical fashion.

Music at GCSE, for example, now incorporates an option in which the student gets let loose on a miniature ⁣50 version of a recording studio. Over a set period of time, he or she will use synthesisers, drum machines and whatever other shiny gimmicks are to hand, to build up a four-track version of an original composition, which is then sent off on cassette to be examined externally at the ⁣55 close of term. In effect, by the time you reach 16, you will be talking about laying down your first track and firing off a demo tape, skills which equip you amply for taking the first steps towards a record deal. The thinking here seems to be that it is all very well teaching classical ⁣60 instruments to Grade Eight but, frankly, pop is where the jobs are.

It might, though, be a sound move to go on to college first. In Carlisle, Rick Kemp has been teaching pop since last September. 'The notion is that the students should ⁣65 learn as much about the business as Elton John knows, but inside two years.' Next term, it's management deals ('very confusing area . . . . no two are alike').

This is all at a considerably disciplined remove from more hallowed rock and roll career practices – from ⁣70 times when a management deal was just a flash of paper, vaguely remembered through a whisky-induced stupor in the dressing-room after an early gig. It's a far cry, too, from days when a degree of musical competence was considered a positive disadvantage. Now the ideal would ⁣75 seem to be a degree *in* musical competence.

Perhaps a proliferation of pop courses is inevitable, given that our own times seem to favour the pop star who knows what he's doing and is quietly but impressively in control of his own business, rather than the cheerfully ⁣80 manipulable slob of old.

PRACTICE

1 The infinitive

A number of infintive forms are possible.
The full infinitive can be used after all parts of speech except prepositions. See line 1 of the text on page 116.
Example:
the surest way to flummox . . .
It may or may not follow the objects of other verbs.

The passive infinitive is used when the action is the subject of the sentence.
Example:
. . . . sent of . . . to be examined . . . (55)

The infinitive without *to* is used after:
1 certain modals.
Example:
. . . . nothing you could call. . . . (7)
2 the objects of certain verbs.
Example:
You can feel the whole building shake.
3 a previous infinitive that has included *to*.
Example:
We're hoping to go and see them on Saturday.
4 *had better . . . , would rather/sooner . . . , why (not) . . . ?*
Example:
You'd better get the tickets today.

The perfect infinitive has a similar meaning to past or perfect tenses.
Example:
We're sorry to have kept you waiting.

The progressive infinitive is used for actions taking place at the time in question.
Example:
It makes a change to be spending the weekend at home.

The negative infinitive always begins with *not*.
Example:
It'd be better not to go.

The use of *to* instead of the complete infinitive avoids repetition.
Example:
I haven't seen them yet, but I want to.

Choose from the following verbs to fill in the correct form of the infinitive in sentences 1–8 below:

move   lose   play   sound   bother
perfect   knock down   overdramatise

1 The Philharmonic made the piece ___ magnificent.
2 The Council won't allow them ___ after midnight.
3 Shall we stay here or ___ nearer the stage?
4 The acoustics were so poor that the whole building had ___.
5 Mozart is said ___ the combination of piano and strings.
6 They managed ___ the finale.
7 Why ___ going if all you can see is a video screen?
8 They seem ___ touch with their musical roots.

2 Reported speech

a Rewrite the following extract from a detective story in direct speech. The inspector talks to Miss Smythe, Mr Bryant, the hotel manager and the night porter. Begin:

INSPECTOR   *Did you see anything unusual last night?*
MISS SMYTHE   *Well, I went to bed early because I had to be up at six this morning.*

'When I asked Miss Smythe if she had seen anything unusual the night before she replied that she had gone to bed early; explaining that she had to be up at six this morning. She suggested that I should have a word with Mr Bryant, seeming surprised that I had not already done so.
He denied having left his room after eleven and objected to being questioned about events after that time. He warned me that his solicitor specialised in cases of police harrassment and told me to leave in an extremely offensive manner.
I asked the manager what time the last guest had signed in but he reminded me that the register had disappeared overnight, although he did promise to find out as soon as possible. Oddly, however, he advised me against talking to the night porter who, he claimed, would not be a reliable witness.
Intrigued by this, I asked him who he had seen after twelve and he informed me that when two men without suitcases arrived, the manager sent him to Miss Smythe's room with an urgent message, ordering him not to reveal the contents to anyone.'

b Write the following sentences in reported speech, choosing the most appropriate reporting verb in numbers 1–8 (all of the verbs are grammatically possible in numbers 1–8).

1 *Well, the truth is I did have a visitor later on.*
   She (implied/agreed/admitted/argued/stated) that ...

2 *Those two men are regular guests here.*
   He (told/advised/assured/informed/promised) me that ...

3 *Let's find somewhere more private to talk about it.*
   He (agreed/implied/proposed/said) that we should ...

4 *I won't answer any more questions until my lawyer gets here.*
   He (promised/offered/threatened/refused/swore) to ...

5 *I'm sorry I didn't tell you this before.*
   She (admitted/apologised for/insisted on/denied) not ...

6 *Can you show me where you found the body?*
   He (advised/asked/encouraged/persuaded/ordered) him to ...

7 *I would be grateful if nobody left the hotel until the murderer is identified.*
   He (requested/begged/invited/recommended) them not to ...

8 *You don't have to look any further than Bryant.*
   He (blamed/stopped/accused/advised) Bryant (for/from/of/against) ...

9 *Do you know who did it, Inspector?*
   He inquired whether ...

10 *What were you doing at one o'clock?*
   He asked him what ...

3 Relatives

In some cases, the only natural place for a preposition is before the relative pronoun.
Example:
*... an option **in which** the student gets let loose on a miniature version of a recording studio (50–51)*

Prepositions are often in this position in formal styles.
Example:
*That is the stage **on which** she performed.*

But in conversational styles, prepositions tend to come at the end of the clause and the relative is often omitted.
Example:
   *That's the stage **which** she performed **on**.*
OR: *That's the stage she performed **on**.*

Determiners can also be placed before relatives.
Examples:
*Waiting outside were hundreds of people, **most of whom** would be disappointed.*
*Touts were demanding $200 for tickets, **all of which** were sold within minutes.*
In more informal styles this sentence might be:
*Touts were demanding $200 for tickets – **all of them** were sold within minutes.*

Join the following sentences, using the above and other stylistically appropriate constructions.
Examples:
May I present the Director.
We are all greatly indebted to her.
*May I present the Director, **to whom** we are all greatly indebted.*
(Both situation and language are formal in this example.)

1 Let's go and see that play.
   Everyone's talking about it.

2 There will now be an interval of approximately ten minutes.
   During this time light refreshments will be served.

3 I'm sure that's the same guy.
   I was speaking to him afterwards in the bar.

4 There would seem to be a trend towards musical productions.
   Many of these have been imported from Broadway.

5 We regret to announce that we are experiencing some difficulties with the lighting.
   Owing to this there will be a short delay.

6 I wrote a strongly-worded letter to the Arts Minister.
   I have yet to receive a reply from him.

7 What they're really trying to do is bring back censorship.
   We've got to fight against it.

8 The first night saw the debut of many unknown actors.
   Two of them had never played in *The Tempest* before.

9 The human condition is again explored in his latest work.
   In it, the playwright parodies submission to conformity.

10 OK, but he forgot half his lines.
   There's no excuse for that.

11 His prolific output included more than forty plays.
   Several of them are still performed today.

12 This is an overlong but ambitious play.
   The best act is undoubtedly the second.

WRITING

1 The informal letter

As letters to friends are written in a style very similar to that of everyday speech, many of the expressions in FUNCTIONS can be used. However, there are certain differences; particularly because of the gap in time between writing and reading, and the factor of distance.

a Match the expressions 1–10 with the writing purposes a)–k):

1 It was a terrible shock to hear that . . .
2 I'm sure everything will go well. . .
3 I'm sorry to have to tell you that . . .
4 It's great to hear that . . .
5 I'd love to come but . . .
6 I'm really sorry for missing . . .
7 Do you by any chance know if . . .
8 How about coming . . .
9 Can I let you know about . . .
10 I should be arriving at about . . .
11 I'd be delighted to . . .

a) apologising	g) hesitating
b) refusing	h) accepting
c) inquiring	i) informing
d) encouraging	j) congratulating
e) inviting	k) arranging
f) commiserating	

b Fill in each of the gaps in the letter to Chris with one of the following expressions:

1 I'm not yet sure of
2 I was very upset to hear
3 The problem is
4 any chance of you coming
5 best of luck with
6 I'm sorry I haven't written sooner
7 it was great to hear that
8 do you happen to know whether
9 you'll be pleased to hear that
10 thanks a lot for the invitation, I'd love to

34, Remington Avenue,
Halifax H19 4JB

22nd October

Dear Chris,

Just a quick note while the others are out and relative calm prevails. Sometimes I wonder when this lot ever sleep – they certainly don't when I'm trying to. So, having (quite unfairly) laid the blame on my flatmates, I really must say (a) ____ – but you know how it is.

Anyway, (b) ____ Angela and Tony are back together again – I can't imagine either of them with anyone else, can you? They asked me to tell you they'll be having a party at Christmas – (c) ____ ? Which reminds me – (d) ____ stay at your place while I'm over – though (e) ____ the exact dates. It all depends on when I get this work finished – (f) ____, I've been so busy going to exhibitions, concerts and the film festival that I've got behind. By the way, (g) ____ that letter of mine ever got published?

Well, that's enough about me – how are things with you over there? (h) ____ about Jenny. It'll take time, but I know she'll get over it – she's that kind of person. On a happier note, (i) ____ you'd done so well in the exam – what will you do now with all that spare time? Don't tell me – I can imagine! Oh, and (j) ____ the interview next week – you'll walk it.

See you soon,
Alex.

---

c Reply to Alex in 200–250 words.

In paper 3 of the Examination, you are instructed:

Fill each of the numbered blanks in the following passage with **one** suitable word.

The key words here are:

'**each**' – Wrong answers do not lose marks – fill them all.
'**one**' – Some Candidates have been known to give answers such as *have to* or *would/should*.
'**suitable**' – Not only in the phrase or sentence, but within the paragraph or text as a whole.

Follow this procedure:

1 **Before** you fill in any blanks, read the text for gist.
2 Look at the immediate context for clues to meaning, part of speech and form.
3 Use your reading skills: look for synonyms, ellipsis, reference words, contrasts, stylistic information, etc. in the wider context.
4 Check that the completed passage now makes sense.

a Read the following passage in one minute only and choose the correct statement below.

The writer's aim is to show that:

1 there is more and more fraud in the art world.
2 experts are over-concerned with the age of works of art.
3 twentieth century art is inferior to that of previous centuries.
4 experts nowadays are only interested in modern art forms.

A few years ago someone sent to an art auction ____
(1) was ____ (2) to be a splendid example of Tudor wood-carving. The experts hailed it ____ (3) enthusiasm and were about to engage in a battle of bids for ____ (4) possession. ____ (5) a village wood-carver, ____ (6) by the turn of events, confessed that he ____ (7) done the carving, and was able to produce evidence to ____ (8) it. When a crestfallen member of the art world, who had enthused about its excellence, was asked what ____ (9) happen to it now, he replied, "Oh, anything. Chop it ____ (10) for firewood, I dare say. It's worth nothing."
To me ____ (11) seemed a dreadful statement. ____ (12) he had believed that a village craftsman of the ____ (13) century ____ (14) produced this work of art he had thought highly of it and ____ (15) prepared to ____ (16) a fortune in it. When he knew that a twentieth century village craftsman had done ____ (17) he considered it ____ (18). The only difference was a ____ (19) of four hundred years. But as a work of art, did it ____ (20) have some intrinsic value or merit?

b Look at these clues to the missing words in the first paragraph and fill in the blanks:

1 A relative; but it cannot refer to *someone* or *auction*.
2 Read on; was it true?
3 The preposition + noun form of *enthusiastically*.
4 The main object of the sentence/*possession*.
5 Contrast with *about to* in the previous sentence.
6 Non-defining relative clause; relative and verb omitted.
7 Reported speech introduced by verb in past tense.
8 What is *evidence* used for?
9 Reported speech, verb in past ⇒ *now*.
10 Phrasal verb; general meaning – *separate into smaller units*.

c For the second paragraph, choose one of the three alternatives:

11 there/that/everything
12 When/Although/Before
13 fifteenth/last/sixteenth
14 has/had/really
15 hardly/was/already
16 invest/waste/pay
17 one/so/it
18 valueless/carefully/art
19 gap/carving/statement
20 might/not/even

LISTENING

1 Pre-listening

a Can you identify these films from the review extracts?

1 Last ship of the silent Chaplin tramp, in 1936, as he and Paulette Goddard walk off hand in hand into the sunset. Beyond (some would say above, some below) criticism. (*b/w*)

2 'Marry me and I'll never look at another horse,' says Groucho to Margaret Dumont; and Marxists won't need reminding of Chico's ice-cream vendor-cum-racing-tipster. Sam Wood; 1937. (*b/w*)

3 Play it again, Sam – and again and again. Somehow the hokum has such durable powers that when Bogie sends Bergman packing (literally) you really believe he would. One of the greats. 1943. (*b/w*)

4 Above all towers Orson Welles, as actor – playing the many ages of the crusading newspaperman who does the dirt on everyone but somehow retains our sympathy to the end – and as producer-director – opening new vistas for the art of film with every dazzling scene. 1951. (*b/w*)

5 Oscar-laden classic about Marshal Gary Cooper searching for support against outlaws against the clock (time-span of film is from 10.40 am to noon). And do not forsake Dimitri Tiomkin's haunting music; 1952. (*b/w*)

6 Gradually this thriller has come to be accepted as a major achievement in the way it pretends, for the first reel, to tell one story, then switches round again, to finish up with one of the most shocking denouements in the history of the cinema. 1960. (*b/w*)

7 True, the dialogue is embarrassing; true, the nerveless borrowing from *Romeo and Juliet* is half-hearted; true, Richard Beymer's acting is laughable and Natalie Wood doll-like. Rita Moreno, George Chakaris are fine, however; the social significance isn't all cop-out, and those ten Academy Awards were not entirely undeserved. 1961. (*c*)

8 Marvellously observed and realised chase thriller with outstanding direction by William Friedkin and convincing performances from Gene Hackman (a little too lovable for his repulsive detective), Fernando Ray (smooth villain), Roy Schneider (tough cop). 1971. (*c*)

b What impression do these movies give of America?

c How are these countries portrayed in films?
1 Italy 2 Germany 3 France 4 Spain
5 The USA 6 Britain
Why?

2 While listening

a Listen and decide whether the speaker's main aim is to criticise:
1 national stereotyping in films.
2 cinema audiences.
3 young film writers.
4 those who propose film censorship.

b Now listen again and answer the following questions.
1 Which countries does the speaker say have become associated with the following stereotyping in films?

Aggressive law enforcement methods.	German
Psychopaths in quiet districts.	the USA
Poor people without hope.	Italy
Power in the hands of the wealthy.	France
Right-wing politics.	Spain

2 Which of these reasons does the speaker give for the negative images?
a) A reaction against the banning of films in Italy.
b) Directors regard patriotism as obsolete.
c) Those who go to the cinema are mainly young.
d) Stories have always contained powerful images.
e) The disparity in wealth within the film industry.
f) Excitement is an essential ingredient of drama.
g) The system of categorising films.
h) Modern films are not works of art.

3 Post-listening

a Choose one of the countries in **2b** and write a short paragraph that gives a fair picture of society there.

b What image is projected of your country by its own film directors and by foreign directors?

4 Discussion

What factors influence you to go and see a film? How big an impact does the poster or music have on you? How effective is the poster below?

GRADING VOCABULARY

Step diagrams show the relationships between different members of 'word families' and are a useful memory aid. This example shows words that describe degrees of voice loudness:

```
                              bellow
                       shout
                  call out
               say
          mutter
       murmur
whisper
```

a In groups, put the following adjectives on the appropriate steps; climbing from worst to best.
Some may be at the same level.

awful	so-so	brilliant
great	appalling	mediocre
passable	poor	superb
outstanding	weak	

```
                              ___
                           ___
                        ___
                     ___
                  ___
               ___
            ___
         ___
```

b Draw step diagrams of about seven words for:
1 The degree of excitement.
2 The intensity of the lighting.
3 How funny the script is.
4 How experienced the director is.
5 How well-known the actors are.

PRAISING AND CRITICISING

1 Classifying

Which of the following quotations were taken from formal reviews?

Praising
What a brilliant movie!
I love the way we're kept in suspense for two hours.
I must congratulate all concerned *on* this fine picture.
I've never seen *a* slicker bit of stunt work *than* this.
I cannot speak too highly of her acting talent.
What I really liked was the twist right at the end.

Criticising
What a disappointment the dialogue *was*!
I am afraid I found the message profoundly depressing.
They *just* stand there reciting the script. Lousy.
The casting *was somewhat less than* inspired.
I was extremely disturbed *by the* gratuitous violence.

2 Discussion

a Look at the table of the most successful films of all time. In pairs, discuss those you have seen. Consider the directors, actors, scripts, characters, photography, plots, settings, soundtracks, special effects, famous lines or any social/political significance.

ALL-TIME FILM RENTAL CHAMPS
(OF US – CANADA MARKET)

Compiled and researched by Variety -to 31 Dec 1987

TITLE	TOTAL RENTALS ($)
1. E.T THE EXTRA-TERRESTRIAL	228 379 346
2. STAR WARS	193 500 000
3. RETURN OF THE JEDI	168 002 414
4. THE EMPIRE STRIKES BACK	141 600 000
5. JAWS	129 549 242
6. GHOSTBUSTERS	128 264 005
7. RAIDERS OF THE LOST ARK	115 598 000
8. INDIANA JONES AND THE TEMPLE OF DOOM	109 000 000
9. BEVERLY HILLS COP	108 000 000
10. BACK TO THE FUTURE	104 237 346
11. GREASE	96 300 000
12. TOOTSIE	95 268 806
13. THE EXORCIST	89 000 000
14. THE GODFATHER	86 275 000
15. SUPERMAN	82 800 000
16. CLOSE ENCOUNTERS OF THE THIRD KIND	82 750 000
17. BEVERLY HILLS COP II	80 857 776
18. THE SOUND OF MUSIC	79 748 000
19. GREMLINS	79 500 000
20. TOP GUN	79 400 000

b Write a review for *The Times* of a film you have seen recently.

ORAL

1 Phonology – Intonation

Falling tones ($\searrow$) are used when the speaker believes he/she is telling the listener something new.

Example:

($\searrow$)
It won an award.

Fall-rise tones ($\vee\nearrow$) are used to refer to information shared by speaker and listener. This may be because of:

1 shared experiences or the immediate context.

Example:

($\vee\nearrow$)
I think this is the best scene.

2 a link with other parts of the conversation. This may be backwards, referring to something already mentioned.

Example:

($\vee\nearrow$)
When you said 'cruise', I thought you meant the actor.

It may be forwards, referring to something yet to come.

Example:

($\vee\nearrow$)
What I want to ask you is why you admire him so much.

a Listen to the following phrases from LISTENING, and repeat.

( )
1 Italy isn't the only other country
( )
2 Professor Stone's
( )
3 a cynical answer
( )
4 reservations remain
( )
5 anyone who remembers Italian neo-realism

b Listen again, mark the tones and say why each is used:

2 Interview

Reading passage

As in the reviews on page 122, the action in films and plays is depicted as 'happening now'. The simple present is used for events while the background is described in the present continuous.

Read the following text and comment on:
1 its probable source.
2 its purpose.
3 whether its purpose is achieved.
4 any unusual features: verb tenses and punctuation.
5 The link with the topic 'Arts and Leisure'.

> At the dawn of mankind, a tribe of apes discover a mysterious monolith. Four million years later, a similar object is found on the moon, beaming signals to Jupiter. A nine-month voyage to follow the signals is launched, with two astronauts manning a huge spaceship and three others in hibernation. The crew is disturbed to discover that Hal, the ship's computer, has a mind of its own . . .

Give your partner marks for; *pronunciation* of sentences, especially intonation; *fluency*.

Discussion

1 Write an introductory synopsis for a very well-known film in less than one minute and in note form. Read it to your partner and see if he/she can guess the title and outline the rest of the story. If not, he/she should invent a brief continuation and ending.

2 You can make informal anecdotes more vivid by using present tenses.
Imagine your response to this situation and continue the story:

> '. . . and then this clown who's lurching around the place manages to empty the contents of his designer beer mug all over me and has the nerve to say 'great party' so I . . .'

The listener should also ask questions in the present tense.

Examples:
You're just having a quiet chat, right?
So what does everyone else do?

REVIEW

1 Intonation

Read these answers aloud and decide which question, a) or b), was probably asked:

(↘)   (↗)
1 We went to the cinema on Saturday.
a) Where did you go on Saturday?
b) When did you go to the cinema?

(↘)   (↘)
2 I was watching videos with John.
a) Who were you watching videos with?
b) Where were you yesterday?

(↗)   (↘)
3 I learnt how to act in the theatre.
a) What did the theatre teach you?
b) How did you become an actor?

(↗)   (↘)
4 It's very sad at the end.
a) What eventually happened?
b) What was the film like?

(↗)   (↘)
5 The critics say it's a shambles.
a) Who says it's a shambles?
b) What do the critics say?

(↘)   (↘)
6 I don't know anyone who's seen it.
a) What have you heard about the new Spielberg film?
b) Hasn't your brother seen the new Spielberg film?

2 Relatives

Complete these sentences using relative clauses. Use each of the following once:

next to which   which ... for   few of them
who ... by   neither of them   instead of which
... from   in spite of which

1 His first 'western' received atrocious reviews ... it was a huge success.
2 Angela Molina and Bob Hoskins were on top form: ... have ever performed better.
3 He should have treated it as a serious play, ... he was going for laughs.
4 Truly a work of incomparable genius, ... others seem very amateurish.
5 There must've been a thousand screaming kids there, ... with tickets.
6 He's the playwright we got the idea ....
7 She played a non-stop three hour set ... was well worth waiting ....
8 It wasn't his song but he didn't say ... it was written ....

3 The infinitive

Complete the answers to the following questions using the appropriate form of the verb in brackets:
1 How do you feel now it's all over?
  It's nice ... (finish)
2 Aren't you coming with us?
  I'd ... (stay)
3 When's their new single coming out?
  It's due ... (release) ... next week.
4 Are you very tired?
  Yes but ... (fall asleep)

4 Vocabulary

Put the following expressions from this unit into **category a**, **b** or **c**. (See STUDY SKILLS on page 17).

uproar   foremost   to play host to   impaired
thrills   to nod off   wisdom   performance
disparaging   sleazy   mishap   sponsorship
touts   overlong   to enthuse about   dazzling
laughable   to think highly of   portrait
to shriek   half-hearted

5 Praising and criticising/Reported speech

Comment on these situations using the appropriate tones – are you telling your partner something new or not?

Get your partner to write down the reported speech versions of your comments.

1 You go to see a contemporary theatre production for the first time (you'd rather have stayed in to watch TV).

2 You're shown a painting which you think is terrible and told the buyer has just paid $50 million for it.

3 Domingo and Pavarotti perform together in Milan for the first time. You are there.

4 You've paid a lot of money to see a rock concert. The band turns up two hours late and only plays for forty minutes.

6 Essay

Write a letter to a student in the class who you don't know very well. Tell him or her how you spend your spare time. He or she should reply to you.

7 Now do the Progress Test for Unit 11 on page 188.

UNIT 12 THE HARD SELL

READING

1 The topic

In groups, discuss these quotations:

> Advertising is the greatest art form of the twentieth century. (Marshall McLuhan)
> The incessant witless repetition of advertisers' moron-fodder has become so much a part of life that if we are not careful, we forget to be insulted by it. (*The Times*)

2 Before reading

What differences have you noticed between TV commercials produced in your country and those made by multinationals or those shown on satellite TV?

3 While reading

a Read the text quickly. Which of the following best sums up the writer's attitude to global advertising?
 1 optimism   2 qualified optimism
 3 qualified pessimism   4 pessimism

b Now, read the text again and fill in each of the blanks with a suitable linking word.

Going for a Song

As advertising is forced to depend less and less on words,
DAVID BERNSTEIN wonders whether global advertisers really can
make beautiful music together.

A   ____(1) we are to speak to global stereotype consumers what language can we use? Music has always transcended borders but words must be few, international and made easily comprehensible by the context. Subtleties are out; local connotations are out; jokes other than visual are out; as are dialogue, spoken expositions and presenters talking to camera.

B   The global ad. would afford us the facility of communicating economically but superficially to a vast common audience rather than communicating expensively but deeply, personally and significantly, to separate audiences. In this trade-off the loser is language.

C   ____(2) visual images and music dominant we are back in the world of silent movies with multitrack replacing the live piano accompaniment. Presumably the stories of silents were *written*. But the screenwriter had to tell the story with little dialogue, a few captions, obvious dumb show and meaningful editing. The constraints created the movie; it became an art form and films crossed borders. Then sound came in – and with it dialogues. The movie became a talkie and the borders closed.

D   Speech which catches the nuances of the location or an ethnic group, dialogue which suggests an emotion in a few colloquial utterances and consequently conveys meaning in the heightened silences, this we shall deny ourselves in the cause of progress.

E   ____(3) should a brand whose advertising is not already 'global' (visual, simple and largely non-verbal) approach the opportunity of satellite? Change its advertising? Entirely, or for satellite only? Or turn away?

F   An advertisement is a relationship between a brand and a consumer. It is usually their first meeting. How do we conventionally describe a satisfactory relationship? 'We speak the same language' says more than 'We understand one another.' The term is exclusive: it connotes sharing and implies a fusion of interest and feelings between the participants.

G   ____(4) will be difficult to use the viewer's language if we aren't allowed to speak – and the only *lingua franca* is a bland adspeak, the marketing equivalent of Eurovision muzak.

H   Is there a role for the writer beyond that of 'ideas man'? With press ads aping television and conventional wisdom assuring us that the average attention span is down to five seconds and shrinking fast, the signs are hardly encouraging.

I   ____(5) television is an uncertain guide. Commercials owe more to cinema. The trade between commercials and television barely compares with that between commercials and feature films. And cinema is undoubtedly more international than television.

J   Can the music say it all? Pop tunes cross borders. The language is simple, the songs get repeated, the words insinuate – meaning of a sort is conveyed. No wonder agencies like to re-use these pre-recorded messages, international hits with all their associated values attached, and fit brands to them. All this must sadden the writer.

---

4 Reading for detail

Which of these questions does the writer answer? How?

1 ... *what language can we use?* (2)
2 ... *approach the opportunity of satellite?* (36–37)
3 ... *a satisfactory relationship?* (42)
4 ... *beyond that of 'ideas man'?* (51–52)
5 *Can the music say it all?* (63)

5 Responding to the text

What does the use of these words tell you about the writer?

1 *we* (1)   2 *us* (9)   3 *we* (48)

As a viewer, how do you feel about the changes predicted in the text?

6 Reference words

What do the following refer to?

1 *this* (14)   2 *the* (23)   3 *it* (25)   4 *this* (32)
5 *it* (44)   6 *that* (60)   7 *these* (67)

7 Sentence completion

Fill each of the blanks with a suitable word or phrase from the paragraph indicated in brackets.

1 Social classifications of consumers ____ . Instead, categories will be based on their interests. (A)
2 I like to make my own mind up ____ to be told what to buy. (B)
3 The difference between 'advertisement' and 'commercial' is a question of slight ____ of meaning. (D)
4 Can't we think of anything original? All we're doing is ____ the worst of American techniques. (H)
5 TV advertising has got so much better. In fact, I'd say some of it now ____ the best programmes. (I)
6 Ads every five minutes? ____ you never watch it! (J)

8 Style and register

The text is probably taken from:
1 a down-market newspaper.
2 a magazine which specialises in broadcasting.
3 a text book on the theory and practice of advertising.
4 a public information leaflet for consumers.

9 Discussion

What is this an advertisement for?

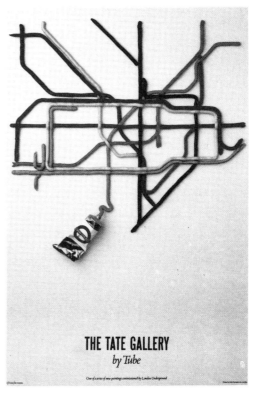

THE TATE GALLERY
by Tube

How effective is it?
Do you think the original was in colour or black and white?
What other types of products are advertised with very few words?
What types of products or services are advertised without pictures?
Which are the most effective, words or images?
In groups discuss other advertisements you find effective.

PRACTICE

1 Introductory *it*

It on line 44 of the READING text refers to *The term*. *It* on line 47 introduces the subject *to use*.

The subject may also begin with *that, what, when, how much, how many* or *whether*.

Examples:
*It's not at all certain **that** what they say is true.*
*It was amazing **how much** they spent on the campaign.*

The subject could also begin with the gerund (usually informal).

Examples:
*It's not much fun **watching** the same ads again and again.*
*It's no use **complaining** about it.*
(*But note: **There's no point in** complaining about it.*)

An object infinitive or *that*-clause can also be introduced by *it*, especially with an adjective.

Examples:
*We consider **it vital to** undercut the opposition.*
*They think **it significant that** sales increased.*

Comment on the diagram by completing these sentences:
1 It's amazing that ...
2 It's fascinating to ...
3 It seems that ...
4 It's incredible how ...
5 It's not clear whether ...
6 It's hardly likely that ...
7 It would be useful to ...
8 It's not worth ...
9 If it's true that ...
10 It's insane spending ...

2 Phrasal verbs

	General sense
through	
We ran *through* the park.	– In one side/out the other
I read *through* the draft.	– Beginning to end
We came *through* the crisis.	– Finish successfully
at	
We arrived *at* the office.	– Exact place
Look *at* the camera.	– In the direction of
She smiled *at* the thought.	– Cause of emotions/ actions
into	
I've moved *into* sales.	– In order to be in
It developed *into* a top agency.	– Change of condition
They ran *into* difficulties.	– Against

Answer the following questions using the verb in brackets and one of the prepositions above.

Example:
What's happened to the car? (crash)
We crashed into a wall.
1 When can I come round? (call) *at*
2 How did you react when he decided that? (protest)
3 What do you think of the magazine? (look)
4 What went wrong with the project? (turn)
5 How did you get here so quickly? (drive)
6 How do you think the exam went? (get)
7 What percentage market share are you after? (aim)
8 How on earth did you get the job? (walk)

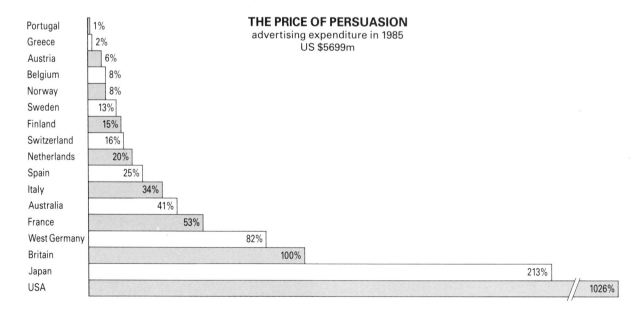

THE PRICE OF PERSUASION
advertising expenditure in 1985
US $5699m

Country	%
Portugal	1%
Greece	2%
Austria	6%
Belgium	8%
Norway	8%
Sweden	13%
Finland	15%
Switzerland	16%
Netherlands	20%
Spain	25%
Italy	34%
Australia	41%
France	53%
West Germany	82%
Britain	100%
Japan	213%
USA	1026%

3 Conditionals

As well as *unless, providing, etc,* other forms are used instead of *if*-clauses. For example, the sentence on lines 47–48 of the text on page 126:

It will be difficult to use the viewer's language if we aren't allowed to speak.

could be re-written:

Without being allowed to speak it will be difficult to use the viewer's language.

Other forms include the following:

Buy that **and** you'll regret it. (informal)
= **If you** buy that, you'll regret it.

Go satellite, **or** you'll be left behind.
= **If you don't** go satellite, you'll be left behind.

Given current trends, we'll have to move up-market.
= **If we take into account** current trends, we'll have to move up-market.

In the event of difficulties, call us right away.
= **If there are any** difficulties, call us right away.

The infinitive can be used as the subject.

Examples:
To take any notice would be a mistake.
Not to have taken any notice would have been a mistake.

a Use one of the above to fill in each of the blanks in the following sentences:
   1 ____ picture loss, re-tune the set. *In the event of . . .*
   2 Come and see us ~~or~~ you'll find what you're *and* looking for.
   3 ____ a good credit-rating, I'm afraid we can't help *Without* you. *реклама (открытка)*
   4 ____ hoardings to appear all over the countryside *To allow* would be crazy.
   5 Don't take too much cash *or* you'll spend it all.
   6 ____ the boom in arts sponsorship, we intend to *given* cut back on subsidies.
   7 ____ any market research would have been very *Not to have done / I* unwise.

b Now complete the following advertising slogans:
   1 Don't delay, or . . .
   2 Buy two, and . . .
   3 Invest right away, otherwise . . .
   4 Without life assurance cover . . .
   5 Send off today, or else . . .
   6 In the event of rain, simply . . .
   7 Not to have bought while prices were high . . .
   8 Given the cost of city centre property . . .?

WRITING

1 Describing objects

Adjectives

In pairs, put these descriptive adjectives (or nouns used as adjectives) into the categories 1–8 below:

money-saving silky bargain rugged
streamlined fine dazzling affordable
interwoven roomy patterned striped
shockproof budget toughened handy
all-purpose brass versatile suede
honeycombed gorgeous stunning rough
tapering exquisite pocket velvety
insulated marble adaptable rawhide

1 Size/shape	2 Material	3 Texture
4 Price	5 Design	6 Usefulness
7 Physical properties	8 Impression	

2 Compound adjectives

These are common in advertising and can be made up of many kinds of word.

Example:
wrap-around = verb + preposition

However, the second half of the compound is often a noun (*all-purpose*), a present participle (*money-saving*) or a past participle (*hand-stretched*).

Compounds may express the complete sense of a phrase.

Example:
leather which is stretched by hand:
hand-stretched leather

Or the approximate meaning.

Example:
we dye the leathers right the way through:
thoroughly-dyed leathers

Match the adjectives below with the pictures opposite.

thirst-quenching   money-saving
easily-loadable   water-resistant
diamond-encrusted   three-hour
personally-engraved   luminous-dial
custom-built   recently-compiled
hard-wearing

3 Colours

Apart from compounds: *blue-black, reddish-brown,* etc, shades are often expressed by adding adjectives or nouns.

In groups, tick the possible collocations in the table. The first one has been done for you.

	YELLOW	ORANGE	RED	GREEN	BLUE	BROWN
Deep			✓		✓	
Light						
Dark						
Bright						
Pale						
Sky-						
Navy						
Olive-						

Work in groups. What colours are these?
Examples:
emerald – *blue/green*   lilac – *purple/blue*

tan   honey   saffron   peach
mauve   sapphire   aquamarine   chestnut
tawny   primrose   turquoise   mahogany

4 Text writing

Write descriptions of 3 of the items from **2 Compound adjectives** that you see opposite. Imagine the colours and use a range of adjectives including compounds (about 50 words each).

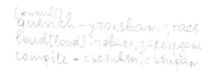

130

LISTENING

1 Pre-listening

a This is the transcript of a radio advertisement.
In groups, discuss the selling techniques used in the
words and expressions in **bold** type.

> As far as home protection is concerned, **burglars** (1) seem
> to have kept up with the times — **or have they?** (2)
> Telecom Security can **now** (3) install a **unique** (4) 24-hour
> **home monitoring system** (5) linked direct to your **existing**
> (6) phone. **Impressed?** (7) Well, you receive not only the
> attention of the police and fire services, but **at the press of**
> **a button** (8), medical assistance too. And at **a price that's**
> **sure to surprise you** (9). Dial 0800 010 999 now, **free of**
> **charge** (10) for more details. **Telecom Security** (11) –
> **they're just down the line when you need them most**
> (12).

b Which of the following tones of voice (or
combination of tones) do you think was used?

enthusiastic	urgent	familiar	humorous
relaxed	seductive	persuasive	contrastive
bullying	caring	forceful	reassuring

c Which tone of voice would you expect to be used in
advertisements for the following?

1 holidays 2 sports cars 3 cigars
4 cut-price carpets 5 toys 6 rock albums
7 political parties 8 beer 9 after-shave
10 soft drinks

2 While listening

a Copy the table below. Listen to the six
advertisements and fill in the missing information.

ADVERTISEMENT						
	1	2	3	4	5	6
Brand name						
Type of product						
Tone of voice						

b Now listen again. Tick which of the following
techniques are used in each advertisement:

	1	2	3	4	5	6
repetition of brand name						
immediate 'need' for action						
'saving' money						
offer subject to conditions						
change in style or pace						
trying to amuse						

3 Post-listening

What type of people were each of the
advertisements aimed at? Consider age, social
group, marital status etc.

b Which, if any, have aroused your interest in the
product?
Why?/Why not?

FUNCTIONS

When we don't know, or have forgotten an expression, we sometimes need to ask for help. Often, the best way is to describe the context by using informal statements or questions.

a Work in groups. Try to identify the words the speaker is looking for in the following sentences.

1 *It's the* background 'music' you hear in supermarkets.
2 *How can you say* 'shopping' as a countable noun?
3 *It's when* a shop charges you too much.
4 *What's the* noun for something that's very good value?
5 *It's a kind of* TV ad which is so quick you don't even notice it.
6 *What's the opposite of* 'retail'?
7 *It's where you* buy something by offering more money than anyone else.
8 *What's the stuff you use for* washing dishes?
9 *It's what you feel when* you've done something wrong.
10 *What's another way of saying* 'shades of meaning'?
11 *It's the thing you use to* change channels from where you're sitting.
12 *Who's the person who* does all the dangerous bits in the commercials?
13 *What do you call the* information and review quotations on the cover of a book?
14 *What's the word for when* you've been sold something you didn't want, for too much money?

b Without telling your partner which you are referring to, explain the meanings of ten of these words and see if he or she can identify them.

Example:
It's when air and water attack a metal. – *rust*

debt	*stereotype*	*leaflet*	*exploit*	*moron-fodder*
grey	*reassuring*	*paradox*	*trailer*	*ever-rising*
rust	*turquoise*	*trade-off*	*seductive*	*self-expression*
numb	*transcend*	*bland*	*lining*	*shoddily-finished*

1 Persuading

a Which of the following expressions would you use when trying to persuade a friend to do something?

1 You must . . .!
2 Don't you see that . . .?
3 Yes, many people say that but . . .
4 You'll never believe . . .
5 Come on! It's not often . . .
6 Just think what you could do with . . .
7 I can assure you that . . .
8 In my experience, people usually . . .
9 If you've never tried . . . you . . .!
10 Can't I persuade you to . . .
11 Go on – it's only . . .
12 There is absolutely no risk of . . .

Which would a salesperson use when trying to sell, for example, a pension scheme?

b Now complete each of the sentences.

c Put these replies as closely in order as possible, from most to least convinced.

a) That's all very well, but . . .
b) No chance!
c) That's certainly a possibility.
d) That seems reasonable enough.
e) Well, it seems like a good idea but . . .
f) That's a good idea.
g) Oh, all right then.
h) But isn't it a fact that . . .?
i) Sounds fine to me.
j) I'd rather not, thank you.
k) That's one way of looking at it, but . . .
l) Well, just for you.

Which is the most formal and the most informal?

d Work in pairs.

Student A You are a salesperson. Try to sell one of the items below to a customer.
☐ life assurance
☐ a used car
☐ home insulation
☐ encyclopaedias

Student B You are a potential customer. A salesman is trying to sell something to you but you want to 'think about it' before committing yourself. Change roles when you have finished.

1 Phonology – Intonation

You will hear rising (↗) and falling (↘) tones.

a Listen and repeat. What impression do the rises give?

b Listen again and mark the tones:

1 as soon as you find out, let me know
      ( )   ( )

2 brought to you in a commercial, by Philips
         ( )   ( )

3 put your finger there and press the button twice
      ( )   ( )

4 you can save an extra £20 on all purchases over
£200
   ( )   ( )

5 if that salesman comes back, don't sign anything
     ( )   ( )

2 Interview

c Now change the rises to fall-rises and say them aloud. What difference do you notice?

EXAM SKILLS THE GROUP INTERVIEW

The group format offers the most realistic context for discussion at all stages of the interview.

Perhaps the best way to avoid any nervousness when taking part is to do your best to help the others. When another candidate is speaking:

1 concentrate on the overall idea being expressed, not individual words.
2 encourage him or her to continue by nodding and smiling.
3 give help if he or she is looking for a word or phrase.
4 don't react negatively (by frowning, etc.) if you notice a mistake.
5 ask questions which require more than a one-word answer.
6 encourage discussion of related topics.
7 ask for more detail, if appropriate.
8 let him or her speak for roughly the same time as yourself.

In groups, look at the pictures.

The 'Examiner' should ask each of the 'Candidates' to describe one of the objects and then let discussion develop. Marks should be given for *fluency* and *interactive communication*.

The 'Candidates' should:

1 use 'open-ended' questions to get each other talking.

Examples:
Why do so many people dream of owning a . . .?
What techniques are used to sell luxury items?
How does a name like Porsche become 'mythical'?
To what extent are people influenced in their likes/dislikes by fashion, advertising, etc.?

2 ask for more details.

Examples:
Could you tell us a bit more about . . .?
I'm interested in knowing more about . . .
How exactly do they . . .?

Discussion

Describe your favourite TV advertisement in your country to your group and see if they can guess which it is.

Now tell the others why yours is the best, using rising tones (hard sell) or fall-rises (soft sell) – or a mixture of both.

Marks should be given for *vocabulary* and *intonation*.

REVIEW

1 Intonation

a Practise this dialogue with your partner:

A 'How much did that cost?' (↘)

B 'About a hundred.' (↘)

A 'A hundred; it can't have done.' (↗) (↘)

B 'I'm afraid it did.' (↘↗)

b Use the same intonation patterns and imagine you have got yourself into the following situations:

1 You mixed up the exam dates.
2 The police caught you speeding.
3 You overslept and missed your plane.
4 You have been sold something totally useless by a door-to-door salesman.

2 Introductory *it*

Choose from these expressions to form sentences using the prompts below.

alarming   not surprising   would appear
quite common   a pity   essential
shocking   no good   outrageous
senseless   well-known   obvious
claimed   sad   totally misleading
occurred to me   great   undeniable

Example:
In the US, advertisers have a lot of influence on programme makers.
***It** was alarming **to** hear that in the US, advertisers have a lot of influence on programme makers.*

1 Advertising sells a materialistic way of life.
2 It stimulates production and creates jobs.
3 Some say it is an art form.
4 A salesman is the last person you want to see.
5 Women are still exploited in many ads.
6 Some TV ads cost more than the programme they interrupt.
7 Some say ads are an insult to the intelligence.
8 Kids are encouraged to demand more and more.

3 Vocabulary

Put the following expressions from this unit into **category a**, **b** or **c**. (See STUDY SKILLS on page 17).

subtleties   screenwriter   constraints
to convey   heightened   to come undone
muzak   span   barely   resemblance
to spot   market research   to tot up
flattery   to put the boot in   rugged
stringent   to acknowledge   to pamper
preoccupied   to get away with

4 Persuading

Roleplay these situations with your partner using expressions from **3 Vocabulary**:

1 You've both been asked to appear together in a TV ad but your friend is a bit shy and not very keen.
2 You've taken up a new sport but your friend thinks it's rather dangerous.

5 Phrasal verbs

Complete the sentences with *at, into* or *through*.

1 They were forced ___ accepting the offer.
2 We laughed ___ the simplicity of the idea.
3 Guess who I bumped ___ on the way here?
4 I've been ___ all the figures so I'm positive.
5 They broke ___ the worldwide market.
6 The firm's in a bad way but I think it'll pull ___ .
7 The idea is for a plane to fly ___ the hoarding!
8 The film crew landed ___ a small airstrip.
9 Eh? I don't know what you're getting ___ .

6 Conditionals

Without using *if*, tell your partner what you'd say in these situations, using an assertive tone where appropriate. Refer to the PRACTICE SECTION on page 129.

Example:
Your friend wants to go and see a second-hand car described as 'needing only slight attention.'
Buy a car like that and you'll have no end of trouble.

1 A salesman keeps calling at your house even though you've told him you're not interested.
2 You sent a cheque (which was quickly cashed) to a mail-order company but you've heard nothing from them since. You have their phone number.
3 You work in a bank and a man asks you what he should do if he loses his credit card.
4 You find a local radio commercial extremely offensive, and believe it is illegal. Ring them up.
5 When you inquire about a job advertised in the paper, you find out that it would entail three hours' daily commuting.

7 Essay

You want to sell two of your personal possessions. In about 60–80 words each, write advertisements for a notice board, making the items sound as attractive as possible.

8 Now do the Progress Test for Unit 12 on page 189.

READING

1 The topic

In groups, make a list of things that can cause depression.
Then suggest solutions for each one.

2 Before reading

Look at the introduction to the article (in bold). Underline the phrases which indicate the text content.

3 While reading

Read the text quickly and select the appropriate subheading below for each part of the text. The parts are marked with a small line.

OUR RESPONSE IS SUBTLE
QUICK RESULTS
NOT A NEW CURE

SAD, but true?

The winter blues, those feelings which can darken many a day at this time of the year, may have a simple and easily remedied cause. Christine Doyle offers a ray of hope to sufferers.

Each year, as Washington's spectacular fall fades into the darkness of long winter evenings, Darlene Barry, a freelance writer in her early thirties with two small children, feels a curious and irresistible depression creep up on her. 5

'Life becomes sort of off-white. I feel duller, less creative and generally inadequate. I just about cope with my children but feel desperately tired. Food is an obsession: for hours I think about cooking and shopping, gaining as much as two stone each winter. 10

As I increase in girth, my energy drains away; I'm like a hibernating bear.' When spring comes Darlene 'wakes up', losing weight and working with recharged vigour. By the time the azaleas are in full bloom, she is her usual energetic, slim self. 15

Darlene suffers from winter depression, an ancient disorder recently rediscovered and aptly named 'seasonal affective depression' (SAD). The cause, according to Dr Norman Rosenthal and his colleagues at the National Institute of Health in Maryland, is lack of sunlight. 20

The researchers' remedy for SAD is to mimic the length of a bright summer's day by using ultraviolet lights with the same spectrum as the sun but which do not, however, tan the skin. Normal artificial lighting is of no benefit, though making the most of winter sun may help. 25

Last winter, Darlene and fellow guinea pigs sat in front of a row of full-spectrum lights, five times as bright as normal indoor lighting, for several hours in the mornings and evenings. The effect was dramatic. 30

———

'After a few days I felt re-energised and while under the lights finished an article I had previously been unable to start. I even felt repelled by a huge chocolate gateau on the cover of a gourmet magazine. The change was so definite I felt as if someone had thrown a chemical switch in my body.' 35

Dr Thomas Wehr, one of the NIH researchers, says: 'Darlene and several others had remarkable remissions: they even felt a little more lively than the rest of us.' The therapeutic effect wears off after a few days so, to keep depression at bay, the lights must be used each day until spring. Now Darlene has installed her own full-spectrum lights at home. 40

In the US publicity is producing hundreds of light-starved volunteers for increasing numbers of studies there. Dr Wehr says: 'When people heard about our work and started to look, they found more and more patients.' 45

———

Psychiatrists first became aware that some people suffered severe depresson as winter progressed more than 50 years ago. But for the most part doctors have forgotten about the condition or do not recognise it,' says Dr Stuart Checkly of the Maudsley. 50

The old Victorian hospitals built to house the mentally ill did have one advantage for patients suffering from depression – huge verandas designed to capture as much light as possible. 'We've had patients who experienced tremendous problems if their offices had no windows: they would even change jobs,' says Dr Wehr. 55 60

4 Reading for detail

Which of the following people/animals are likely to be affected by light changes?
1 Working single parents.
2 Guinea pigs.
3 People working in artificially-lit environments.
4 Those living in areas of poor visibility.

5 Responding to the text

Which of the following should you do if you are suffering from SAD?
1 Go on a diet.
2 Use a sunlamp.
3 Get up early.
4 See a doctor (if it's serious).
5 Buy special lights now.
6 Spend more time in the sunshine.

Another patient, Dr Gary Hill, a 46-year-old pathologist from Maryland, found it almost impossible to concentrate on work during the winter. When he moved to a grey foggy area his symptoms worsened. Now he 65
rises at five o'clock every winter morning and works surrounded by lights for three hours. He repeats this in the evening. When away from home, he runs in the early morning light.

Researchers exploring this new and controversial 70
area are increasingly convinced that its benefits to our emotional health may be considerable.

One key to understanding what happens when light strikes the eye is the pineal gland. The action of this tiny control centre, buried deep within the brain, is still not 75
clear, but it appears to interpret light messages sent to it via the optic nerve. The pineal secretes melatonin, a hormone thought to have a powerful effect on sleep, mood and seasonal reproductive cycles. Levels of the hormone rise at night and subside at dawn. 80

Unlike reptiles and some animals, humans are not obviously responsive to light changes: we do not leap about at dawn and nod off at sunset, or mate only in the spring. Biologists have mostly assumed that we have evolved beyond dependence on environmental 85
triggers.

Nevertheless, melatonin levels do fluctuate over 24 hours and may build up in people who are unusually sensitive to reduced sunlight. Disturbances in the day-night melatonin cycles experienced by some blind 90
people provides further evidence that light affects daily and seasonal rhythms.

These are early days for light research. Those who think they suffer badly from SAD should seek medical help before embarking on a full-scale light treatment. 95
Those of us seeking to ease more trivial discontents should perhaps look no further than a long walk in the wintry sun.

6 Transformation

For each of these sentences from the text, write a new sentence as similar as possible in meaning to the original sentence, but using the word given. This word must not be altered in any way.

1 *The change was so definite I felt as if someone had thrown a chemical switch in my body.* (35–37)
   such
   _____

2 *Psychiatrists first became aware that some people suffered severe depression as winter progressed more than 50 years ago.* (50–52)
   It
   _____

3 *Another patient, Dr Gary Hill, a 46-year-old pathologist from Maryland, found it almost impossible to concentrate on work during the winter.* (62–64)
   concentrating
   _____

4 *When he moved to a grey foggy area his symptoms worsened.* (64–65)
   moving
   _____

5 *One key to understanding what happens when light strikes the eye is the pineal gland.* (73–74)
   struck
   _____

7 Relatives

Fill in each blank with a relative and an auxiliary verb.

Example:
... *depression,* **which is** *an ancient disorder* ...   (16)

1 ... hospitals _____ built to ... (55)
2 ... patients _____ suffering ... (56)
3 Researchers _____ exploring ... (70)
4 ... messages _____ sent ... (76)
5 ... a hormone _____ thought ... (78)
6 Those of us _____ seeking ... (96)

8 Text completion

Complete each of the blanks in the following paragraph with **one** word from the text.

If you find it difficult to _____(1) with life in winter, you may be suffering from SAD – without being _____ (2) of it. Try to make the _____(3) of the brightest part of the day, rather than going out at five o'clock: _____ (4) the light _____(5) the benefit decreases. For the most _____(6) psychiatrists agree that, _____(7) the elderly, you only need thirty minutes' exposure, but this must be a daily 'dose' – otherwise the effect _____ (8) off and depression can build _____(9) again. If you _____(10) find it difficult to get out during the day, at least make sure you work near a window.

PRACTICE

1 Phrasal and prepositional verbs

Like other verbs, phrasal and prepositional verbs can be **transitive** (requiring a direct object); **intransitive** (with no direct object); or **sometimes transitive, sometimes intransitive**. Transitive phrasal verbs are separable, the direct object can go (in some cases **must** go) between the verb and the adverb particle.
Prepositional verbs are inseparable, the object follows the verb and preposition.

Examples:
Transitive prepositional verb:
They suffer from winter depression.
The second part is a preposition if the noun clause is its object e.g. *winter depression* is the object of *from*. In this case the object cannot separate the two parts, although an adverbial can do so:
They suffer every year from winter depression.

Transitive phrasal verb
I put weight on very easily.
weight is not the object of *on*.

Transitive or intransitive phrasal verb:
He wakes up early. – intransitive.
They wake him up early. – transitive
(Personal pronoun objects always come between the verb and the adverb particle.)

If the object of a phrasal verb is very long, it usually comes after the adverb particle:
He woke up everyone in the neighbourhood.

Three-part verbs, e.g. *creep up on* (4), cannot be separated by the object. An adverbial can, however, be placed between the adverb and the preposition.
Example:
*He **crept up** imperceptibly **on** her.*

a Match these rather formal verbs from the text on page 136 with their equivalents on the right.

1	*gain* (10)	a)	ask for
2	*install* (43)	b)	come up against
3	*suffer* (50)	c)	fall off
4	*experience* (59)	d)	get up
5	*rise* (66)	e)	go up
6	*explore* (70)	f)	look into
7	*rise* (80)	g)	put on
8	*subside* (80)	h)	set up
9	*seek* (94)	i)	go through

b Now put the phrasal verbs a)–i) above into the following groups:
1 intransitive (or used intransitively) + adverb.
2 transitive + adverb.
3 transitive + preposition.
4 transitive + adverb + proposition.

c For the group 2 phrasal verbs, rewrite the sentences in the text so that the adverb comes after the object.

d Re-write the sentences putting the words in brackets into the correct position.

1	I don't think it calls for	(drastic action)
2	Would you fill in, please?	(this form)
3	Carry on with	(the course of treatment)
4	It's been getting down a lot	(me/lately)
5	Keep to	(the diet/strictly)
6	I didn't want to bring up	(at a time like this/it)
7	You should cut down on	(considerably/your intake of alcohol)
8	We can rule out	(the risk of any long-term effects/ definitely)

2 Infinitive and gerund

Some verbs can be followed by either the infinitive or the gerund with little or no difference to the meaning, e.g. *started to look* (line 48 of the READING text) is very much the same as *started looking*. But often this is not the case.

With *remember, forget, stop, go on* and *regret*, the gerund is used for something which takes place **before** the action (e.g. of remembering) while the infinitive is for what happens **after**.

Example:
I'll remember telling her . . . = I'll remember what happened . . .
I'll remember to tell her . . . = I'll remember that I should . . .

If we *see, watch* or *hear* something happening using the gerund we are referring to **part** of an action, whereas the infinitive is used for the **whole** event.

Examples:
I watched them testing the theory (when I called in at the laboratory).
I watched them test the theory (over a period of weeks).

When used with the gerund, **want** and **need** mean 'to be in need of' (**need** usually with things, rather than people).
Sometimes, **want** + infinitive can mean 'should'.

Examples:
*The figures **need**/**want** checking.*
*You **want** to spend more time out of doors.*
These uses of **want** are informal.

a Which of the options, a) or b) below, better completes each sentence using the infinitive, and then the gerund?
1 I stopped *to listen/listening* because ...
   a) I was getting bored b) it sounded interesting
2 I saw them *play/playing* chess but ...
   a) he lost as usual b) I don't know who won in the end
3 They need *to study/studying* because ...
   a) they've got an exam b) nobody can explain them
4 I tried *to make/making* new friends but ...
   a) they couldn't help either b) people were too unfriendly

b Complete these sentences:
1 I tried _____ sheep but that didn't work either.
2 I went on _____ about the problem and to suggest solutions.
3 I heard them _____ about me but could only catch a few words.
4 You want to spend less time _____ and more time _____ something about it.
5 I forgot _____ that we'd already finished.
6 I'll go on _____ for a solution but so far I've had no luck.

STUDY SKILLS USING THE DICTIONARY

The dictionary can tell you whether a verb:

1 has irregular past or participle forms (leapt).
2 is transitive (VT) or intransitive (VI).
3 is followed by:
   ☐ the full infinitive (+ *to* – inf.)
   ☐ the infinitive without *to* (+ inf.)
   ☐ the gerund (+ *-ing*)
   ☐ an object and a past participle (+ obj. + *-ed*)
   ☐ a preposition (+ *for*)
   ☐ a *that* clause (+ *that*)
   ☐ certain parts of speech (+ adv./prep./adj./n./pron.)
4 if phrasal, can be separated by its object:
   ☐ look after sb. (somebody)/ sth. (something)
   ☐ switch on sth./switch sth. on
   ☐ hit sb./sth. with sth.

a Use the list on the right to find mistakes in each of these sentences, and correct them using the dictionary entries which follow:
1 I insist absolute silence on.
2 She threatened leaving him.
3 He married with her last year.
4 I succeeded in overcome it.
5 I was refering to the first occasion.
6 I consider a waste of time to carry on.
7 He provided with me the perfect excuse.
8 I dread see him again.
9 He soon got her over and met someone else.
10 I forbid to mention this to anyone.
11 They stole him everything.
12 I lay my cards on the table at our last meeting.
13 I want him to tell immediately.
14 The question raised during the conversation.
15 We prevented him to see it.

consider VT (+ obj. + n./adj.)
dread VT (+ *to* -inf.) (+ *-ing*)
forbid VT (+ obj. + *to* -inf.)
get over VT (get over sb. sth.)
insist on VI (insist on sth.)
lay (laid) VT (+ obj. + adv./prep.)
marry VT/VI (+ obj.)
prevent VT (prevent sb. + *from* + *-ing* sth.)
provide VT (+ obj. + *with* + n./pron.)
raise VT (+ n./pron.)
refer to (-rr-) VT (refer to sb./sth.)
steal (stole, stolen) VT/VI (+ n./pron. + *from* + n./pron.)
succeed VI (+ *in* + *-ing* + n./pron.)
threaten VT/VI (+ *to* -inf.)
want VT (+ obj. + *-ed*)

When you are adding to your vocabulary lists, note down verb patterns in the same way.

SUMMARY WRITING – 4

1 Reading for gist

Read the text quickly and choose a short phrase from each of the second, third and fourth sections as a sub-heading.

Sunset for the sun set!

There is a war being fought on the beaches. The war is between the massed ranks of bikini-clad women and the sun-tan oil manufacturers on the one hand, and the Royal College of Physicians, glossy magazine beauty editors, dermatologists and the avant-garde on the other.

Going brown is bad for you. If smoking is bad for you, so is lying in the sun and soaking up the ultra-violet and going a different colour from the colour you were born with. From honey-gold to deep copper-bronze with all the shades of tan in between, it's BAD for you. So say the merchants of gloom.

And so says the Cancer Research Campaign which yesterday launched a fight against sun tan cancer.

_____

Before World War I, no *lady* EVER got brown. Poets praised women's skin because of its *whiteness*: White as silk, white as milk, white as snow. White skin was a sign not only of beauty, but of breeding.

The first woman to be tall and tanned and young and lovely was the mould-breaker Coco Chanel. Mademoiselle Chanel bobbed her hair. Mademoiselle Chanel threw off her corsets and wore men's vests instead. And Mademoiselle Chanel, on the beaches of Deauville and Biarritz, took off her hat and let the sun shine straight down on to her face.

Mademoiselle Chanel, though, even in 1918, STILL WORE GLOVES while she sunbathed. 'Gloves were essential because sun-darkened hands suffered still more negative prejudice than a tanned face. Neither in public nor in private could a woman of the world risk having her hands look as if they had done manual labour.'

_____

We'll listen to the doctors in the end. We always do. We drink less, we smoke less, we eat less. In ten years we'll sunbathe less. Not that doctors will take all the credit. The truth is that sunbathing as a *fashion* is changing.

Fashion is made from the top. It changes on a whim. Only the leisured rich, the people with either time on their hands or more money than sense, can afford to chuck out what's perfectly serviceable and OK in order to embrace something that's dashingly different.

That's why the only people who know it's fashionable to be a golden shade of pale are a tiny elite. The beauty editors on glossy magazines are talking to the fashionable rich – the rest of us will follow.

Says Alexandra Campbell, beauty editor of *She* magazine: 'Regardless of the warnings, women keep sitting in the sun. What has come about, though, is just that the ultra-brown tan is out – but in the end you cannot shake people's desire to be brown:

_____

What's the first thing that anyone says when someone comes back from a holiday? – 'Oh! You're so brown, don't you look terrific!' Still, all the advice has had some effect because people are settling for a healthy glow or a honey colour instead of a very dark tan.

What is really hitting home is the first generation of people who could afford those package tours to the sun – men and women in their forties – are showing the signs of premature ageing. They are wrinkled and their skin feels like leather.

And it is more a fear of wrinkles than of cancer that keeps people out of the sun a little more than they used to.'

And Penny Farmer, assistant beauty editor of *Woman* magazine, is trying to promote a fairer skin and staying out of the sun. However, she says: 'A pale skin isn't fashionable yet because you cannot get away from the fact that people do like to tan. What is happening is that women are more aware of the dangers and so are using more protective creams and blocks.'

2 Comparing summaries

The summary instructions are:
In a paragraph of 70–100 words, summarise current and future changes in sunbathing habits, and the reasons for them.

You should:
- ☐ show you understand the text.
- ☐ include all the relevant points.
- ☐ be economical with words.
- ☐ use, where possible, your own words.

Which of the following is the best summary?

A

Things have changed radically since the days when women wore gloves on the beach, but it is once again the fashion to remain one's natural colour. This is because of the struggle between those for and against sunbathing. People are copying the light-brown tan of the wealthy, a change long supported by magazine editors and older people who were the first generation to sunbathe abroad. As we took the advice of the Cancer Research Campaign and cut down on cigarettes, so we will reduce the amount of time spent in the sun.

B

Women are more aware of the dangers and so are using better protection and sunbathing a little less. This is more a fear of wrinkles, now affecting people in their forties – the first who could afford package tours to the sun, than of cancer. Beauty editors are talking to the leisured rich, who know its fashionable to be a golden shade of pale. The rest of us will follow; already people are settling for a healthy glow or a honey colour. We'll listen to the doctors in the end, as we always do, and sunbathe less.

C

Women are not staying out in the sun as much and are taking more and more care of their skin. They have seen what has happened to those now in their forties who first had enough money to go abroad and soak up the sun: their skin has been damaged and they are looking much older. Doctors have come out against sunbathing but it will take quite a long time before, inevitably, we do what they say. Beauty editors such as Alexandra Campbell have tried, without much success, to convince women that they should not sunbathe at all, but at least the very dark tan is not in fashion any longer. The example set by the trend-setting rich will be followed by women, with the backing of the magazine editors.

D

Doctors have warned of the cancer risk, but although we will eventually take their advice it is the harm done to the skin of the middle-aged, the first generation to sunbathe in hotter climates, that is having the greatest impact. In time, the lightly-tanned look adopted by high society will catch on; encouraged by magazines whose anti-sunbathing campaigns have led to women spending less time in the sun and improving skin protection as they become more conscious of the hazards.

3 Identifying weaknesses

What is wrong with the other three summaries? Underline the phrases and sentences which could be improved and suggest alternatives.

4 Writing

Study the text again and, in a paragraph of 60–80 words, summarise the changes in attitude towards sunbathing which have taken place this century.

LISTENING

EXAM SKILLS LISTENING –
PREDICTING

In the Examination, there will be a pause in each
part between the instructions and the passage.
You should use this time to predict the content
by looking at the questions, instructions or
statements. This can give you the gist and is
especially important when you are required to
write down a lot of details quickly.

Look at **1 While listening** below.
1 What do *women, ethnic minorities* and *left-
   handed people* have in common?
2 What connotations does *left-handed* have in
   your first language?
3 Make a list of the problems a left-handed
   person might have. Consider domestic
   appliances, work, social life, etc.
4 Make a list of internationally famous people
   who are, or were, left-handed.

1 While listening

Listen to the recording twice and give brief answers
– one word where possible.

a What, according to the speaker, do these people
suffer from?
1 women
2 ethnic minorities
3 left-handed people

b Write down six words associated with left-
handedness.

c Write down twelve practical difficulties
encountered by the left-handed.

d Write down the names of the six well-known left-
handed people mentioned.

2 Post-listening

a How would you describe the speaker's tone of
voice?
1 hopeful   2 resentful   3 satisfied   4 resigned

b Have you formed part of a minority in any way? If
you have, tell your partner:
1 how you were treated by the majority.
2 the words that were used to describe you.
3 any problems it brought.
4 the names of any famous people who have been
in the same situation.

FUNCTIONS

WORRYING, FEARING AND REASSURING

1 Classifying

a Decide which of these expressions are formal, informal and neutral.

Worrying and fearing

. . . is giving cause for concern.

. . . scare/terrify/petrify me.

I'm worried in case . . . + *present tense* . . .

I'm worried sick about . . .

I am extremely anxious about/regarding . . .

I'm afraid/terrified/frightened to death of . . . + *noun/gerund*

What if . . .?

I've got a fear/terror/dread of . . .

One never knows what might happen if . . .

The very thought/idea of . . . + *noun/gerund* . . . makes me . . .

(Just) imagine (if) . . .

I've got a nasty/strange/uneasy feeling that . . .

I'm scared stiff of/that . . .

I am concerned lest . . . (should) *infinitive* . . .

(Just) suppose/supposing (that) . . . +

Reassuring

There's no need to/you needn't worry about + *noun/gerund*

There's nothing at all to worry about.

There is absolutely no cause for alarm/anxiety/concern.

It'll all turn out fine/be all right in the end.

You may rest assured that . . .

Take it easy./Calm down./Don't panic./Relax.

It wouldn't be the end of the world if . . .

I can assure you that you need have no fears about . . .

I should like to assure/reassure you that . . .

Don't lose any sleep over/get so worked up about . . .

Cheer up! It's not as bad as all that!

There is no reason whatsoever to be apprehensive about . . .

b Work in pairs.

Student A Read through the stressful events listed below. Imagine some of them are happening to you.

Talk about your worries and fears.

Student B Try to reassure your partner.

Change roles when you have finished.

WHAT AMERICANS FIND STRESSFUL

Rank	Life event
1	Death of spouse
2	Divorce
3	Marital separation
4	Jail term
5	Death of close family member
6	Personal injury or illness
7	Marriage
8	Fired at work
9	Marital reconciliation
10	Retirement
11	Change in health of family member
12	Pregnancy
13	Marital difficulties
14	Gain of new family member
15	Business readjustment
16	Change in financial state
17	Death of close friend
18	Change to different line of work
19	Change in number of arguments with spouse
20	Mortgage over $100,000
21	Foreclosure of mortgage or loan
22	Change in responsibilities at work
23	Son or daughter leaving home
24	Trouble with in-laws
25	Outstanding personal achievement
26	Partner begins or stops work
27	Begin or end school
28	Change in living conditions
29	Revision of personal habits
30	Trouble with boss

c Which of the following frighten you? Tell your partner why.

☐ confined spaces

☐ the dark

☐ deep water

☐ flying

☐ heights

☐ lifts

☐ loneliness

☐ public speaking

☐ spiders and insects

1 Phonology – Low Key intonation

The pitch of the voice sometimes falls, and remains low, during part of a sentence. When this happens, speech is often quicker and quieter.

a Listen to the following sentences from the LISTENING text and underline the low key words:

1 the person, the man or woman, was using his or her right hand
2 and dextrous, right-handed, means capable and skilful
3 a right-hand man, that's a very common phrase, is someone who
4 cameras, another thing, not that I'm a great photographer, but the button

b What kind of information do these words contain?

c Listen again and repeat.

d In the following sentences underline the low key words and read the sentences aloud to your partner:

1 no-one would wish, by choice, to use the right hand
2 it's not easy being left-handed, you know, there are all sorts of problems
3 over the ages, of course, people have been persecuted
4 and I agreed, which I should never have done, to use my right hand

Discussion

Make a list of twelve questions about yourself which you would enjoy answering.

Example:

What grade did you get at First Certificate? (If you got an 'A'.)

Think of your successes, interests, opinions, likes, dislikes, preferences, childhood, ambitions, amusing or frightening experiences, and personal details.

Give the list to the others in your group and get them to ask you the questions. They should give you marks for; *pronunciation*, sentences, particularly your use of low key intonation; *vocabulary*.

REVIEW

1 Low key intonation

a Listen, and fill in the low key words:

1 means capable and skilful, _____. I mean it's always ambidextrous
2 you can't be a violinist, _____, because you might bump someone
3 because they're left-handed, _____, my own mother
4 but, _____, perhaps the necessity to conquer

Read the sentences to your partner.

b Fill in the blanks with information your partner probably already knows, or words spoken to yourself as an aside:

1 My favourite rock band, ____ is playing here soon.
2 Doing lots of homework, ____, is essential.
3 I had a nightmare, ____, about something like that.
4 I'm staying with the same family, ____, in August.
5 And I thought, ____, he was telling the truth!
6 I'd read about SAD, ____, somewhere before.

Read the sentences to your partner.

2 Vocabulary

a Respond to the following sentences using the phrasal verbs in brackets.
Example:
Didn't you use to smoke? (give up)
Well I did, but I managed to give up.

1 She's a lovely person; so unlike her father. (take after)
2 Didn't you warn him? (point out)
3 How did you lose so much weight? (keep away from)
4 You could do with a quiet holiday somewhere. (fix up)
5 He looks so unhealthy; is he eating properly? (live on)
6 Do you like living with your parents? (get on with)

b Put the following expressions from this unit into **category a**, **b** or **c**. (See STUDY SKILLS on a page 17.)

freelance	dull	to keep sth/sb at bay
disorder	trigger	trend-setting
to ease	gloom	to look no further than
to soak up	whim	to chuck out
regardless	wrinkles	to come about
to hit home	backing	to settle for
hazards	full-scale	to come out against

3 Infinitive and gerund

Tell your partner about the following, using expressions from **2 Vocabulary** if possible (see PRACTICE).

1 Things you mustn't forget/must remember to do this week.
2 What you remember about an accident or illness you've had.
3 Something you regret doing.
4 A worry or phobia and what you've tried to do about it/tried doing.
5 Something you should stop doing.
6 Anything you stopped to do on the way to the lesson.
7 Things that need/want doing at home.
8 Something you'll never forget doing.
9 What you've seen/watched/heard people do/doing lately.

4 Worrying, fearing and reassuring

In pairs practise the dialogues in these situations, using low key intonation where appropriate:

You've got a powerful motorbike and have offered to give someone a lift home from a party. Everyone knows how fast you ride and there are icy patches on the roads. Your partner is not sure whether to accept.

You are in the most dangerous part of a big foreign city. You can both sense the violence in the atmosphere and want to get back to your hotel – but you've just found out that public transport stopped running at 10 pm. Your partner is beginning to panic.

You are the Public Relations Officer of a multinational which dumps toxic waste in the sea. Your partner is the spokesperson for local fishermen and environmentalists.

5 Summary writing

Look back at the text on page 136 and, in a paragraph of 80–100 words, summarise the effects of seasonal affective depression and its remedies.

6 Now do the Progress Test for Unit 13 on page 190.

UNIT 14 RIGHTS AND WRONGS

READING

I know my rights!

1 The topic

Which are the most basic rights that people have, or should have? What order of importance would you put them in?

2 Before reading

Look at the title of the text.
Why should 'children's rights' be described as folly?
Which children's rights would be different from adult's rights?

3 While reading

Decide whether the following statements are TRUE, FALSE, or NOT STATED.
The Convention on the Rights of the Child:

1 was approved and signed by 20 governments.
2 will suggest punishments for cruel parents.
3 was probably written by adults.
4 only protects English-speaking children's rights.
5 says nothing about television.
6 bans abortion.
7 guarantees financial aid for pregnant women.
8 is similar to a convention that protects mothers.

Germaine Greer on the folly of 'children's rights'

A One of the most significant achievements of the last months of the Eighties was that the 44th Session of the General Assembly of the United Nations unanimously agreed to adopt a United Nations Convention on the Rights of the Child. ₅ It had taken 30 years to gather the 54 Articles of the draft Convention from more than 80 international declarations and treaties. The Convention will pass into international law when 20 governments have ratified it; they will then be ₁₀ expected to write it into their own legal instruments.

B … The Convention applies mainly to the treatment of children by adults, but rather than drawing up a system of prohibitions and penal- ₁₅ ties for adults who oppress and abuse children, it prefers to use the woolly pseudo-democratic rhetoric of rights, rights which children themselves have not enunciated and are powerless to enforce. ₂₀

C … Though the Convention states that a child has a right to decide its own affairs, it seems very unlikely that children were consulted about what should go into it. If British and American children had drafted the Convention, ₂₅ there would probably be Articles according children the right to go to bed when they want to, and to choose their own food, and to watch the kind of television they want as much as they want, and to tie up the telephone for as long as ₃₀ they feel they need to, and setting minimum rates of pocket money and pay for household chores. Most of the children in the world, however, would not make the kinds of demands that rich kids persecute their parents with. ₃₅

D … Obviously a new-born child cannot decide its own good, yet many of the Articles of the Convention apply to it, and even to the rights it should have enjoyed before it was born. The child is entitled to 'appropriate legal ₄₀ protection before as well as after birth'; this wording was arrived at after long deliberation. It is justified, by UNICEF at any rate, as adumbrating a first right of the child, the right to a healthy mother. Herein lies the awkwardness ₄₅ at the centre of the notion of a charter of children's rights, for if the mother's right to health had been respected, if she had the right to conceive and give birth when, where and how she wanted, if her own development had not been ₅₀ distorted by malnutrition, by daily toil, by infectious disease, by poverty, she could be securing her own rights rather than having them by proxy, as it were, just because she is carrying that international commodity, a child. ₅₅

E … It is not after all children who should have adequate health care, food and clean water, but people. Most of the mothers in the world are already going short in order to feed and clothe their children, but a UN Convention on ₆₀ the Rights of the Mother has never been mooted, and would not have had the smooth if glacier-slow passage of the Convention on the Rights of the Child if it had been.

146

4 Responding to the text

Do you think the UN Convention on the Rights of the Child will be useful? Why / Why not?
Do you think the author's tone is serious and academic or mocking and ironic?
Why has she chosen this tone?

5 Reference words

What do these words refer to?

it 6   its 22   it 24   they 27   this 41   It 43
she 49   them 53   their 60   it 64

6 Style

Match the formal expressions 1–8 on the left with the neutral expressions a)–h) on the right. Why does the author use these formal expressions?

c 1 legal instruments   a) in this
f 2 enunciated   b) giving an outline of
e 3 according   c) laws
g 4 deliberation   d) hard work
b 5 adumbrating   e) giving
a 6 herein   f) put forward for discussion
d 7 toil   g) careful consideration
fh 8 mooted   h) claimed

7 Sentence completion

Fill each of the blanks with the appropriate form of a word or phrase from the paragraph indicated in brackets.

1 The safeguards do not _apply to_ those convicted of political 'crimes'. (B)
2 A law cannot be _enforced_ if everyone ignores it. (B)
3 They told her to look after her _own affairs_ rather than interfere in other people's. (C)
4 The government abolished the accused's _right to_ remain silent. (C)
5 Keep quiet about it; not because I'm involved but for your _own good_. (D)
6 It took them weeks of discussions to _arrive at_ a decision. (D)
7 Despite the complications, she _gave birth_ to a healthy 7 lb boy. (D)
8 If the crops fail, millions will _go short_ of food. (E)

PRACTICE

1 Infinitives as relatives

Like the -*ing* form (line 26 of the READING text:
... *Articles according* ... = 'Articles which accord')
and the past participle, the infinitive can have a
similar function to a relative.

Examples:
The first country to ratify it was Sweden.
= *The first country which ratified it was Sweden.*

The action to be taken must succeed.
= *The action which will be taken must succeed.*

The people to talk to are the NCCL.
= *The people you/one/victims etc. should talk to are the NCCL.*

for + a subject can be added in this construction.
Example:
The people **for you to talk to** are the NCCL.

Expand the following notes into complete
sentences using infinitives as relatives.

Example:
The first state/enfranchise women/New
Zealand/1893.
The first state to enfranchise women was New Zealand in 1893.
1 The only ones/prosecuted/given a small fine.
2 The best place/them/go/a nursery.
3 The main issue/discussed/responsibility sharing.
4 The worst cases/reported/countries at war.
5 The two/not/legalised abortion/Ireland and
   Malta.
6 There aren't enough inspectors/every case/
   looked into.
7 The cleverest thing/done/that situation/been/get
   out.

2 Introductory there

Apart from in standard *there is/are* forms, *there* is
used:

a) in literary or formal styles, before verbs which
   express existence or the action of appearing.
   Example:
   There *now exists a new political wing within the
   Democratic Party.*

b) in similar styles, but after adverbials.
   Example:
   Into the courtyard **there** *marched his escort.*
   In this construction, however, 'there' is often
   omitted.

c) before *seem* or *appear*.
   Example:
   There *seems/appears to be some mistake.*

d) with *to be* or *being*.
   Examples:
   We don't want **there** *to be any more rumours.*
   I was surprised at **there** *being no-one around.*

e) Before the following structure using *for*.
   Example:
   There'*ll be nothing for us to do.*

f) With certain verbs, *no* + -*ing*.
   Example:
   There'*s no knowing what might happen next.*

Finish the following sentences using forms a) – f)
twice. The first one has been done as an example.

Example:
1 There would seem to have *been some confusion.*
2 There was nobody ...
3 To the left of the judge sat ...
4 We would prefer ...
5 There lived ...
6 There appears to be little hope ...
7 There's no telling who ...
8 We insist ...
9 On top of the hill ...
10 There is no evidence ...
11 There approached ...
12 There's no denying that ...

3 Adjective order

If there are a number of adjectives before a noun, they should be placed in a certain order.

Put three or four adjectival forms from this list before each of the nouns in the table.

The first one has been done as an example.

army   black   bright   brown
cotton   dark-haired   denim
European   evil   foreign-backed
foreign-made   freedom
government-condoned   green   grey
hideous   human rights   international
investigating   latest   murder
muscular   newly-formed   physical
plastic   prison   prisoners of conscience
purpose-built   South American   small
spring   stone   stunning   timing
top-security   United Nations   warm
well-intentioned   widespread   woman

1 number, opinion, size, shape, age, temperature, etc.	2 colour	3 origin	4 material	5 defining	6 noun
A *small*	*black*	*foreign-made*	*plastic*	*timing*	device.
A					morning.
					campaigners.
					uniforms.
A					committee.
A					prison.
					cruelty.
A					fighter.
A					jacket.
An					squad.
The					report.
A					leader.

WRITING

In *Section B* of the **Use of English** Paper, you are asked to write your own answers to questions about a text. Your aim is to understand and interpret concisely.

DO

☐ read for gist and then think of a title.

☐ look for contextual clues.

☐ infer by looking for clues in more than one part of the text.

☐ use your own words where you can, but there is no harm in using individual words from the text.

☐ check for language mistakes in your answers.

DON'T

☐ Add to the information in the passage.

☐ Re-write the question at the beginning of your answer; you should keep it as brief as possible.

☐ Be satisfied with only one point if more are possible, for example in *Why . . .?, How . . .?* or *What . . .?* questions.

☐ Try to define expressions as a dictionary would; you should explain them as they are used in the context.

☐ Forget to leave yourself time for the summary at the end.

---

a Read the following passage, then choose the best answers to the questions which follow it.

'To everything there is a season, and a time for every purpose under the heaven,' wrote Ecclesiastes. There was only one time when Amnesty could have been born, and that was in the exhilarating, brief springtime in the early Sixties, when after rebuilding the cities we set about reshaping the world.

Our hopes were encouraged by the fortuitous conjunction of three forward-looking world leaders, John F. Kennedy, Nikita Khrushchev and Giovanni Roncalli (John XXIII). As Dante had written, *'Mi sembrava un riso dell'universo'* (All nature seemed to wear an unusual smile). Amnesty's goal is to bring persecution to an end. Lofty idealism would not have brought support without the practical mode of operation suggested. This was based on a structure to adopt 'Prisoners of Conscience', the term was coined to describe those who neither advocated nor used violence but were imprisoned because their ideas, religion or race were unacceptable. Groups were to be formed which would adopt three 'Prisoners of Conscience', one from each of the three parts of the world.

There are now 3,600 groups in 55 countries. Adoption involves taking every reasonable step to secure the prisoner's release and in sending financial support to his dependants until his release and until his reintegration in his own country or one of asylum. In practice, these steps involve writing, and persuading 'opposite numbers' to write to anyone with influence in the imprisoning country, to the family and, of course, to give hope to the prisoner; time and time again released prisoners have testified that letter-writing campaigns have brought improvement in their conditions and sometimes their early release.

Amnesty's concern is never with a country's politics but only with the penal laws enforced to limit or crush freedom and with the torture and killings. Amnesty never seeks to intervene in the political or economic structures which each country must choose according to its tradition, philosophy or religion. But freedom to live in dignity without fear and to speak or worship without reprisals are the concern not of one culture but of the entire human race; they are as essential as the air we breathe, the food we eat or the water we drink.

It now has 500,000 members in more than 140 countries. There is no Government which does not take Amnesty seriously, though some occasionally use bitter words. And, most important of all, there is no Government that is today prepared either to admit or defend torture.

Yet if the horizon of freedom is brighter, the smoke from the fires of ethnic conflict pricks the eyes of humanity. Self-determination is the yeast of freedom. If the brow-beaten people of the Earth were rescued from their daily fear, terrorism would sink to insignificance. Given their situation, what have they to lose by setting off bombs?

If my renewed call against persecution finds an echo, the address and telephone number of Amnesty International is in the directories of most capital cities and of many towns. If other commitments preclude active participation, money (from any but governments and political parties) is needed for food parcels, for central investigation, for publication and for tracing and prosecuting torturers.

If the people of goodwill – of whom there are more in the world today than ever before – work together, we can and will stop persecution anywhere and everywhere.

Choose the best answer to each of these questions. Decide what is wrong with the other two answers in each case.

1 Which prisoners does Amnesty International help?
a) Those against violence but persecuted for their ideas, beliefs or skin colour.
b) Those against violence but persecuted for their ideas, beliefs or skin colour, and those facing execution.
c) Non-violent ones subject to religious or racial discrimination.

2 What does the word *one* refer to on line 30?
a) release   b) reintegration   c) country

3 What expression could be used instead of *seeks to* on line 41?
a) looks for   b) asks for   c) tries to

4 How does the writer justify the activities of Amnesty groups in countries which are not their own?
a) Rights have no frontiers and are a basic human need.
b) Amnesty has members in nearly every country.
c) The writer justifies the activities of Amnesty groups in countries which are not their own as rights have no frontiers and are a basic human need.

5 Why does a country choose a particular political and economic system?
a) Because of its customs, thought or beliefs.
b) Because of internal and external pressures.
c) Because of its tradition, philosophy or religion.

6 Explain the phrase *the smoke from the fires of ethnic conflict pricks the eyes of humanity* on lines 56–58.
a) The damage caused by racial strife hurts our eyes.
b) Racial strife worries everyone.
c) We try to ignore racial strife.

7 What is meant by *Self-determination is the yeast of freedom* on lines 58–59?
a) Self-determination leads to freedom.
b) Self-determination is one aspect of freedom.
c) Freedom leads to self-determination.

8 Explain what the passage says about terrorism.
a) It would end if we stopped the oppression which makes people feel things could scarcely get worse.
b) Amnesty tries to stop it, but terrorism would hardly exist if we could end the constant oppression of people who feel that things could not get worse.
c) If people did not live under constant oppression, feeling that things could hardly get worse, terrorism would virtually disappear.

9 Give another phrase for *If other commitments preclude active participation*. (lines 67–68)
a) If you are a politician or party member.
b) If your beliefs are not compatible with Amnesty's.
c) If you are too busy to take part in Amnesty's work.

10 What should you do if you feel Amnesty is a good cause?
a) Join and attempt to change the political system in foreign countries.
b) Contact them; give practical help if you can but send money if you can't.
c) If you can't give practical help, send money for food, research, printed materials and action against torturers.

b) Now answer the following questions using the clues in brackets:

1 What does the word *springtime* (line 5) mean in the passage and why is it appropriate here? (*exhilarating/Sixties* – quotation at beginning)

2 When was Amnesty founded and why was that the best time to do so? (*could have been* – national and international situation)

3 What word or phrase could be used in place of *lofty* (line 15)? (contrast in the same sentence)

4 What was *based on a structure to adopt 'Prisoners of Conscience'* (lines 17–18)?

5 Give another expression for *coined* (line 18). ('*Prisoners of Conscience*' in inverted commas)

6 Explain the *steps* (line 30) that Amnesty takes. (not only after *in practice*, but also before)

7 What evidence is there that Amnesty has been successful? (end of fourth paragraph and part of the sixth)

8 What is meant by the word *crush* (line 40)? (Will it be weaker or stronger than *limit*?)

9 Why does the writer describe his call as *renewed* (line 64)? (beginning of text – use of the first person)

10 Explain the phrase *finds an echo* (lines 64–65). (What is the purpose of the reference to addresses and telephone numbers?)

151

LISTENING

1 Pre-listening

You are going to hear a discussion about computerised information and the privacy of the individual.

Discuss the following questions and then fill in the table with your own opinions.

	YES	NO	IT DEPENDS
1 Could computerised data be used by the state to form a complete picture *of* everyone?			
2 Does the state need this information to fight crime and terrorism?			
3 Do law-abiding citizens have anything to worry about?			
4 Should doctors ever reveal details about their patients?			
5 Does the financial system need records of people's transactions and credit ratings?			
6 Should records be kept of political extremists?			

2 While listening

a Listen and write down five of the sources of information mentioned.

Example:
The Police

b

Listen again and tick the speakers who agree with the following statements.

The speakers are:
1 Mark – a civil liberties spokesperson.
2 Stephen – a civil servant.
3 Amanda – a financial services executive.
4 Penny – an ordinary member of the public.

	1	2	3	4
1 Everyone has a right to privacy.				
2 Only criminals need to worry about computerised records.				
3 Computerised information ensures the efficient functioning of society?				
4 The public should know who holds information.				
5 Secretly held records could hold wrong information.				
6 Computerised records infringe individual liberty.				

Which of the speakers' views are closest to your own?

3 Post-listening

What expressions do the speakers use to interrupt? How do they avoid being interrupted?

INTERRUPTING AND COUNTERING INTERRUPTIONS

Here are some expressions you can use to interrupt someone or to avoid being interrupted.

1 Classifying

In which situations would you use the formal ones: when would you use the informal ones?

Interrupting formal → informal

If I might just come in/make a point here, . . .
I'd like to add something here, if I may, . . .
If I could make a point here, . . .
Sorry to interrupt but . . .
I'm sorry, but I don't think that . . .
Yes/OK/Right, but let me ask you . . .
Just/hold/hang on a minute/moment!, . . .
Now (you) listen to me!, . . .

Countering interruptions formal → informal

If I could explain that at the end, . . .
If you will allow me to continue, . . .
Just a moment, please, I won't be long, . . .
I'll deal with that point in a moment, . . .
If you'd just be patient, . . .
If you'll just listen!
Let me finish!
Don't butt in!

2 Reading for gist

Read the text 'Data Users' and say where you think it is taken from.

3 Role play

Work in pairs.

Student A
You suspect that Data Users have broken some of the Principles in ways that directly affect you. You have decided to speak to a representative of one of the organisations. Try to interrupt (on a falling tone at the end of a phrase or sentence).

Student B
You represent a Data User which has broken some of the Principles. Be very evasive and rather pompous, trying to avoid being interrupted.

Change roles when you have finished.

DATA USERS

How can you see what is held about you?

Write to Data Users – that's what the Act calls organisations or individuals who keep information about you on computer – and ask if they hold any personal data about you. They must reply to you.

What Data Users will give you

Data Users must:
- tell you if they hold any data about you,
- give you a copy of the information.

The Data Protection Principles
(Remember 'personal data' is information about you held on computer).
Computer users handling personal data must:
- obtain and process information lawfully.
- register the purposes for which they hold it.
- not use or disclose the information in a way contrary to those purposes.
- hold only information which is relevant and not excessive for the purposes.
- hold only accurate information and, where necessary, keep it up to date.
- not keep information longer than necessary.
- give individuals access to information about themselves and, where appropriate, correct or erase the information.
- take appropriate security measures.
If you suspect that any computer user has broken a Principle, you can complain to the Registrar who can investigate.

Will you always be able to see records about yourself?

There are a few exceptions to your right to subject access.
Some important exceptions concern data held for the purpose of:
- preventing or detecting crime
- catching or prosecuting offenders
- assessing or collecting tax or duty.
But the exceptions only apply if access to the data could hinder one of these purposes. Data Users have to be prepared to justify any decision to withhold data to the Registrar or to the Courts. Your right to see health and social work data may also be restricted. Data Users do not have to tell you that they are withholding data under an exemption. They may reply along the lines of 'I do not hold any personal data which I am required to reveal to you'. It may not always be clear whether information has been withheld. If you think information is being wrongly withheld, complain to the Registrar.

ORAL

1 Phonology – high key intonation

The pitch of the voice sometimes rises on a prominent syllable to express a contrast.

a Listen to the following from the LISTENING text and underline the high key words in the second sentence of each (shown in italics):

1 ... if you haven't broken the law you have nothing to fear ... *Well, that's not strictly true ...*

2 ... and therefore the police have access to it. *Now, you can make up your own mind from what you've heard tonight ...*

3 ... we need the information, it's it's ... *Could I, could I just for a second continue what I was saying ...*

What kind of contrast is expressed in each?

b Listen again and repeat the part in italics.

c Underline the high key words and syllables in the following and then practise each of them with your partner as part of dialogues.

1 ... the public should be more aware of these things.
Could I just change the subject slightly ...

2 ... but they will have some details on you, yes. It sounds as if they'll have an incredible amount to me.

3 ... so I'm glad you agree that access to records is vital ...
Wait a moment! I was talking about ...

STUDY SKILLS   DEFINING TERMS

Before discussing a statement, it helps to define the terms used.

Look at the following quotation.

We must accept some loss of freedom in the fight against terrorism. (Prime Minister)

☐ *We must* could refer to the:
1 government.
2 government and people.
3 people.

☐ the *loss of freedom* may be

for:
1 terrorists.
2 their sympathisers.
3 people identified with them.
4 more than one of these.
5 everyone.

in force:
1 until things improve.
2 until *the fight* is won.
3 indefinitely.

of:
1 speech.
2 association.
3 movement.
4 the right to remain silent.
5 a number of these and/or others.

from:
1 arbitrary arrest.
2 state surveillance and data usage.
3 searches of the person and property.
4 torture and execution.
5 more than one of these and/or others.

☐ *the fight* could be:
1 political.
2 social.
3 economic.
4 violent.
5 a number of these and/or others.

☐ *terrorism* might be directed against:
1 an ethnic, social, economic, political or religious elite.
2 a larger sector of society.
3 everyone.

Think about the questions below this statement:

The human rights record is worse in the East than in the West.

1 Which *human rights*?
2 Does *record* mean past, present or both?
3 Is *worse* used qualitatively, quantitatively or both?
4 Does *the East* just mean communism?
5 Does *the West* include past dictatorships?

Use the same approach with the terms in essay titles.

---

2 Discussion

Look at the quotation opposite. Before you discuss it, define the key terms in bold:

*'If **society fits** you **comfortably**, you call it **freedom**.'* ... (Robert Frost)

REVIEW

1 High key intonation

Reply to these comments using the words in brackets in high key:

... there is absolutely no cause for concern ...
(if I could)
I believe you had a bad time over there. (horrific)
There are no political prisoners in our jails. (hundreds)

2 Introductory there

Rewrite these sentences using *there*.
1 We had no-one to turn to.
2 We would like an official observer to the present.
3 A heated argument ensued.
4 Thousands of refugees poured into the camp.
5 It seems that nobody can suggest an answer.
6 It's impossible to say when steps will be taken.
7 Certain dangers to civil liberties have arisen.
8 What's the point of having unenforceable laws?

3 Adjective order

Imagine you are in prison in an oppressive country. How would the following look to you?

Use several adjectives in each case.

1 The cell and its furniture.
2 Your cell-mate.
3 The food.
4 The chief interrogator.
5 Your girlfriend/boyfriend during visits.
6 The countryside on the day of your release.

4 Infinitives as relatives

Rewrite these sentences using the infinitive with *to*.
1 The thing you should do is give a false name.
2 The last people who went there disappeared.
3 The only news which has come out is that he's well.
4 There's nothing we can do except wait and hope.
5 The only people who didn't know were the cardholders.
6 The worst cases that have been verified were the attacks on civilians.
7 Data which will be held may be accessed by the police.
8 There's just one way we can fight back.
9 A fear that has been voiced is the misuse of information by employers.
10 The document everyone should read is the *Universal Declaration of Human Rights*.

5 Vocabulary

Put the following expressions from this unit into **category a**, **b** or **c**. (See STUDY SKILLS on page 17.)

scourge   unwavering   take precedence over   sheer   misguided   widespread   mayhem   heartening   to fall short of   to overwhelm   flogging   to indulge in   to reshape   brow-beaten   to trace   persecution   prosecution   to disclose   to hinder   to withhold   along the lines of

6 Interrupting

Choose one of the following statements, define the key terms with your partner and discuss it using expressions from **5 Vocabulary**.
If you feel he or she is not keeping to the agreed definition, or talking too much, try to interrupt using high key intonation.

Your partner should try to avoid being interrupted if he or she thinks you are being unreasonable.

1 All murderers should be executed.
2 Those whose ultimate aim is the suppression of free speech should not themselves be allowed that right.
3 Only those who have something to hide will not welcome these essential data-collection measures.

7 Essay

Define the key terms in this title and write a balanced composition of about 350 words:

'Well-meaning but naive human rights campaigners should not meddle in the internal affairs of sovereign states.' Discuss.

8 Now do the Progress Test for Unit 14 on page 190.

UNIT 15 TALKING MONEY

excruciatingly? } very embarassing

embarassing }

READING

1 The topic

In groups, discuss the following quotations:

> Money doesn't talk, it swears.
> (BOB DYLAN)

> Money is better than poverty if only for financial reasons.
> (WOODY ALLEN)

2 Before reading

Look at the subheadings in the text. What do you think the source, purpose and content of the text will be?

> When I was young I used to think that money was the most important thing in my life; now I am old, I know it is. (OSCAR WILDE)

> Money can't buy friends but you can get a better class of enemy. (SPIKE MILLIGAN)

_____(1), investing in the Stock Market has meant going against their principles.

_____(2), there are over 900 unit trusts to choose from.

_____(3) there was no single unit trust which specialised in investing in companies whose products, services and operations actually benefit the community.

_____(4), many people opted for putting their money into building societies or bank deposit accounts.

There it earns a safe, but modest return.

_____(5), the Stewardship Unit Trust now offers you an alternative means of putting your money to work.

How to Invest for Profit Without Lowering Your Standards

_____(6) carefully selecting and monitoring the companies in which we invest, The Stewardship Unit Trust has successfully bridged the gap between financial gain and social obligation.

The Trust aims to invest, as far as practicable, in companies whose products or services make a positive and healthy contribution to society.

_____(7), we do not invest in companies involved in the arms trade or gambling.

_____(8), we make every effort to avoid investing in the tobacco industry, in alcohol, and in countries with dictatorships or oppressive regimes.

We seek out companies with healthy track records in labour relations, pollution control and environmental protection.

_____(9) these broader considerations, the objectives of the Trust are to achieve long term capital appreciation and increasing income.

Just how successful this approach has been can be seen from the results:

_____(10) its start on June 1st 1984 the value of the investments in The Stewardship Unit Trust has grown to over £56 million.

It must be stressed that the price of units, and the income from them, can go down as well as up, and past experience is not necessarily any guide to future growth or rate of return.

_____(11), we believe that investing in companies with enlightened managements can often pay better dividends than investing in 'profit only' companies.

A Proven Approach

_____(12) 'socially sensitive investment' is relatively new in Britain.

In the United States, it has been available for more than a decade.

_____(13), results show that investing in 'socially concerned' companies, both large and small, often gives a better return than investing in the general market.

_____(14) concerned companies are usually operated by diligent and concerned managements and this shows up in their robust financial performance.

Experienced People Looking After Your Kind of Investment

The trust is run by experienced Investment Managers who care about your financial investment. They receive overall guidance from a Committee of Reference who scrupulously research the suitability of companies in which the Trust invests.

There are two types of units available: Distribution Units which give the investor a half-yearly income in cash, and Accumulation Units which automatically reinvest your income and thereby increase the value of your holding. The price of both types of unit may go up or down so should be considered as longer term investments.

Find Out More

_____(15) full details on the Stewardship Unit Trust and how you can invest, phone Friends' Provident Unit Trust Managers Limited.

roulett wheel

156

3 While reading

Read the text opposite and fill in the blanks with the following expressions:

At the same time   But   By   For
For example   For many people   Nevertheless
Not surprisingly   Since   Subject to
Thankfully   There   True
We admit that   We further believe that

4 Reading for detail

Answer the following using the clues below each question.

1 What made many people invest in building societies and banks? (See lines 1–2 and 5–8)
2 What are the main objectives of the Trust? (Lines 22–24 and 34–36)
3 Why should 'companies with enlightened managements' (47) be better investments? (Lines 59–62)
4 What are 'profit only' (49) companies?
5 What is meant by 'concerned companies' (59)? (Lines 23–24 and 25–26)
6 Who decides where your money is invested and how the companies are chosen? (Lines 66–70)
7 Why is it important for investors to realise that units 'may go up or down' (42–45)? (Lines 75–78)

5 Responding to the text

Consider these observations on 'ethical investments'.

☐ Fund management companies want to break into a new market, ie people who have not invested in the Stock Market before.
☐ If gambling is immoral could it not be argued that investing in the Stock Market is in itself gambling?
☐ In both the US and UK ethical trusts have generally been more successful than 'general market' funds; this remained the case after the October 1987 crash.
☐ Companies can legally keep details of overseas subsidiaries secret; the trusts and their unit holders may not know where their money is being invested.

6 Register

Match the following expressions from the text (in italics) with the definitions a)–f) below:

1 *unit trusts* (5)   2 *building societies* (10)
3 *capital appreciation* (36)   4 *rate of return* (45)
5 *dividends* (48)   6 *holding* (74)

a) Percentage of profits paid to shareholders.
b) Increase in value of assets.
c) Percentage interest received from an investment.
d) Group of shares owned.
e) Organisations which invest in stocks and shares on behalf of small investors.
f) British financial institution that pays interest on deposits and lends money for house purchase.

7 Transformation

For each of these phrases and sentences from the text, write a new one as similar as possible in meaning to the original, but using the word given in bold.

1 True, there are over 900 unit trusts to choose from. (3)
choice
_____

2 How to invest for profit without lowering your standards. (16–17)
principles
_____

3 Just how successful this approach has been can be seen from the results. (37–38)
show
_____

4 We admit that 'socially sensitive investment' is relatively new in Britain. (51–52)
novelty
_____

5 The Trust is run by experienced Investment Managers . . . (65–66)
charge
_____

8 Text organisation

List the lines of the text that refer to *conscience*, those referring to *profit* and those which refer to both. What kind of pattern do you notice?
Why do you think the text has been organised in this way?

PRACTICE

1 Phrasal verbs

Many compound nouns are formed from phrasal verbs by attaching the adverb or preposition to the beginning or end of the verb.

Example:
*money which **comes in** = income*

Complete the sentences below using the prompts given.

Example:
The government has blocked the proposed takeover.
Our company has been taken over by a multinational.

1 She announced the breakup of the huge conglomerate.
'The huge conglomerate has ____ *broken up*', she announced.
2 The firm was sold at a giveaway price.
The price was too low, the firm ____ *gave away*.
3 The poor figures were due to an accounting slip-up.
The accountant ____ *slipped up* and made the figures look worse than they were.
4 Lack of demand has brought about factory shutdowns.
Factories have had ____ *shut down* because of lack of demand.
5 The unexpected rise in inflation is seen as a setback to progress.
Progress ____ *set back* the unexpected rise in inflation.
6 Major cutbacks in capital expenditure are foreseen.
We forecast the need to ____ *cut back* considerably.
(2 possibilities)

2 Gerund and infinitive

Here are some more forms which can be followed by either the infinitive or the gerund.

love, hate and *prefer* can take both in most cases.

Example:
I love to dabble/dabbling on the stock market.

But they tend to take the infinitive when referring to a single occasion.

Example:
I hate to bring this up, but I must tell you now.

In comparative sentences, *prefer* should be followed by the gerund.

Example:
They prefer taking risks to settling for modest returns.

mean with the infinitive means 'intend', while with the gerund it means 'involve' or 'entail'.

Examples:
We mean to take them over by acquiring a block of shares.
Taking them over means acquiring a block of shares.

afraid to do something and *afraid of doing* something are usually interchangeable, but for unexpected and unwelcome events the gerund is used.

Example:
We're afraid of losing our savings; who knows what might happen in world markets?

interested to is used for events which have already happened, whereas *interested in* refers to (possible) future actions.

Examples:
I was interested to see that prices rose after the sale.
I'm interested in buying stock.

sorry to refers to the present or immediate future, while *sorry for* is used for the past.

Examples:
Sorry to bring bad news, but I must tell you . . .
Sorry for bringing bad news, but I had to tell you . . .

certain to, or *sure to* means 'definitely', but *certain/ sure of* refers to what somebody (maybe mistakenly) thinks is definite.

Examples:
He is certain/sure to make a fortune as their value has already trebled.
He was certain/sure of making a fortune but then their gains were suddenly wiped out.

a Read the following text and choose the correct form of the verb in brackets, adding the appropriate preposition where necessary:

> Investigators said they were interested (speak) to the broker who was paid $10m for his advice. This would mean (liaise) with their Wall St counterparts. It is felt that he is likely to prefer (hand) over his records to (fight) court injunctions ordering him to do so.
>
> He has said that although he hated (reveal) information given to him in confidence, something he had never done before, and was sorry (harm) ILF's reputation, he had already cooperated as he was afraid (damage) his own firm's standing.
>
> The growing scandal seems certain (lead) to a drop in takeover activity on both sides of the Atlantic.

b Complete the following sentences using an infinitive or a gerund:
1 As stockbrokers, we love _____ prices constantly rising.
2 I meant _____ you know but I forgot.
3 I looked at the figures and was interested _____ that there had been a sharp rise.
4 I'm sorry _____ you but I'm afraid I can't.
5 They're sure of _____ cover their losses.
6 People are afraid _____ in equities after the recent big fall.

STUDY SKILLS DICTIONARY EXAMPLES

Good dictionaries give examples of words in context, either in an appendix, the entry itself or both. They show grammatical patterns in relatively simple language, which consists of expressions commonly used with the word you are looking up.

Examples:

risk VT
He risked his life savings trying to make a fortune.
I can't risk wasting any more money on this idea.

assist VT/VI formal
They assisted him to make the right decision.
She is assisting him in negotiating the deal.
We may be able to assist you with your financial planning.

For the next lesson, imagine you are writing to someone you do not know very well. This person has not paid you back some money you lent him or her. Study the examples in your dictionary of the verbs used in the letter and complete it with suitable linking words.

> Dear ....
>
> I do not enjoy ....
> .... I am not used to ....
> .... you promised ....
> ..... I am not accusing ....
> .... I do not like to keep ....
> .... I suggest ....
> .... I would much prefer .....
> .... if you agree ....
> .... I would rather avoid .... you to court,
> .... I regard this ....
> If you .... then I apologise ....
> ..... to you like this and look forward ....
>
> Yours sincerely,
> ....

159

WRITING

DESCRIBING CHARACTER

1 Text appreciation

Look at the following extracts from *The Quiet American* by Graham Greene and answer the questions below.

A | Pyle was very earnest and I had suffered from his lectures on the Far East, which he had known for as many months as I had years. Democracy was another subject of his – he had pronounced and aggravating views on what the United States was doing for the world.

B | He looked more than ever out of place: he should have stayed at home. I saw him in a family snapshot album, riding on a dude ranch, bathing on Long Island, photographed with his colleagues in some apartment on the twenty-third floor. He belonged to the skyscraper and the express elevator, the ice-cream and the dry Martinis, milk at lunch, and chicken sandwiches on the Merchant Limited.

C | Not that Pyle was very important. It wouldn't have done to cable the details of his true career, that before he died he had been responsible for at least fifty deaths, for it would have damaged Anglo-American relations, the Minister would have been upset. The Minister had a great respect for Pyle – Pyle had taken a good degree in – well, one of those subjects Americans can take degrees in: perhaps public relations or theatrecraft, perhaps even Far Eastern studies (he had read a lot of books).

D | Pyle was quiet, he seemed modest, sometimes that first day I had to lean forward to catch what he was saying. And he was very, very serious. Several times he seemed to shrink up within himself at the noise of the American Press on the terrace above – the terrace which was popularly believed to be safer from hand-grenades. But he criticized nobody.

E | Perhaps I should have seen that fanatic gleam, the quick response to a phrase, the magic sound of figures: Fifth Column, Third Force, Seventh Day. I might have saved all of us a lot of trouble, even Pyle, if I had realized the direction of that indefatigable young brain. But I left him with arid bones of background and took my daily walk up and down the Rue Catinat.

F | I wondered how Pyle over the years would stand that hard core, for Pyle was a romantic; but then of course in his case there would be a good settlement, the hardness might soften like an unused muscle when the need for it vanished. The rich had it both ways.

G | All the time that his innocence had angered me, some judge within myself had summed up in his favour, had compared his idealism, his half-baked ideas founded on the works of York Harding, with my cynicism. Oh, I was right about the facts, but wasn't he right too to be young and mistaken, and wasn't he perhaps a better man for a girl to spend her life with?

1 Which extract indicates the narrator's nationality?
2 Which imply that he is poorer than Pyle?
3 Which extracts probably came first and last in time?
4 Which implies regret about the past?
5 Which phrase in F is a simile?
6 Which extract focuses on Pyle's education?
7 Which refers to his social background?
8 Which phrases in G are metaphors?
9 Which extract expresses irritation with Pyle?
10 Which implies a certain admiration for him?
11 In which extract does the narrator attempt to be objective?
12 Which extracts are written partly in an informal style?
13 Which extract is the most cynically expressed?
14 Give the opposites of these words, as they are used in the extracts:

   a) *earnest, aggravating* (A)
   b) *quiet, modest, serious* (D)
   c) *indefatigable* (E)
   d) *romantic* (F)
   e) *innocence, cynicism* (G)

2 Description

In about 150 words, describe someone you've met who is very different from Pyle. Think about:

First impressions

Examples:
. . . (one of) the most . . . I've ever met.
She seemed/looked as if . . .
He gave the impression of being . . .

Personality

The *qualities* on page 112, those you added, their opposites and the adjectives formed from them.

Influences

Family, educational, social and economic background.

Idiosyncrasies

Examples:
She's always . . . -ing . . .
He'd never dream of . . . -ing . . .
I've never known her to . . .
The (more) he . . . the (less) he . . .

If you have read one of the prescribed texts thoroughly, and enjoyed it, you may wish to answer question 5 of the **Composition** paper and discuss the book during the **Interview**.

Essay titles usually focus on one, or possibly two, of the following:

1 the plot.
2 the theme.
3 characters.
4 an event.
5 the writer's style.
6 the setting.
7 objects.
8 the writer.
9 a quotation from the text.
10 your response.

a Match each of the above with these past Proficiency essay titles:

   a) Shakespeare – *Macbeth*
       Give some examples of the ways in which the special atmosphere of this play is created.
   b) Scott Fitzgerald – *The Great Gatsby*
       What does this novel tell us about American life in the 1920s?
   c) Jane Austen – *Persuasion*
       Why does Captain Wentworth eventually marry Anne and not Louisa?
   d) George Eliot – *Silas Marner*
       Explain the part played by gold in *Silas Marner*.
   e) Robert Graves – *Goodbye To All That*
       'The First World War was a tragic story of waste and futility.'
       How does *Goodbye To All That* illustrate this statement?
   f) Margaret Drabble – *The Millstone*
       Why is the book called 'The Millstone'?
   g) Patricia Highsmith – *The Talented Mr Ripley*
       Do you agree that because we know who committed the murders there is no suspense or excitement in this novel?
   h) John Arden – *Serjeant Musgrave's Dance*
       What is Serjeant Musgrave's plan and why does it fail?
   i) John Osborne – *The Entertainer*
       What difference is there between Archie Rice on stage and Archie Rice at home?
   j) D.H. Lawrence – *Selected Tales*
       'One thing which Lawrence really understands is the suffering in women's lives.'
       Discuss how true you think this statement is in relation to two or three of the stories.

Follow the following guidelines for preparation and writing:

DO

☐ make notes under headings 1–10 above as you read.
☐ look up expressions if the context does not help and they are essential for overall understanding.
☐ discuss aspects of the book, such as the characters, with other people.
☐ read any published notes on it.
☐ try to see a theatre or film version and compare it with the book.
☐ read the book again just before the examination.
☐ read the question carefully and underline the key words.
☐ use your descriptive, discursive and narrative writing skills, where appropriate, to maximum effect.
☐ interpret the meaning of the text and illustrate this with examples and quotations.

DON'T

☐ spend too much time on the book if your work in other language areas is likely to suffer.
☐ choose question 5 in the examination if it seems more difficult than other titles.
☐ refer to other books, whether or not they are by the same author.
☐ state the obvious by using phrases such as 'James Joyce is a well-known writer'.
☐ include irrelevant quotations just because you have memorised them.
☐ write quotations at all if you can't remember them exactly.
☐ misspell the author's name, the title or the names of the characters.
☐ repeat yourself, especially in the conclusion.
☐ leave yourself short of time for the other essay; the marks given are the same for both.

b Basing your answer on your reading of one of your prescribed texts, answer one of the following (in about 350 words).

1 What part does money play in the text?
2 'This novel must have been written from personal experience.' How true do you think this is?
3 How relevant is the text's message to the 1990s?
4 Describe a major event in the story and its consequences.
5 What does the text tell us about young people's attitudes in the place and at the time it was set?
6 How do you account for the text's continuing popularity?

LISTENING

1 Pre-listening

For each of the comments 1–8 below, choose one of these words to describe your reaction:

amused	angry	irritated
bored	complacent	delighted
incredulous	disapproving	disgusted
enthusiastic	resigned	surprised
contemptuous		

1 Young people nowadays are only interested in money.
2 Money-making is a basic human instinct.
3 Money and sex are two of men's favourite topics of conversation.
4 People should be proud of becoming rich by hard work.
5 Human nature is essentially cooperative, not competitive.
6 Free market economics bring about a freer society.
7 Economic growth merely increases the demand for imports.
8 Society is contemptuous of those who are not competitive.

'But I thought they built the M25 so we wouldn't have to see that sort of thing'.

2 While listening

a Listen and decide whether the following statements are true or false.

From the tones of voice used by the speakers, we can infer that:
1 from the outset, the speakers dislike each other.
2 the man feels he is superior to the woman.
3 the woman finds the subject boring.
4 they gradually become more relaxed.
5 the man is better informed about the subject.
6 the woman feels intimidated.
7 the woman thinks the man is a liar.
8 in the end they understand each other better.

b Look back at comments 1–8 in Pre-Listening and in the table below. Listen for the expressions below.
   1 Write the appropriate word from the list in Pre-listening which best describes the attitude of the speaker.

COMMENT	WORDS USED	ATTITUDE
1	*Oh really, that's not true at all!*	incredulous
2	*Look, taboos perform . . .*	
3	*Well, be that as it may . . .*	
4	*Oh, nonsense! . . .*	
5	*I'm sorry, I have to disagree.*	
6	*I don't know how . . .*	
7	*Oh no, for goodness sake . . .*	
8	*I don't think that's true . . .*	

3 Post-listening

Discuss the economic trends in your country, making your attitudes clear by your tone of voice.

FUNCTIONS

EXPRESSING SURPRISE, IRRITATION AND ANGER

1 Classifying

a Match the mainly informal expressions below with the following headings and complete the sentences as examples.

  a) SURPRISE
  b) IRRITATION
  c) ANGER

  1 You're forever/constantly ... + -ing ...
  2 Who'd ever have imagined that ...!
  3 They will (every time) ...
  4 This is starting to really + verb ...
  5 I'd never've guessed that ...!
  6 You just ... (all the time).
  7 I'm fed up with/sick of + noun/-ing ...
  8 Surely they can't have + past part ...?
  9 He keeps (on)/never stops ... + -ing ...
  10 Now look here, you + (adj +) noun, ...
  11 Fancy ... + -ing ...!
  12 Why do they have to ...?
  13 I've just about had enough of + noun/ing ...
  14 If ... hadn't + past part ... I wouldn't ...
  15 Why don't you just + verb ... (and + verb) ...

b Reply to the following comments using some of the expressions above.

  1 Hey! You've won first prize in the lottery!
  2 I'm sorry, but you know I don't get paid till Friday.
  3 You've just got another parking ticket!
  4 She says she's bored stiff, as usual.
  5 He's been left a fortune by an aunt he's never even met!
  6 All you think of is money. Now back in the Sixties ...
  7 We'll give you the loan, but at 95% monthly interest.
  8 The phone bill's gone up again.
  9 I didn't tell you, but I've got my own plane.
  10 Look, I've told you – foreigners pay double to come in.

2 Role play

Work in pairs.

Student A
You are the male speaker from LISTENING. Continue the dialogue by expressing your feelings about the information in the pie chart and the other speaker's point of view.

Student B
You are the female speaker from LISTENING. Continue the dialogue by expressing your feelings about the information in the pie chart and the other speaker's point of view.

Change roles when you have finished.

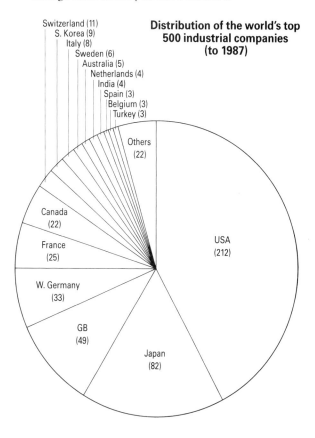

Distribution of the world's top 500 industrial companies (to 1987)

Switzerland (11)
S. Korea (9)
Italy (8)
Sweden (6)
Australia (5)
Netherlands (4)
India (4)
Spain (3)
Belgium (3)
Turkey (3)
Others (22)
Canada (22)
France (25)
W. Germany (33)
GB (49)
USA (212)
Japan (82)

ORAL

1 Phonology – Elision and linking

In rapid, less formal speech, certain sounds which you would expect to be pronounced are missed out.

a Listen to these extracts from Units 10, 14 and 16. Follow the transcript and cross out the consonants that are omitted from the words in italic.
The first one has been done as an example.

1 under a *communist* system
2 frequently performed *acts*
3 as far as I'm *concerned* Penny
4 I'd *just* like to
5 who's always *going to* be straight
6 you've *got to* let people go

Now read the extract aloud quickly to your partner.

2 Interview

Photograph

With your partner, choose two of the people who are talking to each other and using your imagination, discuss:

1 the first impressions they give you.
2 what their backgrounds might be.
3 what their characters might be like.
4 how each person is likely to react to the other.
5 what emotions they are probably expressing.

Now roleplay the conversation with the person your partner has chosen.

Give marks for; *vocabulary*, particularly descriptive expressions; *pronunciation* of individual sounds, especially those at the ends of words.

Reading passage

The purpose of this text is to report. But it also contains the message: 'The very rich are very mean.'

> Harry and Leona Helmsley, who are worth $1.4 billion and own the Empire State Building, have been accused of leaving unpaid car rental bills and of demanding 'free goods and services' from contractors.

Read the following passages.
What could be asked about their contents?
What is the message of each one?

> 1 The Ministry of Agriculture gave the World Rabbit Association £24 last year. But despite exhaustive searches through the Ministry no trace could be found of the organisation.
>
> 2 Commenting on her brother's bequest of all his money to the government, Mrs Daphne Stamp said, 'Wilfred Chinner was a complete fool. He left £90,000 to help pay off the national debt which is £185 billion.'
>
> 3 A street mugging ended with a new twist yesterday when the victim's stolen wallet was returned intact. The victim was continuing his walk home when the muggers caught up with him, returned his wallet and said, 'Sorry mate, wrong bloke.'
>
> 4 The latest fashion appears to be prison-made shirts which can sell for up to £25 each. They are wanted so much by the fashion-conscious that two men staged a raid on Sudbury Prison, Derbyshire, to steal six striped shirts.

Discuss

What is the connection between the messages of texts 1 and 2, and between texts 3 and 4?

164

REVIEW

1 Elision and linking

a Listen to these extracts from the listening tape. Cross out the consonants you do not hear in the words in italics.

1 he poured *cold* water on the idea
2 I was very *pleased* with it
3 but it *disrupts* everything!
4 they *asked* for three
5 does he *want to* come or not?

Read the extract to your partner.

b Look back at extracts 1–4 on the previous page and those above. Which letter do the 'missing' consonants often follow?

2 Gerund and infinitive

Tell your partner about the following:
1 what you hate/love/prefer doing/to do in class, and one activity you prefer doing to another.
2 anything you're afraid to do/of doing.
3 something you mean to do this week.
4 what is certain/sure to happen before the year 2000.
5 things in the past, present or future which you should apologise for.
6 what someone you both know is certain/sure of doing – but about which you are more sceptical.
7 what passing the Proficiency exam will mean doing.
8 things you are interested in doing after you've passed.

3 Vocabulary

a Finish each of the following sentences using the compound noun form of the verb in **bold**.

Example:
What's **held** the merger **up** for so long?
Why . . .
*Why has there been a **hold-up** in the merger?*

1 Didn't the entire staff **walk out**?
   Wasn't there . . . ?
2 Will someone be **standing in** for you while you're away?
   Will you . . . ?
3 Is stock still **building up**?
   Is there . . . ?
4 Did many shareholders **turn out** for the meeting?
   Was there . . . ?
5 We'll be **getting together** at my place soon.
   We'll . . . .
6 The company has been **taken over**.
   There has . . .

b Put the following expressions from this unit into **category a, b** or **c**. (See STUDY SKILLS on page 17.)

to opt for	track record	to bridge the gap
enlightened	long term	to accord with
counterpart	injunction	it wouldn't do to
aggravating	gleam	half-baked
hard core	rampant	to trickle down
urge	a new twist	subject to
mugging	to stage	to catch up with

4 Surprise, irritation and anger

What would you say in the following situations? Use expressions from **3 Vocabulary** and speak quickly, eliding and linking consonants where appropriate.

1 You've had your brakes repaired but the garage has done such a bad job that you've had to take the car back. This time the bill is even bigger.
2 Whenever you go out in the evening, one of your friends manages to find an excuse to leave just before it's his/her turn to pay for a round of drinks.
3 Looking through a catalogue, you suddenly realise that some of the stamps you collected as a child are now worth a small fortune.
4 A group of older people you know seem to spend half their time reminiscing about the 'good old days' of the alternative society, and the other half boasting about how much they've made out of house-price rises.
5 You're in the middle of a crowd when suddenly you notice that someone is trying to pick your pocket. You grab his arm just in time.
6 You know somebody who is rich, famous and who you think is the most attractive person you've ever met. One day you get a letter saying that he or she feels the same way about you.

5 Essay

Think of a novel you have read (in English or your first language) which is written in the first person singular. In about 200 words, describe the narrator's character from the point of view of someone else in the story.

6 Now do the Progress Test for Unit 15 on page 191.

READING

1 The topic

a Look at the people in the photographs. Why was each person successful? What did each do personally to achieve success?

b What are your aims in life?
How will you use your intelligence to achieve them?

2 Before reading

Look at the title and sub-title of the text. In what way do you think the article will be interesting?

3 While reading

Read the text quickly. How does the writer answer the question in the first sentence?

He looks very intense. He's raising his eyebrows.
furrow - grooven/broken on his brow (read)

bulbous - kauba toe

PERSPIRATION BEATS INSPIRATION

Geniuses may be made rather than born. But dilettantes will lose out – only people with an obsessive interest in a subject have a chance to turn intelligence into genius.

MICHAEL HOWE

A Can anybody be a genius? After investigating the causes of exceptional abilities, I am no longer so sure that the correct answer is an unequivocal 'No'. What strikes us most forcibly about people of genius is how different they are from everyone else. Their brilliance is dazzling: their exceptional powers of creativity make them seem like a race apart, not only superior but inherently superior to other people. But a preoccupation with the sheer extraordinariness of outstanding individuals can be counterproductive. It forms as obstacle to understanding excellence, and hinders our efforts to explain how a few people become capable of remarkable achievements.

B   Take the case of Mozart, a genius if ever there was one. Even as a young child, according to some accounts, he was not only a brilliant performer, but also an accomplished composer. The conclusion that the cause of his achievement lay in powers that were innately exceptional seems inescapable. Surely, someone like that must have been born with special gifts or talents. Yet a closer examination of Mozart's life suggests otherwise. It establishes that, as Thomas Edison put it, there is no substitute for hard work, not even for as dazzling a creative genius as Mozart. Even the abilities that underlie the greatest human achievements are acquired, not inherent. For example, Mozart produced none of his lasting compositions until the twelfth year of his musical career. During those 12 long years of hard training, music was his whole life.

to raise - to run
It's head and shoulders picture.—
I didn't catch that – Statiepeie! Could you put it in another way?

4 Reading for detail

Answer the following, in your own words where possible, using the clues below each question.

1 Why do geniuses *seem like a race apart* (7)?
   (See lines 5–9 and 40–45)
2 What is meant by *hinders* (12)?
   (Lines 11–14)
3 What is implied about Mozart's childhood compositions in the second paragraph?
   (Lines 16–18 and 28–30)
4 Give an alternative expression for *mastering the craft* (37).
   (Lines 30 and 32–34)
5 Explain the expression *innately talented* (52).
   (Lines 18–22)
6 What is the part played by *luck and chance* (57)?
   (Lines 57–63)

5 Responding to the text

a Note down the factors which play a part in outstanding achievement and compare notes with your partner.

b How could they be applied in practice in your own career?

6 Sentence completion

Complete each of the blanks with a suitable word or phrase from the paragraph indicated in brackets.

1 She got it done in the end, just by ____ hard work. (A)
2 You can't deny that ____ a success story, that was it. (B)
3 I don't believe it! ____ you haven't done it already? (B)
4 You can make it. If anyone ____, ignore them. (B)
5 Everything will need to ____ drastic changes if we are to get ahead. (C)
6 While doubts may have existed in the past ____ they have now got their priorities right. (E)
6 Though we differ in our methods we are ____ believing that the aim is sound. (F)

7 Transformation

Complete each of the following sentences so that it is as similar as possible in meaning to the sentence in the text.

Example:
Lines 3–4
It . . .
It is how different they are from everyone else that strikes us most forcibly about people of genius.

1 Lines 28–30
   For example, not until . . .
2 Lines 35–37
   Every composer . . .
3 Lines 37–39
   Neither . . .
4 Lines 46–49
   Only . . .
5 Lines 57–61
   No-one . . .

C   An analysis of the early careers of 70 eminent composers showed that they all had to undergo a similarly long period of arduous musical education. No composer has created a great work of music without having dedicated at least 10 years to mastering the craft. There are no short cuts to genius, either in music or in any other field of endeavour.

D   However, the belief that individuals of genius are set firmly apart from ordinary people persists – perhaps because it is so hard to imagine how anyone without extraordinary powers could be capable of the most remarkable of all human achievements.

E   People can acquire special abilities, but only after a lengthy period of training and there is every reason to suppose that the same is true of those people who create works of genius. Conversely, there is no reason to decide that an exceptional intellectual feat justifies the belief that the person who performs it must be innately talented. There also seems to be almost no limit to what most people are capable of achieving, if their experiences of life and their opportunities for learning are rich enough.

F   What causes a person to produce works of genius? The contribution of luck and chance appears to be too substantial for anyone to possess the kind of knowledge about the causes of genius that would make precise predictions about particular individuals possible. Similar reasons rule out the possibility of deliberately manufactured geniuses. At the same time, it is worth noting that people accepted as geniuses are alike in being intelligent and knowledgeable (as we would expect), and that they are single-minded, often to the point of obsession.

PRACTICE

1 Phrasal verbs: passive use

Compare the following active and passive sentences:

Similar reasons rule that possibility out.
That possibility is ruled out for similar reasons.
Their genius sets such individuals firmly apart from ordinary people.
Such individuals are set firmly apart from ordinary people by their genius.

Complete these sentences then change them to the passive form.

Example:
Unforeseen difficulties have held the project ____.
a) *Unforeseen difficulties have held the project up.*
b) *The project has been held up by unforeseen difficulties.*

1 Haven't they worked a solution ____ yet?
2 If it looks as if it'll work, you should try it ____.
3 They turned massive losses ____ consistent profits.
4 How can she follow her triumph ____?
5 They shared the rations ____ as fairly as possible.
6 Only a genius could've thought an idea like that ____.
7 To avoid publicity, we'd better play our victory right ____.
8 They put its growth ____ mainly ____ new innovations.

2 Conditionals

In more literary styles, the phrase on lines 54–55 of the READING text could be written:
. . . ***should*** *their experiences of life and their opportunities* ***be*** *rich enough.*

The contracted form is not possible in the negative:
. . . ***should*** *their experiences . . .* ***not be*** *rich enough.*

Similar forms include:

Were he to + *inf.* (literary) = If he were to + *inf.*
Had I + *past part.* = If I had + *past part.*
But for + *noun/pron.* = Without + *noun/pron.*
Were it not for + *noun/pron.* (literary)
= If it were not for + *noun/pron.* = Without
Had it not been for + *noun/pron.* (literary)
= If it had not been for + *noun/pron.* = Without

a Complete these sentences using the structures above:
1 Should . . . call again . . .
2 But for . . . from my family . . .
3 Had we . . . their advice . . .
4 Were I not . . . the prize . . .
5 Had it not . . . my perseverence . . .
6 Were it not . . . our teacher . . .
7 Were they . . . me the job . . .
8 Had I not . . . single-minded . . .
9 Should there . . . another recession . . .
10 Were there . . . no demand for my skills . . .

b Imagine you are writing your memoirs to date. Look back at the events 2–10 below and write a sentence for each.
1 a move to a new school/university/job

Example:
Had I not looked for the positive aspects, it would have been very depressing.

2 a cultural or sporting event in which you did not do as well as you had expected
3 an illness or accident
4 a difficulty overcome
5 money worries
6 an academic achievement
7 family problems
8 meeting somebody special
9 a relationship which did not work out
10 reaching Proficiency level in English

c Now imagine how you would cope with these or similar events if they were to occur in the future. Write six sentences.

168

1 General

Once you have completed stage 3 on page 103, you should:

☐ Work out a revision timetable – a certain number of hours per day – that allows you to study unhurriedly. Leave time for relaxation and do not include the day before the exam.

☐ Look back through the book and at all your notes. While you are doing so:
  – underline, or highlight, essential points.
  – draw vertical lines against important sections.
  – put an exclamation mark (!) against vital material.
  – put a question mark (?) against anything that needs checking.

☐ Work for two hours at a time, and on some days do three such sessions. This prolonged concentration will provide practice for the day of the written Papers.

☐ Do the final Test Paper in the Practice Book.

☐ Explain difficult points to other students, discuss them and listen to their explanations of other problem areas.

☐ Run quickly through everything you marked in the book and in your notes a few days before the examination.

2 Language areas

a Naturally, some areas will need more attention than others. Put these aspects of grammar in order of difficulty, as they seem to you:

. . . conditionals	. . . the subjunctive
. . . other verb tenses	. . . the passive
. . . word order	. . . reported speech
. . . linking words	. . . modal verbs
. . . relatives	. . . prepositions
. . . introductory *it/there*	. . . ellipsis
. . . phrasal verbs	. . . inverted forms
. . . verbs + *ger./*inf.	. . . other areas

b Now list the aspects of the following which you find the most difficult:

Phonology   Vocabulary   Style/Register

3 Individual items

When you need to check individual items, the table of contents and the index in the book will be very useful; as well the headings and sub-headings in your notes.

Look at the following questions and write the answers. Then, check them.

1 Complete the tense sequence:
   I'm really enjoying myself – it's the first time . . .
2 You're listening to a friend telling a story. What expressions would you use to encourage him or her to continue?
3 What is the meaning of *at* in this sentence?
   She wondered at her own meteoric rise to the top.
4 Is the preposition in this sentence correct?
   We spent a week at Paris.
   Why/Why not?
5 What is a *unit trust*?
6 Underline the stressed words in this sentence:
   It was the last day of the race and we were first in a field of twenty-five.
7 Put these adjectival forms in the correct order:
   A car/grey/Japanese/slim phone.
8 You've been asked by the Examiner what you think of a book you've read. You enjoyed it; what would you say?
9 How could you begin the last paragraph of a discursive essay, apart from writing *finally*?
10 You can't remember the word *guilty*. What would you ask your partner(s)?
11 What can you predict from this introduction?
   You will hear a radio programme in which the 'person of the year' is interviewed.
12 Is it correct to separate the two parts of this verb?
   *They **rewarded** him **for** his bravery.*
   Why/Why not?
13 Complete this sentence:
   So quickly . . . make an impact . . . he was promoted.
14 Write out this sentence:
   /ɪt wəz tə hɪm ən ɪz brʌðə juː ʃʊd əv sent ðəm/

4 Skills

To improve your language skills further:
☐ Read anything that is of interest to you.
☐ Listen to radio programmes.
☐ Write about your hobbies and interests, trying out new ideas.
☐ Speak to anyone you can.

1 Beginnings and Endings

The opening sentences of a narrative/descriptive essay should create an initial interest in the story, while the aim of the closing sentences is to make readers think about what they have just read.

a Look at the following techniques and match them with the jumbled examples 1–10 below.

Beginnings

a) Describing the background.
b) Making a provocative statement.
c) Arousing interest in the plot.
d) Arousing interest in a character.
e) Relating to the reader's own experiences.

Endings

f) Adding a twist to the story.
g) Linking to the introduction.
h) Giving an explanation.
i) Leaving a mystery unsolved.
j) Raising a moral issue.

---

1 And when she at last plucked up the courage to open that door, what she saw was beyond anything she had even remotely imagined.

2 The monitor showed clearly what was in his hand luggage, yet the security man seemed not to notice.

3 So that was it then. All along, they'd watched, waited and kept their hands clean. Once we'd taken out the local dealers they would quietly move in.

4 You've probably thought a thousand times that it couldn't happen to you. This was my thousand and first.

5 In a way, then, that peaceful summer's evening was to become the background to a chain of events that would change my lifestyle out of all recognition.

6 But did he really have to drag his wife and children down with him, while others feathered their architect-designed nests, just to prove he was a man of principle?

7 If there were two ways of doing something, Tanya instinctively chose the illegal one.

8 It was one of those mornings when the clouds looked as if they had been washed in the *ordinary* soap powder from the TV ads.

9 I'd always thought the terms 'military intelligence' were mutually exclusive; now I'd got the proof.

10 Yet something still troubled him. Hadn't he been there when they shot him? Hadn't he also witnessed, from a respectful distance, the burial and the genuine sorrow on the faces of friends and family? In that case, who had sent the coded message *ten days later*?

---

homework

b Write a story entitled *If at first you don't succeed, try, try again*. Use the questions as prompts and add your own beginning and ending. The answers to the questions must be contained within the text. *350 words 1 hour*

Paragraph 1

Where did the action take place?

Paragraph 2

What did he/she look like?
What sort of person was he/she?
Who else was involved?

Paragraph 3

What did he/she want to do?
What was going on while he/she tried?
Why did he/she fail?

Paragraph 4

Why did he/she try again?
What added complications were there?
How did he/she look, before and after succeeding?

Paragraph 5

Had he/she failed this time, what would have happened?

c Now give your essay to your partner and get him or her to answer the questions.

d Write a similar set of questions as an essay framework. Your partner should write the story for homework.

Tick the points which already form part of your approach.

General
- Read the instructions very carefully – don't assume they will be the same as on previous papers. ☐
- Write in the time you've allocated next to each section, title or question. (Not Paper 4) ☐
- Do the simpler questions first – don't get stuck and fail to reach some you could have done easily. ☐
- Leave time for checking and clarify anything which is illegible. ☐
- Make sure you have spelt words which appear in texts, questions and instructions correctly. (Not Paper 1) ☐

Paper 1 – Reading Comprehension
- In *Section A*, imagine the situation in which the sentence is spoken. (Also *Section A* of Paper 3) ☐
- Always choose one of the alternatives – wrong answers are not penalised. (Also Paper 4) ☐
- One mark is given for each correct answer in *Section A*, two marks in *Section B* – spend more time on the latter. ☐

Paper 2 – Composition
- You're writing for a reader, not a computer, so make your essays interesting and entertaining. ☐
- Don't aim for perfection in one essay at the expense of the other – the marks required to reach pass standard are much easier to get than those higher up the scale. ☐

- If it should happen that your mind 'goes blank' when you look at the question, underline the key words and note down anything connected with the title – then you'll have got started. ☐

Paper 3 – Use of English
Section A:
- As it carries more marks, allow more time for this part than *Section B*. ☐
- Never give more than one answer; both must be right for the mark to be awarded. ☐
- Write what you can for each item; marks may be given for part of the correct answer. ☐

Section B:
- If you decide to add an extra point, put an asterisk* where it should go and write it at the end next to another *. (Also Paper 2) ☐
- If you are running out of time write in note form, particularly in the summary. ☐

Paper 4 – Listening Comprehension
- If you have any practical difficulties, e.g. you cannot hear the recording properly, tell the invigilators immediately. ☐
- Look at the questions for each part before you listen to it; there won't be time to look at the whole test before the tape begins and there is no common theme anyway. ☐
- When each piece begins, make sure you're looking at the right page. ☐
- Only $\frac{1}{2}$ a mark is given for True/False, Yes/No and other 'alternative' questions; spend less time on these. ☐

How many did you score?
If you totalled 16 or more, you have most of the Exam Skills needed for success.

LISTENING

1 Pre-listening

You will hear a conversation between two people, Ivanka and Vicent who recently passed Proficiency.

(The woman) speaks and writes fluently, and when she is reading or listening to English finds it easy to get the general idea without understanding every expression. Nevertheless, she does tend to make mistakes when speaking or writing, and sometimes misses specific points when she reads or listens.

(The man) has studied grammar and phonology carefully, and has a wide vocabulary reflecting his frequent use of dictionaries. He concentrates on everything he reads or listens to. His conscientiousness, however, can lead to hesitation when speaking, a lack of spontaneity when writing and over-concern with detail when reading or listening.

How do you think they felt during each part of the exam? Fill in the table with suitable adjectives.

	Ivanka	Vicent
1 Reading Comprehension		
2 Composition	—	
3 Use Of English		
4 Listening Comprehension		
5 Interview		

2 While listening

The first time you listen, check your predictions above and correct them where necessary.

Listen again, and choose one of the answers A, B, C or D.

1 Which of them felt that the oral examiner helped him or her?
A Ivanka   B Vicent
C Both of them   D Neither of them.

2 Vicent thinks that candidates will do well in the interview if they
A are asked simple questions
B give simple answers
C explain and give examples
D ask the examiner questions.

3 Which of these points are **not** made about Paper 4?
A The language used in the texts is too complicated.
B The questions are difficult.
C In some questions, none of the options seem to be correct.
D You can't listen as many times as you would like to.

4 Which of them wrote a narrative and a discursive essay?
A Ivanka   B Vicent
C Both of them   D Neither of them.

5 Either Ivanka or Vicent suggests that you should
A find out what the exam is really like by taking it.
B study less hard.
C practise your timing.
D think only about passing the exam.

3 Post-listening

Do you think they passed Paper 5 of the exam? Why/Why not?
Which of the speakers is more like you in approach?
Note down what you have learnt from his/her experiences.

in great spirits, calm, self-confident uncertain

FUNCTIONS

EXPRESSING OPTIMISM, PESSIMISM AND SATISFACTION

Here are some ways of expressing these emotions. Think of other ways of putting them into words and write them down.

Optimism

I don't see how anything can go wrong. (informal)
I'm sure it will be a success. (neutral)
I have every confidence in our ability to . . . (formal)

Pessimism

Anything that can go wrong, will go wrong. (informal)
I'm not at all confident that . . . (neutral)
I have my doubts/misgivings about . . . (formal)

Satisfaction

It's all worked out just as I wanted it to. (informal)
I'm really thrilled about . . . (neutral)
It gives me great pleasure to . . . (formal)

Consider the issues below:

Inequality at home and abroad.
Looking after the environment.
A war or other disaster.
A current scandal.
A general election.

Discuss them with your partner. One should be the optimist, the other the pessimist.

Use a number of situations, for example:
☐ taking part in a serious debate.
☐ talking to an acquaintance at work or college.
☐ chatting to a close friend.

EXAM SKILLS   THE INTERVIEW

Look at the 20 points below and underline those you need most practice at. Work on them during the interview on the next page.

General

1   Relax and be friendly to the Examiner(s), and other Candidates if you are doing the interview in a group. Look people in the eye during the conversation.
2   Choose the style of language appropriate to the kind of people you are speaking to (as you would in your first language).
3   Don't mumble or give many one-word answers; if you don't show the Examiner what you are capable of you won't be given the benefit of the doubt. You must talk.
4   Don't be afraid to express your own opinions. Give reasons for them and ask other Candidates for theirs.
5   If a question is not clear, ask the other person to repeat it or explain it.
6   If you can't think of a word you need, explain it, if it's an object describe its uses, what it's similar to etc.
7   Try to use a wide range of vocabulary, structures and functional language.
8   Don't worry about slips of the tongue or small mistakes – everyone makes them.
9   If you are not familiar with the topic, try to guide the conversation to one (within the general theme) that suits you better.

The photograph

10   Look at the picture carefully and think of the language you will need to describe the scene.
11   Study people's physical appearance, facial expressions and actions.
12   Speculate about their ages, social background and personalities.
13   Consider what led up to the scene and what might come after it.
14   Predict the questions which may be asked (including *What would happen if . . .?* questions) and any related topics which could be discussed. What would you ask?

Reading passage

15   Read the text quickly to form a general impression.
16   Think about its source, purpose, content, link to the theme, message and any unusual features.
17   Quote from the passage if you wish.

Communicative activity

18   Study rolecards for clues to the relationship that exists between the participants.
19   Imagine the situation and convince yourself that you are really there.
20   To prepare a talk, don't try to write a script; just note down headings (for/against, introduction/main points/ending, examples etc.) and key words.

Finally, remember that even if you had an 'off day' you could still pass in the exam: you don't have to pass every Paper.

ORAL

1 Phonology – assimilation

In ordinary rapid speech, a sound at the end of a word may be affected by the sound which begins the next word.

Examples:
... but he drives a hard bargain ... = /ha:ba:g n/

... and she's won ten points ... = /tempoɪnts/

Listen to the following extracts, concentrate on the words in italics and underline the consonants which change their sound.
Write in the appropriate symbol above each.
/f/   /k/   /ʃ/   /ʒ/   /dʒ/   /ŋ/

1 *this* should mean the end
2 it *was* your idea
3 didn't even *have* to try
4 I *don't* quite see
5 the *right* question to ask
6 that *made* you sweat!

Read them aloud quickly to your partner.

2 Interview

Think of questions to interview your partner using the following material and give marks.

Photograph

Give the 'Candidate' time to study the photograph below, then initiate discussion.

Reading passage

Ask the 'Candidate' to study one of these passages and then invite comment.

> 1 The work ethic, far from having been discarded, has merely been reshaped by the rich for their own purposes; not, this time, to serve as a model of iron discipline to the workers in industry, but as a decoration, an impressive and plausible facade for themselves, which will conceal the uselessness, or even the downright noxious nature, of their avocations.
>
> 2 Besides inventing the scissors and designing an aeroplane, this Renaissance athlete, composer, architect, poet, anatomist, mathematician, sculptor and philosopher could write with both hands on different subjects simultaneously while talking about a third, and many of his scientific notes were written from right to left. But it is as a painter that he is best known.
>
> 3 It seems, then, that when we decribe ourselves as talented in certain areas and not talented in others, what we are *really* describing is those areas of our potential that we have successfully developed, and those areas of our potential that still lie dormant, which in reality could, with the right nurturing, flourish.

Discussion

a) Short talk
Invite the 'Candidate' to give his or her views on this statement:
No-one is born lucky; in life you make your own luck.

AND/OR

b) Roleplay
Assign one of these roles to the 'Candidate' and take the other yourself:

> A number of teachers are absent from the language school you attend. You and your partner are asked whether you could stand in for two of them and teach classes of ten young beginners.
> 1 You are confident that you can do so.
> 2 Your partner is not keen on the idea.

Optional reading

Ask the 'Candidate' to choose two or more of these topics to discuss with you:
1 Which of the main characters do you find the most interesting? Why?
2 What part do success and failure play in the plot?
3 Do you think the writer likes the location where the book was set? Give reasons.
4 Do you have a better insight into society of the period after reading the text? Why/Why not?
5 A theatre or cinema production of the text.
6 How does the author create the feeling of hopelessness which runs through the text?

REVIEW

1 Assimilation

a Listen to the following extracts and write the appropriate symbol above each consonant that changes its sound using one of the following:

/ʃ/ /p/ /ʒ/ /tʒ/ /ŋ/

1 found it *quite pleasant*
2 *this* young woman's work
3 and he *says yes*
4 he *won't make* that mistake
5 *might you* be interested?

Read them aloud quickly to your partner.

b Look back at the extracts on the previous page and those above. Which letters change their sound? Before which letters?

2 Phrasal and Prepositional verbs

Finish each of the following sentences so that it corresponds to the one before it. Use the verb in brackets plus an adverb or preposition.
Example:
The theatre has sold all the seats for the premiere.
All the seats (book)
*All the seats for the premiere have been **booked up**.*

1 Everybody is discussing that book.
   That book (talk) ...
2 His landlady evicted him from his lodgings.
   He (turn) ...
3 The doctor warned me about the risk.
   The risk (point) ...
4 People recognise celebrities wherever they go.
   Celebrities (stare) ...
5 They have cancelled his debts.
   His debts (write) ...
6 They started the company in 1964.The company (set) ...
7 If the prototype is less than perfect the manufacturers will reject it.
   The prototype (throw) ...
8 It's no good trying to persuade them as they will already have decided.
   Their minds (make) ...

3 Vocabulary

Put the following expressions from this unit into **category a**, **b** or **c** (see STUDY SKILLS on page 17.)

dilettante   to reshape   sheer
accomplished   gifts   counterproductive
underlie   lasting   short cut   lengthy
feat   less than perfect   to discard
single-minded   unhurriedly   all along
move in   award   facade   flourish

4 Optimism, pessimism and satisfaction

What would you say before and after the following events? Speak quickly, assimilating consonants where appropriate.

1 A friend has been offered a grant to study in the USA, but thinks it will be hard to adapt to life there.
2 You are at an important conference. A person confides that he or she has to make a speech but is secretly terrified.
3 You are in a lift when it suddenly stops between floors. Someone you don't know very well starts to panic.

5 Conditionals

Not everyone, of course, can make a success of everything. Explain how this unfortunate man could have avoided the sequence of disasters.

Example:
Had he taken precautions the pipe would not have burst.

THE LEAST SUCCCESSFUL HOME REPAIRS

Home repairs offer immense scope to the right sort of person. Mr Brian Heise, of Utah, showed the way when he woke to find a burst pipe flooding his house.

Deciding to hire a pump, he went out to his car only to find that a tyre was flat. Returning indoors to make a phone call, he received an electric shock so great that he was hurled across the room and ripped the telephone out of the wall.

He then found that dampness had caused the floor to swell and the front door was jammed so he could not get out. A seminal figure in the world of home repairs, he spent some while screaming through the window for help. Only when a neighbour smashed down the front door did Mr Heise notice that his car had been stolen.

Having informed the police, hired a pump, sealed the leak and cleaned up his flat, Mr Heise felt that the moment had come to relax. Displaying an impressive versatility, he went off to a nearby civil war pageant and within minutes of arrival he sat on a bayonet.

---

6 Essay

Write a story entitled 'Money cannot buy happiness'. (about 350 words)

7 Now do the Progress Test for Unit 16 on page 192.

8 A final thought
Everything yields to success, even grammar.
Victor Hugo

Index of Functions

Expressing *ability* 48
Accepting invitations 120
Giving advice 13, 15
Agreeing with dislikes 83
Agreeing with likes 83
Agreeing with opinions 53, 84
Making *arrangements* 120
Asking about likes and dislikes 83
Asking about preferences 103
Asking for advice 48
Asking for information 74, 120, 133, 134
Asking for opinions 53, 74
Expressing *anger* 163
Apologising 62, 120, 158
Talking about *causes* 49
Expressing *certainty* 73, 158
Changing the topic 113
Checking understanding 93
Clarifying 93
Commiserating 120
Expressing *condition* 28, 29, 38, 71, 89, 99, 108, 128, 168
Confirming understanding 93
Congratulating 120
Connecting speech 111
Expressing *contrast* 50, 88
Criticising 123
Describing
    first impressions of people 33, 34, 160
    people's actions 34
    personality 160
    position 34
    processes 30
    scenes 43
Disagreeing with dislikes 83
Disagreeing with likes 83
Disagreeing with opinions 53, 84
Expressing *dislikes* 83, 158
Expressing *dissatisfaction* 59
Emphasising 32
Encouraging 120
Talking about the *future*
    asking hypothetical questions 29
    hypothesising 28, 29, 71, 99, 108, 168
    expressing optimism & pessimism 173
    predicting 69, 71, 73, 75
    reacting to predictions 73, 75
    sequencing 71
    wishing 59
Expressing *indifference* 103
Giving information 62, 120
Giving permission 48
Hesitating 113, 120
Expressing *inadvisability* 48, 63
Initiating & developing conversation 114
Interrupting & countering interruption 153
Introducing arguments 81
Inviting 120
Involving other speakers 113, 134
Expressing *irritation* 163
Expressing *lack of necessity* 48
Expressing *likes* 83, 158
Expressing *necessity* 48
Expressing *obligation* 48, 63
Expressing *opinions* 53, 94
Expressing *optimism* 173
Talking about the *past*
    asking for information 43
    asking hypothetical questions 43
    contrasting with the present 43, 44
    hypothesising 38, 89, 168
    regretting 59
    reporting speech 118
    expressing satisfaction 173
    sequencing events 18, 43
    speculating 78
Persuading 133
Expressing *pessimism* 173
Expressing *possibility* 48
Praising 123
Expressing *preferences* 103, 158
Talking about the *present*
    asking hypothetical questions 29
    contrasting with the past 44
    hypothesising 28, 29, 108, 168
    sequencing 30
    wishing 59
Expressing *prohibition* 48, 63
Reacting to persuasion 133
Reassuring 143
Refusing 120
Repeating information 32
Requesting 13, 62
Responding to a story 23
Talking about *results* 49
Expressing *satisfaction* 173
Sequencing 18, 30, 43, 50, 71
Telling a *story* 23, 43
Summing up 32, 50
Expressing *surprise* 163
Threatening 63
Wishing 13, 59
Worrying & fearing 143, 158
Writing letters
    of *application* 61
    to the *editor* 60/61
    to *friends* 120

Index of Structures

Adjective order 149
Adverbials
    positioning 19
    of sequence 32, 43, 50
    inversion after 109
all the same 88
although 50
always (criticism of habit) 160
and
    result 49
    conditional 129
are (etc) to 63
as (cause) 49
as a result 49
as opposed to 103
as soon as 18, 43
as/though . . . are (etc) 88
because 49, 79
better (you'd etc) 63
bound to 73
by the time 18
can 48, 78, 163
Conditionals
    second 13, 28, 63, 71, 73, 103, 134, 143

as/so long as 29
providing/provided (*that*) 29
on condition (*that*) 29
unless 29, 31, 63
whether . . . or not 29
whatever etc 29, 31
no matter what etc 29, 31
third 38
without *if* 63
and/without/ (*not*) *to do/* (*not*) *to have done/given/or/in the event of* 128/9
mixed forms 89, 133, 163
were to/if + should/if + happen to 99
should/were I to/had I/but for/were it not for/had it not been for 168
consequently 49
conversely 81
could 48, 73, 78, 153
dare 63
either . . . or (*else*) 63
enough/too (result) 49
even so 88
even though 88
fancy -ing 163
for (cause) 49
forever/constantly -ing 163
Future simple 10, 62
Future perfect 69
Future perfect progressive 69
Gerund 143, 163
Gerund or infinitive 99, 138, 158
    after *start/remember/forget/stop/go on/regret/see/watch/hear/want/need/try* 138
    after *love/hate/prefer/mean/afraid/interested/sorry/certain/sure* 158
have to 48, 163
hence 49
however 50, 81
if only 59
Imperative 63, 68, 143
in case 143
in contrast 50
Infinitive
    with passive 28
    as relative 62, 148
    full/passive/without *to*/perfect/ progressive/negative/*to* only 118
    as subject of conditional 129
    or gerund: see "Gerund or infinitive"
in spite of the fact that 88
instead 50
Introductory *it* 81, 128, 135
Introductory *there* 148
it isn't as though 108
it's not as if 108
it's no use -ing 128
it's (*about/high*) *time* 108
it wasn't until . . . that 43
just 163
keep doing 123, 163
lest 143
may 48, 68, 78, 113, 143, 153
might 48, 68, 73, 78, 81, 153
much as 88
must 48, 73, 78, 123, 133
need to 48
nevertheless 88
on the one hand 81
on the other hand 50, 81
ought to 48
Passive 28

with/without agent 28
intransitive verbs 28
stative verbs 28
using *get* 28
+ infinitive 28
+ perfect infinitive 28
Past perfect 18
Past perfect progressive 18
Past progressive 18
Perfect infinitive 118
    with passive 28, 118
    as subject of conditional 129
Perfect participle (cause) 49
Phrasal verbs
    with *off/on/away* 68
    with *round/out/up* 88
    with *back/down/over* 108
    with *through/at/into* 128
    separable and non-separable 138, 168
    three-part verbs 138
    compound nouns from 158
    passive use 168
Prepositions
    of place 39, 68
    dependent *on/with/about/at/from*
Present participle
    cause 49
    as relative 62
Present perfect 62, 71
Present perfect continuous 10
Present simple
    state/repeated action 10
    future use 71, 143
    narrating past events 124
(*would*) *rather* 103, 108, 109, 133
rather than 103
Relatives 78, 137
    defining and non-defining clauses 78, 121
    omission of pronoun 78
    positioning of prepositions and determiners 119
Reported speech 58, 118
Reporting verbs 110, 118
should 48, 68, 99, 143, 168
Simple past 10, 18
since (cause) 49
so (cause/result) 49
so. . .as 43
so. . .that 43, 49, 50
(*would*) *sooner* 103
sorry for 120
such. . .that 49
surely 163
that is why 49
the first time 71
there's no point in 128
therefore 49
though 50
thus 49
used to 15, 43, 145
    would 43
Verbs
    stative and dynamic 28
    transitive and intransitive 138
    consider/dread/forbid/get over/insist on/lay/marry/prevent provide/raise/refer to/steal/succeed/threaten/want 139
    risk/assist 159
while (contrast) 50
whereas 50
will (criticism of habit) 123, 163
wish 59
(*and*) *yet* 88

PROGRESS TESTS

UNIT ONE

Paper 1: Reading Comprehension

In this section you must choose the word or phrase which best completes each sentence. On your answer sheet indicate the letter A, B, C or D against the number of each item 1 to 15 for the word or phrase you choose.

1 You'll never __B__ what happened yesterday!
   A think   B guess   C tell   D estimate
2 The __D__ of the negotiations will be known tomorrow.
   A outline   B output   C outlook
   D outcome
3 That __C__ me of the time we were on holiday abroad.
   A remains   B recalls   C reminds
   D remembers
4 I'm looking for the __C__ edition of the book.
   A unadulterated   B undivided
   C unabridged   D unmitigated
5 This year's sales show that non-alcoholic drinks are our most important ___ area.
   A growth   B grower   C grown
   D growing
6 The police were ___ the countryside for the killer.
   A brushing   B sweeping   C combing
   D trimming
7 They tried to __B__ the truth from the public.
   A occult   B conceal   C reserve
   D shelter
8 They've been working harder than ___ recently.
   A ever   B never   C always
   D generally
9 The government has __B__ new instructions to the police.
   A ordered   B issued   C delivered
   D emitted
10 To __D__ a long story short, we couldn't find them anywhere.
   A make   B say   C explain   D cut
11 At that time, physics was not very advanced compared to __C__ science.
   A actual   B nowadays   C present-day
   D newly-coined
12 There is a wide __A__ of theories about the origins of the language.
   A range   B number   C scale   D class
13 The large number of ___ is leading to near-monopolies in some industries.
   A takeaways   B takeups   C takeovers
   D takeoffs
14 He really believed those people __B__ .
   A almost   B in the pub   C seldom
   D stupidly
15 Several people were __C__ in the road accident.
   A wounded   B harmed   C injured
   D pained

Paper 3: Use of English

Fill each of the blanks with a suitable word or phrase.

Example:
*The local produce is not on **a par** with the best imports.*

1 In the dictionary, a 'hint' is _term of_ an 'indirect suggestion'.
2 After they _were_ researching for years, they at last found the answer.
3 We left the car and _went on_ foot as far as the waterfall.
4 The suspect they were chasing just disappeared ___ air.
5 She ___ better when she had a sudden relapse.
6 Almost everyone I know has given _up_ smoking.
7 They seem to understand it but it doesn't ___ any sense to me. _make_
8 He _was_ dismissed by the time his name was disclosed.
9 The word 'hopefully' has _a_ mean 'I hope'.
10 It suddenly dawned ___ that I'd made a big mistake. _on ?_

UNIT TWO

Paper 3: Use of English

a Fill each of the numbered blanks in the passage with one suitable word.

The candidate began his speech by ~~saying~~ (1) he had ever promised that direct taxes would be reduced, and said the Government had completed its five-year ~~pla~~ (2) in office successfully. He was more concerned, he claimed, with looking ~~aft~~ (3) the weaker members of society by increasing ~~all~~ (4) payments to the poor, disabled and elderly.

He appealed to ____ (5) not to take too much notice of the ~~opi~~ (6) polls currently being published in what he described as 'extreme ____ (7) newspapers owned by ultra-conservative interest ____' (8). He went on to run ____ (9) the main points of his party's ____ (10) manifesto – an alternative to the ~~whol~~ (11) enterprise system based on socialist ____ (12) of common ownership ~~programme~~ (13) than a mild version of ____ (14) market economics, ____ (15) so fashionable ~~am~~ (16) some circles.

He summed ~~up~~ (17) by referring to the Government's achievements and ~~fut~~ (18) programme, adding that none of the promises made would ever be ____ (19) – something he could guarantee as he would soon be ~~the~~ (20) ~~elected~~ Secretary of State by the Prime Minister.

b Finish each of the following sentences in such a way that it is as similar as possible in meaning to the sentence printed before it.

Example:
He doesn't usually get up before 10.
*He's not **in the habit of getting up before 10**.*

1 He can wait like everyone else, whoever he is.
No *matter who is he, he can wait like everyone else.*
2 It is believed that he was kidnapped by terrorists.
Terrorists are . *believed to be his kidnapper*
3 We'll definitely go unless anything unexpected crops up.
We'll definitely go as . *far anything . . .*
4 Even if you don't win I'll still support you.
Whether *you win or loose, I'll still . . .*
5 The police caught them trying to sell heroin.
They got . *caught selling . . .*
6 I'd stand for election only if I had a chance of success.
Provided *that I had . . ., I'd stand for . . .*
7 It'll take about the same time, whichever road you choose.
No *matter which road you choose, it'll . . .*
8 If you don't get a move on we'll be late.
Unless *you move on, we'll be late.*

9 Reliable reports state that she escaped yesterday.
She is . . .
10 He's highly unlikely to be invited, but if he is I think he'll come.
I think he'd come if . . .

UNIT THREE

Paper 3: Use of English

For each of the sentences below, write a new sentence as similar as possible in meaning to the original sentence, but using the word given in bold. This word must not be altered in any way.

Example:
I'm sure nothing will go wrong.
turn
I'm sure everything will turn out well.

1 You are legally required to complete this form.
   law
   ~~You are required by law to...~~

2 It reminded me of the time we first met.
   memories

3 There have been accusations that he stole the money.
   accused
   ~~He has been accused of stealing the...~~

4 She gives me the impression of being a bit snobbish.
   seems
   ~~She seems to be a bit snobbish.~~

5 I'm sorry but I've been too busy to fix it.
   found

6 I'll always remember the time you told him what you thought of him.
   forget
   ~~I'll never forget the time you...~~

7 He only stayed at university for a year.
   dropped
   ~~He dropped out of the u. after~~

8 I wouldn't mention this to anyone if I were you.
   quiet

9 It was the funniest thing I'd ever seen.
   funny

10 You'll be in trouble if this behaviour continues.
   go

Paper 1: Reading Comprehension

In this section you must choose the word or phrase which best completes each sentence. On your answer sheet indicate the letter A, B, C, or D against the number of each item 1 to 15 for the word or phrase you choose.

1 They're living on an isolated farm in the __B__ of nowhere.
   A centre   B end   C middle   D back

2 As soon as he saw the article, he sued the paper for __D__ .
   A slander   B damages   C outrage   D libel

3 Have I ever told you about the people who __C__ live here?
   A use to   B was used to   C used to   D would

4 Reports say the gang tried to ____ the chief security officer.
   A induce   B bribe   C grease   D reward

5 There was an age __D__ of six years between my sister and me.
   A distance   B range   C interval   D gap

6 At the age of seventeen, she began work as a __A__ manager.
   A a trainee   B an apprentice   C a learner   D a trainer

7 We have some questions __B__ the disappearance of your wife.
   A relating   B concerning   C referring   D connecting

8 The government has set up a __A__ committee to monitor hygiene.
   A watchdog   B guard dog   C lapdog   D stray dog

9 The police went through the __C__ of the car looking for clues.
   A leftovers   B rests   C wreckage   D rubble

10 He was __D__ for spraying graffiti on the school walls.
   A ejected   B discharged   C evicted   D expelled

11 The ____ attacker will go on trial next week.
   A alleged   B presumed   C certified   D confirmed

12 We have no __B__ to see a repetition of such a scene.
   A want   B desire   C care   D lust

13 Many have called for blood sports to be __D__ illegal.
   A come   B done   C called   D made

14 You should be ashamed __B__ yourself for making her cry like that.
   A with   B of   C about   D for

15 His sensual voice and __A__ good looks made him a star.
   A striking   B shocking   C hitting   D flashing

UNIT FOUR

Paper 3: Use of English

a Fill each of the numbered blanks in the passage
with one suitable word.

On the ____ (1) Chicago was much as I'd expected;
but ____ (2) come straight from my own small town
everything seemed to be on ____ (3) a huge scale
that, to *be* (4) honest, I felt overwhelmed by it. In
the first ____ (5), the airport – O'Hare, the world's
busiest – is more *like* (6) a city than a place for
planes to land. People *who* (7) live there and never
used ____ (8) to leave the terminals for years on end, ____
(9) just about everything you need *to* (10) be
found there.

  As ____ (11) downtown Chicago, well, there
____ (12) be more skyscrapers in New York but ____
(13) are taller, and here you see buildings not quite
high ____ (14) to fall into this category making ____
(15) for the real thing.

  To ____ (16) to the river, I wondered at first why
____ (17) is that it runs 'backwards'. A helpful
Chicagoan explained that it used to carry *too* (18)
much pollution into the lake that the city council
reversed its flow. As a ____ (19), all the muck now
ends up somewhere else, but it is an example of
what you ____ (20) call big thinking in a very big
town.

(margin note: instance)

b Fill each of the blanks with a suitable word or
phrase.

Example:
*As long as certain criteria **are met** flight dates can be
changed.*

1 I've always been quite keen ____ by train. *(note: on travelling)*
2 As there's a bus strike, you ____ come to school
   till 10 tomorrow. *(note: can't)*
3 I see what ____ when you say it's busy here in
   July! *(note: you mean)*
4 If you can't go to the meeting, I'll speak ____ your *(note: on)*
   behalf.
5 Don't you think people ____ try to smile a little
   more often? *(note: should)*
6 I hope you'll be more careful in future. That's
   the second time I've got you ____ trouble.
7 Don't waste time talking about things which
   have nothing ____ with the subject. *(note: in common)*
8 I know a lot of people like photography, but
   as ____ I'm concerned it's just boring.
9 You'd better face up to ____ you aren't suited to
   this job.
10 I've told you before; you ____ knock before you *(note: must)*
   come in!

UNIT FIVE

Paper 1: Reading Comprehension

In this section you must choose the word or phrase which best completes each sentence. On your answer sheet indicate the letter A, B, C, or D against the number of each item 1 to 15 for the word or phrase you choose.

1 The programme ____ with the inner-city housing shortage.
   A covers B deals C focuses D concentrates

2 They can't play a note, _C_ write their own songs.
   A let alone B not to mention C less likely
   D never to say

3 The suspect tins have been _D_ from supermarket shelves.
   A retired B withheld C retracted
   D withdrawn

4 We decided to ____ the argument by tossing a coin.
   A settle B compromise C mediate
   D reconcile

5 The Minister for Foreign _B_ has been replaced.
   A Matters B Affairs C Issues D Business

6 The manager has been given a ____ hand to improve efficiency.
   A free B heavy C firm D open

7 We are _B_ a person aged 20–30 for this well-remunerated post.
   A wanting B seeking C searching
   D looking

8 His speech was full of ____ references to little-known authors.
   A dark B murky C obscure D shadowy

9 Their policies have led the country to the ____ of bankruptcy.
   A line B rim C brink D ledge

10 He was fined $100 for _A_ public property.
   A damaging B hurting C wounding
   D injuring

11 I would like to ____ the issue of equal opportunities.
   A rise B bring C raise D state

12 The ____ of violent fans are often in their late twenties or thirties.
   A cheerleaders B bandleaders
   C teamleaders D ringleaders

13 I will never give my _B_ to such a crazy idea.
   A consent B permission C allowance
   D permit

14 They have all been _C_ with handling stolen goods.
   A accused B incriminated C charged
   D implicated

15 She said there could be no _B_ of an amnesty for terrorists.
   A probability B question C likelihood
   D answer

Paper 3: Use of English

Finish each of the following sentences in such a way that it is as similar as possible in meaning to the sentence printed before it.

Example:
'I saw him just five minutes ago,' she shouted.
*She shouted that **she had seen him just five minutes earlier.***

1 It really is a pity we left the cassette deck in the car.
   If only . . .
2 Will you please give her this message.
   I would . . .
3 'I was thinking about it yesterday,' he remarked.
   He remarked that . . .
4 If you come any nearer I'll scream the house down.
   Come . . .
5 You're always leaving dirty dishes in the kitchen.
   I wish . . .
6 All recruits must report at 0730 sharp.
   All recruits are . . .
7 I don't think it would be very sensible of you to go there now.
   I wouldn't . . .
8 'Incidents are being reported and further measures will have to be taken,' said a spokeswoman.
   A spokeswoman said that . . .
9 He told the children to go into the playground.
   'Into . . .
10 If you don't leave at once I'll call the police.
   Either . . .

UNIT SIX

Paper 3: Use of English

a Fill each of the blanks with a suitable word or phrase.

Example:
*The plane takes **off** at noon.*

1 By next year the price will probably ____ up a lot.
2 People on the beach were cut ____ by the rising tide.
3 Let's go for a meal after the show ____
4 Somebody should ____ that an accident was going to happen one day.
5 They managed to get ____ from the men chasing them.
6 By the next century, the world's temperature will ____ for some time.
7 Why don't we get ____ the car and go for a walk.
8 She just carried ____ reading as the phone rang.
9 We mustn't make a move until the time ____ right.
10 It's not ____ an invention as a complete technological revolution.

b For each of the sentences below, write a new sentence as similar as possible in meaning to the original sentence, but using the word given in bold. This word must not be altered in any way.

Example:
Heavy industry in Europe has little future.
numbered
The days of heavy industry in Europe are numbered

1 I'm certain things will get better soon.
bound

_____

2 They should have arrived by now.
supposed

_____

3 You can't be serious!
joking

_____

4 These days the railway line is not in use.
longer

_____

5 We can't possibly pay that much.
question

_____

6 I refuse to listen to this nonsense.
prepared

_____

7 We're quite sure there won't be any growth this year.
chance

_____

8 To a certain extent the two processes are quite similar.
respects

_____

9 The theory's all right, but it won't work if they actually try to do it.
practice

_____

10 Shipbuilding in this town disappeared long ago.
since

_____

UNIT SEVEN

Paper 1: Reading Comprehension

In this section you must choose the word or phrase which best completes each sentence. On your answer sheet indicate the letter A, B, C, or D against the number of each item 1 to 15 for the word or phrase you choose.

1 The crowd stayed on their feet ___ the race.
  A as B belong C while D throughout

2 There was some amazing climbing gear on ___ at the exhibition.
  A display B parade C sight D ceremony

3 Once again the American national ___ rang around the stadium.
  A hymn B song C anthem D melody

4 He's so obsessed with physical ___ that he's never out of the gym.
  A form B fitness C shape D soundness

5 You're going to have to ___ your studies more seriously, David.
  A do B make C take D work

6 I'm afraid I was on the ___ side yet again.
  A lost B failed C losing D failing

7 They're running the ___ of being relegated to the second division.
  A danger B risk C peril D hazard

8 He retired from rugby on the ___ of chronic shoulder trouble
  A basis B reasons C results D grounds

9 I don't think ___ of the teams playing in the final this year.
  A often B much C deeply D well

10 We'd better ___ a start on this job before nightfall.
  A make B have C do D take

11 A report the year before had ___ of the danger of fencing fans in.
  A alerted B shown C advised D warned

12 Ladies and gentlemen, the time ___ to announce the name of this year's winner.
  A comes B is coming C has come
  D has been coming

13 The referee looked at his watch but told the teams to play ___.
  A on B up C off D along

14 Don't you ___ all the extras very expensive?
  A think B meet C find D buy

15 If the manager had ___ sense he'd sack the lot of them.
  A a B his C any D much

Paper 3: Use of English

Fill each of the numbered blanks in the passage with one suitable word.

The news that Ben Johnson, the Olympic 100 metres champion and world-record ___ (1), had been stripped of his gold medal shocked the world, but for some other competitors ___ (2) was merely confirmation of what they already felt to be the truth: that the dramatic improvement ___ (3) his performance since the preliminiary rounds ___ (4) have been drug-induced.

Despite all the unconvincing excuses – that the samples ___ (5) have been mixed up, that it was sabotage, that the analysis itself ___ (6) not have been reliable, and ___ (7) on – the IOC took the ___ (8) that Johnson had been using an anabolic steroid and disqualified him.

He was sent home ___ (9) disgrace and ___ (10) for life from the Canadian team. He ___ (11) certainly have lost millions of dollars in sponsorship and other deals, but even ___ (12) must surely hurt less than losing the respect of ___ (13) team mates, one of ___ (14) replied, when asked about Johnson: 'Ben who?'.

On the other ___ (15), voices were raised against unscrupulous coaches ___ (16) administer muscle-building drugs without the athletes' knowledge. There were also accusations of hypocrisy, some ___ (17) that their use was so widespread that it was unfair to single one man out, while others wondered ___ (18) no gold-medal winners from the major sporting nations had failed tests. But ___ (19) common the use of illegal substances is, the fact remains that Johnson admitted in 1989 that he had been using steroids ___ (20) years.

UNIT EIGHT

Paper 3: Use of English

a Finish each of the following sentences in such a way that it is as similar as possible in meaning to the sentence printed before it.

Example:
The aid workers returned to a warm welcome.
*The return **of the aid workers was warmly welcomed**.*

1 We can't do much; all the same it's better than nothing.
   In spite . . .
2 Depending on the country, the priorities are different.
   The priorities differ from . . .
3 We would very much like to help, but there is little we can do.
   Much as . . .
4 We saw terrible suffering whenever we went there.
   If . . .
5 The situation is desperate; even so there are some hopeful signs.
   Desperate though . . .
6 It's a transport problem, not a cash problem.
   It's a problem not . . .
7 There isn't enough food now because there was a drought last year.
   If . . .
8 They are well aware of the situation, yet overseas aid has been cut.
   Even though . . .
9 It's just as well we built up stocks as I think there's going to be a poor harvest.
   If . . .
10 Livestock farming may be wasteful, nevertheless it's the West that buys the meat.
   Wasteful as . . .

b Fill each of the blanks with a suitable word or phrase.

Example:
*Why don't you get **rid of** that useless old car?*

1 Every effort was made to put ____ the raging forest fire.
2 We aim to provide every family ____ food to last the summer.
3 I think at last the problem can be solved once and ____ .
4 It's hard to account ____ a huge difference in the figures.
5 Trade has picked ____ considerably since the recession ended.
6 It's unclear whether they are capable ____ the situation.
7 The programme had a tremendous impact ____ opinion everywhere.
8 Why don't you both call ____ for a drink after work?
9 Far ____, production has actually increased this year.
10 He was referring more to capital goods ____ consumer goods when he called for increased imports.

UNIT NINE

Paper 1: Reading Comprehension

a In this section you must choose the word or phrase which best completes each sentence. On your answer sheet indicate the letter A, B, C, or D against the number of each item 1 to 15 for the word or phrase you choose.

1 Water was ___ slowly from the burst pipe.
A leaking B filtering C emitting
D spilling

2 For a ___ moment, I thought I'd found the answer.
A fleeting B split C flying D passing

3 Now let's ___ to the other highly topical issue on tonight's show.
A go B look C turn D see

4 If it serves our ___ there's no reason why we shouldn't use it.
A purpose B plan C aim D intention

5 In a ___, the temperate zones are to blame for desertification.
A manner B sense C direction D nature

6 Other parties have been getting on the ecology ___ since the Greens' electoral successes
A roadshow B stagecoach C bandwagon
D driveway

7 If it ___ everyone, let's meet again at eleven.
A fits B pleases C suits D agrees

8 I've got a ___ suspicion that we've not been told the truth.
A hard B strong C tough D harsh

9 The school ___ was always beating up smaller children.
A yob B hooligan C mugger D bully

10 Something tells me that trouble is ___ over there.
A boiling B rising C brewing D causing

11 The major TV ___ are competing for the rights.
A networks B complexes C chains
D mazes

12 The dramatic rise in world population is ___ credible.
A little B only C rarely D barely

13 We called in at a ___ village to stock up with food.
A near B close C nearby D next

14 There's no way of knowing the ___ of the top-level talks.
A outcome B outlook C outbreak
D outburst

15 You'd better ___ before you say something you'll regret.
A freeze over B ice up C cool down
D chill slightly

b For each of the sentences below, write a new sentence as similar as possible in meaning to the original sentence, but using the word given in bold. This word must not be altered in any way.

Example:
The cultivable land has been reduced to half.
down
The cultivable land is down to half.

1 There's been a fall of over 60% in sales of aerosols.
fallen

_____

2 They certainly put their time there to good use.
most

_____

3 I couldn't care less whether they build it or not.
same

_____

4 You are admitting defeat by taking no action.
amounts

_____

5 Which would you rather do, camp or stay in hostels?
appeals

_____

6 I wasn't all that convinced by the points they made.
convincing

_____

7 It is unlikely, but if I saw one I would tell you right away.
were

_____

8 I like the idea of sailing much more than flying.
sooner

_____

9 Where do all the waste products go?
happens

_____

10 They didn't think about the fauna when they burnt it down.
thought

_____

UNIT TEN

Paper 3: Use of English

a Fill each of the numbered blanks in the passage with one suitable word.

Friends and relatives of those caught up in religious cults are often unaware ____ (1) the fact that the Information Network Focus on Religious Movements (Inform) is now there to help. It is not ____ (2) advice was ____ (3) unavailable; several organisations have been cult-watching for years, but they have a ____ (4) to dismiss the possibility that the recruit ____ (5) have found something positive. Deprogramming, at ____ (6) rate according to one sociologist, either fails and people go ____ (7) to the cults more fanatical ____ (8) ever, or it ____ (9), but then they become ____ (10) kind of true believer. She accuses some of the cultbashers ____ (11) having ____ (12) too far by insisting that in ____ (13) circumstances ____ (14) they ever speak to cult officials, claiming it would be as if they ____ (15) 'Communicating with the Devil'. The founders of Inform feel that it is time people ____ (16) objective, value-free information and although it is not, strictly ____ (17), a totally independent body – the government recently handed ____ (18) a sizeable grant – the costs of conducting research and amassing data from world-wide ____ (19) must somehow be ____ (20).

b Finish each of the following sentences in such a way that it is as similar as possible in meaning to the sentence printed before it.

Example:
The pressure was so intense that he collapsed.
*So **intense was the pressure that he collapsed.***

1 There isn't a bigger community centre in any other city.
   In no ...
2 The solitary figure trudged back down the lane.
   Back ...
3 He has little idea of what is in store for him.
   Little does ...
4 People began to whisper as soon as we arrived.
   No ...
5 It hurt so much that he passed out.
   Such was ...
6 She very rarely appears on stage these days.
   Hardly ...
7 My preference would be for you to make an early start.
   I would rather ...
8 He won't be satisfied until the job is finished.
   Only ...
9 A glistening black shape emerged from the depths of the heaving seas.
   From ...
10 There wasn't a soul to be seen on the ill-lit streets.
   Not a ...

UNIT ELEVEN

Paper 1: Reading Comprehension

In this section you must choose the word or phrase which best completes each sentence. On your answer sheet indicate the letter A, B, C, or D against the number of each item 1 to 15 for the word or phrase you choose.

1 Tomorrow we're ____ to the mountains for a week.
   A on   B over   C off   D along
2 We would like to meet with a ____ to finalising the contract.
   A hope   B purpose   C view   D motive
3 It was supposed to be completed by now, but they've ____ to begin work on it.
   A yet   B never   C already   D always
4 The subsidy is good news for manufacturers and consumers ____.
   A two   B alike   C just   D both
5 We witnessed the all ____ familiar scene of police attacking peaceful protesters.
   A too   B excessively   C very   D horribly
6 After losing his job, he began to get ____ with the rent.
   A back   B behind   C after   D arrears
7 They all think very ____ of her in the office.
   A highly   B well   C much   D greatly
8 Please ____ us know your decision as soon as possible.
   A make   B allow   C let   D tell
9 I was astonished ____ everyone get up and walk out.
   A see   B to see   C seeing   D having seen
10 The so-called comedy hardly ____ a smile.
   A rose   B lifted   C raised   D upheld
11 They survived ____ water from the radiator when the jeep broke down.
   A to   B on   C by   D in
12 He ____ to be known as the leader of his generation.
   A came   B developed   C became   D turned
13 The band made a brilliant ____ album and then split up.
   A farewell   B departure   C ripoff
   D withdrawal
14 The refugees were safe ____ attack within the embassy compound.
   A to   B from   C of   D for
15 The final decision was put off until ____ date.
   A another   B a later   C a further   D a blind

Paper 3: Use of English

Fill each of the blanks with a suitable word or phrase.

Example:

*I must congratulate you **on your** recent success.*

1 We demand that those responsible ____ punished.
2 The portrait is of the king, ____ whom the artist was later imprisoned.
3 The tiny flat is ____ cry from the mansion he lived in when he was famous.
4 You're not experienced enough yet. I'd advise ____ attempting it for the moment.
5 I've been asked ____ reveal the information to you or anyone else.
6 The standard of his work leaves ____ desired.
7 It's all ____ saying 'let's make an album', but who's going to record it?
8 It's quite an experience ____ working with the big names.
9 The ceremony was attended by his old friends, many ____ had travelled thousands of miles to be there.
10 The best examples are to ____ in his earlier works.

Paper 3: Use of English

a Finish each of the following sentences in such a way that it is as similar as possible in meaning to the sentence printed before it.

Example:
The signs are hardly encouraging.
*We **are hardly encouraged by the signs***.

1 We can't set up the business if we don't raise more capital.
Without . . .
2 Prices had gone up so much that I was astounded.
It . . .
3 The film won't fit onto the video cassette if you don't stop the tape for the commercials.
Stop . . .
4 If you go out with her I'll never speak to you again.
Go . . .
5 Standing here's a complete waste of time.
It's . . .
6 We'll probably have enough if we allow for 5% inflation.
Given . . .
7 I think shopping around is very sensible.
I think it . . .
8 We'll miss the plane if you don't hurry up.
Either . . .
9 If the place is empty there's no point in going there.
It's . . .
10 Sponsorship will be considered, should there be a fall in revenue.
In . . .

b For each of the sentences below, write a new sentence as similar as possible in meaning to the original sentence, but using the word given in bold. This word must not be altered in any way.

Example:
It's not so much a crisis as a temporary slowdown.
rather
It's a temporary slowdown rather than a crisis.

1 You don't have to pay for repairs.
charge
_____

2 There was no-one I less wanted to see than John.
last
_____

3 The printer hasn't been working properly.
wrong
_____

4 He's well known in business circles.
world
_____

5 When we last added up, there were ten of them.
count
_____

6 She looks rather like someone I used to know.
resemblance
_____

7 All you have to do to get help is press a button.
at
_____

8 Only the *Daily Mirror* has the story!
exclusive
_____

9 The amount of time people spend watching TV is gradually going down.
less
_____

10 Specially-designed tyres make the new model much safer.
for
_____

UNIT THIRTEEN

Paper 3: Use of English

a Fill each of the numbered blanks in the passage with one suitable word.

An artificial gill may sound like something ___ (1) of a Jules Verne novel but an American company has succeeded in ___ (2) one. Aquanautics of California has designed a 'gill' which can extract 80% of the oxygen dissolved ___ (3) seawater. The prototype can produce one-tenth of a litre of pure oxygen ___ (4) minute. Last month Ministry of Defence officials went to California to see the gill ___ (5). ___ (6) interest was not only in a piece of apparatus that would ___ (7) a man to work underwater without an air supply, but ___ (8) in providing submarines ___ (9) oxygen.

The Aquanautics gill is simple ___ (10) principle and borrows much ___ (11) the real thing. Seawater is run over thousands of tiny tubes. Flowing inside these tubes ___ (12) a special liquid with properties similar to blood. It contains 'carrier' molecules that pluck oxygen ___ (13) the seawater, across the tube walls, and carry ___ (14) off to an electrochemical cell. In the cell, electrons are removed ___ (15) the carrier molecules and pure oxygen is released. The tiny tubes are made ___ (16) of a poly-propylene with pores just the right size to allow gas through, but which ___ (17) water out. The carrier molecule was designed and engineered ___ (18) the haemoglobin molecule ___ (19) carries oxygen in our blood. The artificial version is smaller and more efficient because, ___ (20) haemoglobin, carrying the oxygen is all it has to do.

b Fill the blanks with a suitable word or phrase.

Example:

*The children were forbidden **to go near** the old mine.*

1 He's terrified in case the boss ___ what really happened.
2 Anyone who has that amount stolen ___ house must have more money than sense.
3 He threatened ___ unless they left at once.
4 The very thought of a ___ up my arm makes me shiver.
5 She's quite unable to cope ___, particularly since her illness.
6 I remember ___ to him once but I can't think where.
7 There's no need to worry about your condition ___ worse, Mr Jones, as long as you keep to the diet.
8 I stopped ___ the sun after I saw that documentary on what it can do to you.
9 Doctors launched another ___ on smoking.
10 The police prevented people ___ until the bomb disposal experts declared it safe.

UNIT FOURTEEN

Paper 1: Reading Comprehension

a In this section you must choose the word or phrase which best completes each sentence. On your answer sheet indicate the letter A, B, C, or D against the number of each item 1 to 15 for the word or phrase you choose.

1 As soon as we'd finished cleaning the kitchen, we set ___ tidying the bedrooms.
   A to B about C off D up
2 Congress refused to ___ the troop reduction treaty.
   A comply B ratify C uphold D consent
3 There was a big fall in ___ prices on the stock exchange.
   A commodity B goods C item D assets
4 You can vote by ___, if you are abroad when the election is held.
   A order B substitute C request D proxy
5 I'll ___ with your enquiry in a second.
   A treat B sort C deal D handle
6 It took him hours to decide on the exact ___ of the letter.
   A wording B styling C sentencing D expressing
7 Even the right to vote, as it ___, is not guaranteed.
   A is B be C could D were
8 This is just a ___; the final document won't be ready until next week.
   A sketch B draught C trial D draft
9 Our job is to ___ information on cases of injustice from all over the world.
   A recollect B gather C hoard D stash
10 News of the disaster brought the celebrations to ___ end.
   A the B an C some D their
11 Our main ___ is to prevent people starving.
   A concern B worry C interest D anxiety
12 Cleaning, ironing and other ___ just take up so much time.
   A chores B labour C shifts D homework
13 He asked his parents for more ___ money.
   A allowance B change C pocket D wallet
14 Those who originally come from another country are a ___ minority.
   A prosecuted B pestered C persecuted D pursued
15 We've asked ___ again to be allowed to visit them.
   A on and on B ever and ever C more and more D time and time

b For each of the sentences below, write a new sentence as similar as possible in meaning to the original sentence, but using the word given in bold. This word must not be altered in any way.

Example:
They just criticize other people all the time.
forever
They're forever criticizing other people.

1 It'll definitely be ready by Friday.
sure
_____

2 The company's objective this year is to double its profits.
aims
_____

3 Losing his nerve at the last moment is what frightens him.
afraid
_____

4 I've rarely met such an intelligent person.
most
_____

5 I spoilt your evening; I really do apologise.
sorry
_____

6 It came as a complete surprise to learn you were sisters.
guessed
_____

7 What she said later aroused my interest.
interested
_____

8 It's always been my intention to move out of the city.
meant
_____

9 You'd make things a lot easier for us if you cooperated.
save
_____

10 He'd rather save up than borrow money.
prefers
_____

Paper 3: Use of English

Finish each of the following sentences in such a way that it is as similar as possible in meaning to the sentence printed before it.

Example:
Sharon and Gary were the first guests who arrived.
*The first guests to **arrive were Sharon and Gary**.*

1 They're going to build an office block which will be 600 feet tall.
The office block to . . .
2 It appears that there has been an accident.
There . . .
3 The little shop under the bridge is the place you should go to.
The place to . . .
4 I'm not happy about so many people being here.
I'm not happy about there . . .
5 We would have nothing to say to each other.
There . . .
6 A single cry came from the bleak moors.
From . . .
7 I'd like the room to have bigger windows.
I'd like there . . .
8 Jane is the person you should meet.
The person for . . .
9 Certain difficulties arose in the signing of the treaty.
There . . .
10 The facts cannot be disputed.
There . . .

UNIT FIFTEEN

Paper 3: Use of English

Fill each of the numbered blanks in the passage with one suitable word.

How many of us are fed ___(1) with sales? Every January and June the battle to seek ___(2) bargains ___(3) struggling through a chaos of cut-price tickets and ___(4) than appealing merchandise. Every year TV ___(5) on showing the same old scenes of the storming of the big stores ___(6) the First Day of the Sales. And every year – ___(7) it isn't my imagination – it seems ___(8) if the sales start earlier and drag ___(9) longer, presenting an increasingly unappetising prospect.

The cleverest and most self-controlled shoppers are ___(10), perhaps, who stay ___(11) altogether. They are the 'wise virgins' who have ___(12) their clothes shopping early and selectively, ___(13) there is fresh and abundant merchandise to choose ___(14). They are the odd ones who feel the urge ___(15) swimwear in March and coats in August; but for most of us it would mean going ___(16) the grain of common sense.

A prime rule is to avoid ___(17) anything at a marked-down price that ___(18) not have tempted you at full whack, but the ultimate cleverness – worth making ___(19) effort to achieve and the stuff of sales-trip fantasies – is ___(20) able to buy something from last season that will come into fashion in the next.

UNIT SIXTEEN

Paper 3: Use of English

a Finish each of the following sentences in such a way that it is as similar as possible in meaning to the sentence printed before it.

Example:
He wouldn't have lost out if he'd just made that extra effort.
*Had **he just made that extra effort he wouldn't have lost out**.*

1 It would be a very ordinary book without the fine characterization.
But for . . .
2 We need to think this matter over carefully.
This matter . . .
3 Should the stranger ever return, vengeance would await him.
Were . . .
4 I am very pleased to announce the name of the winner.
It gives . . .
5 The conflict would have lasted decades without his far-sighted intervention.
Had it . . .
6 I'm not at all happy about your choice of career.
I have . . .
7 We would be in trouble now if they hadn't given us their unequivocal support.
But for . . .
8 They've ruled further action out at this stage.
Further . . .

b Fill each of the blanks with a suitable word or phrase.

Example:
*He discovered the cause in a sudden **flash of inspiration**.*

1 There'll be no limit ___ you can achieve once you've graduated.
2 The village had changed out ___ recognition since we were last there.
3 His ideas are quite clear but he sometimes finds it hard to put ___ words.
4 Mr Williams is off sick today. Could you stand ___ for him, please?
5 What struck me ___ was his amazing memory.
6 He has a very relaxed attitude, sometimes to the ___ laziness.
7 He got an excellent job without ___ to university.
8 Singapore's growth has been spectacular and the same is ___ the other so-called New Japans.
9 So you're taking a month's holiday just before your exams; isn't it about time you ___ priorities right?
10 As somebody once ___ it: 'Nothing succeeds like success'.